Defining Literary Criticism

Defining Literary Criticism

Scholarship, Authority and the Possession of Literary Knowledge, 1880–2002

Carol Atherton

First published 2005 by
PALGRAVE MACMILLAN
Houndmills, Basingstoke, Hampshire RG21 6XS and
175 Fifth Avenue, New York, N.Y. 10010
Companies and representatives throughout the world

PALGRAVE MACMILLAN is the global academic imprint of the Palgrave Macmillan division of St. Martin's Press, LLC and of Palgrave Macmillan Ltd. Macmillan® is a registered trademark in the United States, United Kingdom and other countries. Palgrave is a registered trademark in the European Union and other countries.

ISBN-13: 978–1–4039–4679–9
ISBN-10: 1–4039–4679–5

This book is printed on paper suitable for recycling and made from fully managed and sustained forest sources.

A catalogue record for this book is available from the British Library.

Library of Congress Cataloging-in-Publication Data
Atherton, Carol, 1972–
    Defining literary criticism : scholarship, authority, and the possession of literary knowledge, 1880–2002 / Carol Atherton.
       p.   cm.
    Includes bibliographical references (p.) and index.
    ISBN 1–4039–4679–5 (cloth)
    1. English literature—History and criticism—Theory, etc.   2. English literature—Study and teaching (Higher)—Great Britain.   3. Criticism—Great Britain—History—20th century.   4. Criticism—Great Britain—History—19th century.   I. Title.
    PR27.A86 2005
    920—dc22
                                                                         2005045415

10   9   8   7   6   5   4   3   2   1
14   13   12   11   10   09   08   07   06   05

Printed and bound in Great Britain by
Antony Rowe Ltd, Chippenham and Eastbourne

Contents

Acknowledgements

A number of individuals and organisations helped me to find and consult the archival materials on which parts of this book are based. Extracts from this material have been reproduced by courtesy of the Keeper of the Archives, University of Oxford; the Syndics of Cambridge University Library; the Archives at King's College, London; Manuscripts and Special Collections, University of Nottingham; and the Director and University Librarian, the John Rylands University Library, University of Manchester. Sue Usher, librarian at the English Faculty Library, University of Oxford, helped me in my initial search for material. Merton College, Oxford, awarded me a Schoolteacher Fellowship in August 2000, which enabled me to carry out research at the Bodleian Library. Owen Hartley of the University of Leeds helped me to locate both E. M. W. Tillyard's *The Muse Unchained* and F. R. Leavis's *Education and the University: A Sketch for an 'English School'*.

Part of my research for Chapter 2 was presented as a paper on 'Institutionalising English: The Study of Literature in the Late Nineteenth Century' at 'The Organisation of Knowledge in Victorian Britain', the Conference of the Centre for Research in the Arts, Social Sciences and Humanities, at the University of Cambridge in May 2002. A revised version of this paper will be published in *The Organisation of Knowledge in Victorian Britain*, a forthcoming British Academy Centenary Monograph. Chapter 6 is based, in part, on my paper 'The Literary: Theory, Education, and Academic Knowledge', delivered at the 'Post-Theory: Politics, Economics and Culture' conference at De Montfort University in September 2001, and on my article 'The New English A-Level: Contexts, Criticism and the Nature of Literary Knowledge', published in *The Use of English* in Spring 2003. The ideas expressed in this chapter were also explored in 'Firm Foundations? The Condition of English at A-Level', delivered at the English Subject Centre's conference 'The Condition of the Subject' at the University of London in July 2003, and in my article 'Critical Literature? Context and Criticism in A-Level English Literature', published in *English Drama Media* in January 2004.

This book has benefited from the advice, encouragement and kindness of Josephine Guy, Philip Smallwood, Ron Carter and Robert Eaglestone. Brian Sudlow, Sean McEvoy and Martin Fisher read and commented on drafts of various chapters and helped me to sharpen my thinking on a variety of points: I am also extremely grateful for the friendship and support of Richard Cave, Jess Day, Dermot Fitzsimons, Jan Flanagan, Linda Hill, Simon Mozley, Janet Nevin and Georgia Redpath. Finally, I owe an enormous debt to Matthew Hartley for his continuing patience over what must have seemed a very long period of time.

Introduction

In October 2002, 80 teachers from the west of England were invited to attend a conference on the teaching of English and history, held at Dartington Hall in Devon. Organised by the Prince of Wales, the conference included speeches by the poet Andrew Motion, the historian Simon Schama and 14 other writers and academics. The weekend was intended by the Prince to provide an opportunity for 'all of you teachers of English and history who do value our culture [...] to enrich your teaching despite the unavoidably narrow straitjacket of the examination system', particularly at a time of mounting uncertainty about the growth of an 'exam culture' in British schools: according to the Prince, such a culture could lead to the creation of 'an entire generation of culturally disinherited young people'.[1]

The Prince of Wales's concern for education, and for English in particular, was nothing new. In 1989, he stated that English was taught 'bloody badly', adding his voice to what Deborah Cameron has described as a period of 'moral panic' over the teaching of grammar and Standard English.[2] Cultural disinheritance and the narrowness of education were also the theme of his 1991 Shakespeare Birthday Lecture, in which he lamented the fact that 'thousands of intelligent children leaving school at 16 have never seen a play of Shakespeare on film or on the stage, and have never been asked to read a single word of any one of his plays'.[3] Such concerns reflect the manner in which the teaching of literature can be said to have generated a 'moral panic' of its own, distinct from Cameron's purely linguistic version yet drawing on a similar fear of cultural dislocation and disorder. Yet the Dartington weekend can also be linked to a much broader set of debates about the academic discipline of English, involving not only the issue of literary heritage, but also the very nature of literary knowledge.

In 2000, post-16 education in England and Wales underwent a series of reforms that included the introduction of an additional set of public examinations and an increase in the number of subjects studied in preparation for university entrance.[4] These reforms also represented a revision of the discourses that governed certain subjects, marking a philosophical change in what was to be considered 'valid' academic knowledge and how this knowledge was to be quantified and assessed. It was perhaps inevitable that English Literature – one of the education system's most complex and problematic subjects – should fall into this category. In fact Peter Buckroyd, chief examiner in English Literature at the Northern Examinations and Assessment Board, went so far as to comment that students would fail the new exams if schools continued to teach English literature in 'conventional' ways.[5] The new English was to be dynamic, rigorous and theoretically informed: students would need to show an understanding of cultural and historical contexts, literary traditions and movements, and 'the ways in which texts have been interpreted and valued by different readers at different times'.[6]

The reform of A-level English Literature has provoked a number of debates – about the defining qualities of literature, its place in forming the individual sensibility and the elitism involved in making its study more complex and specialised – that highlight the contested nature of English in the early twenty-first century. In schools, philosophies of English range from the heritage-driven literary canon of the National Curriculum to the 'critical literacy' promoted by organisations such as the National Association for the Teaching of English, drawing on new technologies and the popular media to create a version of the subject that reflects pupils' own experiences of texts and language. In universities, English exists in a number of diverse and often competing forms, with the popularity of some of these forms – cultural studies, postcolonial literature, feminist theory – threatening the existence of other, more traditional specialisms in less fashionable centuries and genres.[7] Furthermore, as if a lack of internal consensus were not enough, English and its practices are frequently attacked by sceptics outside the discipline's boundaries. Many of these attacks focus on literary criticism, the process of analysis and evaluation that seems to epitomise the subject's intangibility. This process – or so one popular strand of thought goes – is all about making texts mean whatever one wants them to mean, seeing in them things that are not actually 'there': what it emphasises is not knowledge, but interpretation. This seems to prove almost incontrovertibly that the discipline of English lacks an objective body of knowledge, a core of material that can be taught and tested. And if

English is subjective, based only on opinions, there seems to be little to separate the reading produced by a seventeen-year-old student from that of a schoolteacher or university professor, or indeed the person who has never studied English literature in any formal sense. In the words of Martin Amis, the study of literature has always possessed a 'historical vulnerability', in that 'it has never seemed difficult enough [...] Interacting with literature is easy. Anyone can join in.'[8] The effect of such beliefs is to deny the discipline's claim to expert knowledge – hinting that its very status as a discipline is built on false assumptions.

The new version of A-level English Literature that was introduced in September 2000 initially seemed to counter some of this vulnerability. One of the ways in which it tried to achieve this was by demanding a close analysis of the contexts in which texts are produced and interpreted, meaning that the study of historical and cultural backgrounds, and of literary criticism, would become more explicit and systematic. It was perhaps not surprising that many of the objections to these reforms focused on their perceived threat to the 'specialness' of literature, with historical and critical scholarship being seen as intrusive and unnecessary. While the new focus on contexts and interpretations gave English a factual dimension that would help to regulate the assessment of knowledge, this also seemed to detract from more idealistic subject philosophies that emphasised personal growth and spiritual development. The acquisition of factual knowledge therefore came into direct conflict with the more complex and less tangible matter of the individual's relationship with the text.

What is most interesting about these debates is their echoing of arguments that were circulating over a hundred years ago, when English literature first became an academic subject in English universities.[9] Objections to English, then as now, focused on its perceived lack of academic weight and the belief that it was bound up with judgements rather than knowledge, making it difficult to assess for academic purposes. English struggled to gain acceptance at Oxford and Cambridge, and was excluded from the remit of the British Academy when it was founded in 1901, with Henry Butcher, one of the Academy's early Presidents, stating that it represented a 'genius' which 'cannot be organized'.[10] Its supporters therefore had to demonstrate that it was possible to formulate an appropriate academic methodology for English – to set down what the study of English literature was to involve, the kinds of knowledge it was to produce and why these were to be considered valuable, within a wider social context as well as in academic terms.

This desire to codify the study of literature for academic purposes was part of a set of changes in intellectual life that took place during the nineteenth century, usually seen in terms of the related processes of professionalisation and specialisation and the changes that they brought about in the nature of intellectual authority. In the early Victorian period, such authority was invested in the 'man of letters' or 'sage', a figure who made a living by writing and possessed a general and wide-ranging awareness of issues from history, politics and religion to literature, philosophy and natural science. The man of letters published widely (and for a broad and generalist audience) and was recognised as a popular source of authority, with this authority often assuming a moral as well as an intellectual dimension. However, such men were replaced, over the course of the century, by professional academics. This new class of intellectual workers wrote for specialist audiences – in other words, their professional peer-group – and were governed by professional codes, structures and methodologies. This situation was made possible by changing perceptions of knowledge itself, including how this knowledge was to be accumulated, organised and used, and what purpose it was to serve. It was also hastened by the increasing fragmentation of the reading public that had been brought about by the spread of literacy and developments in print technology, meaning that reading – in particular, of new fictional genres such as the romance and the detective story – was brought into the domain of the mass market and its very different needs and demands.[11] Late-Victorian intellectuals could not rely on the existence of a socially homogenous public sphere of readers who shared both their cultural values and the type of knowledge on which their work was based. Instead, they turned to the universities to provide them with a new kind of intellectual community.

As intellectual life became a profession, the knowledge it involved had to be regulated and defined according to professional codes, governing matters such as progression, validity and social utility. For some disciplines of knowledge, assimilation into professional structures was relatively straightforward. The natural sciences, for instance, readily adopted norms of specialisation, precision and the avoidance of bias, and the use of 'scientific' methodologies subsequently assisted the professionalisation of disciplines such as history. This process was aided by the establishment of university departments and courses at both Honours and postgraduate level, and by the existence of institutions such as the British Academy and the Royal Society, which conferred additional status on their members, supported research and provided a forum for professional discussion.

It seems to have been much more difficult, however, to make the study of English literature fit these new professional paradigms. For one thing, there was strenuous resistance to the idea that the subject could be an academic discipline. Its detractors argued that it lacked rigour and was too subjective and 'gossipy', requiring no specialised skill beyond that of mere reading – which, as one Dr Mayo at the University of Cambridge argued, was a skill that should be gained in the nursery, not the university.[12] Even those who were convinced of the benefits of reading were sceptical, believing that literature possessed qualities that could not be reduced to the level of a science. While literary study had gained enormous popularity in the adult education movement, and was seen within that sector as something of a 'poor man's Classics' because of its perceived capacity to civilise and humanise, its entry into the universities was to be more complex.

The present volume – a contribution to the growing field of the 'history of the book' – is an attempt to trace some of the arguments that have surrounded the study of English since it became a professionalised academic discipline in English universities in the late nineteenth century. Central to this attempt is an account of the form that English took in the late nineteenth and early twentieth centuries in a range of English universities: Oxford, Cambridge, Manchester, Nottingham and King's College, London. Such an account builds on the work carried out by D. J. Palmer in *The Rise of English Studies* (1965), which offers a chronological history of the institutionalisation of English and the debates over the subject that took place at Oxford in the 1880s. It also reaffirms the value of a documentary approach to intellectual history after a period in which studies of the discipline of English have often been highly politicised, focusing on the rhetoric that surrounded the subject rather than the institutional forms it eventually took. The desire to 'rewrite' the study of English that emerged from the Marxist revisionism of the early 1980s drew much of its impetus from the claims made on behalf of the subject's capacity to humanise and civilise, found abundantly (although not exclusively) in the work of critics such as Matthew Arnold and John Churton Collins. Yet while such claims were powerful, they did not offer a form of English that could be shaped to fit the developing norms of academic professionalisation. The early professors of English needed to address these norms in order to construct an academic methodology that was appropriate to the study of English literature, countering the claims that literature was an unsuitable topic for academic study. In order to gain credibility as a discipline, English had to be rigorous and systematic: what it had to demonstrate was not the civilising power of literary study, but its intellectual validity.

What emerges from this documentary history is a strong sense of what Marjorie Garber has termed 'disciplinary libido', or the desire of one academic discipline to become its near neighbour.[13] English secured its disciplinary status not because it was unique – in the way that its nineteenth-century proselytisers wanted it to be – but because its early institutional forms drew on the same kinds of factually based knowledge as other, more established subjects such as history, Classics and philology. Students on these early courses were examined on sources and contexts, metre and verse-forms, and the development of genres: they were asked to paraphrase and quote at length, and put lists of texts in chronological order. Much of their set reading consisted of poetry, rather than prose fiction. Most of this poetry was pre-Romantic: at Oxford, this historical bias was even more apparent, with over half of the university's English degree being given over to the study of medieval and Anglo-Saxon literature. Yet literary *criticism* was largely absent. The evaluative process that would seem to lie at the heart of criticism, with all its connotations of subjectivity and personal opinion, was difficult to reconcile with the demands of professionalisation. Instead, the early courses in English literature focused on kinds of knowledge that were easy to teach and assess, and were therefore comparable with the form and content of other professionalised disciplines.

Yet while such methods enabled English to take up its place in the universities, they did not pass unchallenged. One feature of the wider development of literary criticism in the late nineteenth and early twentieth centuries is the way in which some writers resisted the practices and values of academic study even as these practices were being established: either explicitly, in denying that literary criticism could be 'taught' in a scientific, codified way; or implicitly, in a refusal to adopt the methods that were coming to be accepted elsewhere as part of an academic discipline. The advent of academic professionalisation may have limited the days of the amateur scientist or historian, but literary criticism continued to be produced outside the universities, often in direct opposition to the emerging norms of scholarship. Moreover, these norms were questioned not just by outsiders, but by the very people who might be expected to be most vociferous in upholding them: the early professors and academics, who frequently occupied an ambivalent space between the values of the amateur and the institutional status of the professional.

The resulting debates about the nature of criticism form an important part of the disciplinary history of English. In essence, these debates are about a problem of definition: the issue of what literary criticism was, who it was written for and what kind of skills it drew upon. Should literary criticism ever devote itself solely to an audience of specialists, or was it to retain its older function of explaining texts to a wider group of less knowledgeable readers? Could it ever rely on the kind of knowledge that could be taught and examined, or did it depend instead on the personal sensibility of the individual critic? In short, did one have to study English at a university in order to be an effective literary critic – however 'effectiveness', in this context, was defined?

The main body of this book covers a period from the 1880s – when debates about the status of English at Oxford, fuelled by the work of the critic John Churton Collins, were at their height – to 1969, when F. R. Leavis, in *English Literature in Our Time and the University*, stated the need for criticism to keep alive 'the long creative continuity of our culture'.[14] Yet this is not where the book ends. My own work as a teacher of English Literature at secondary level has shown me that the most significant feature of these early debates about literary criticism – about its nature and methods, its underlying values and its social utility – is their persistence. Modern commentators on the discipline of English Literature in schools are discussing exactly the same issues as their nineteenth-century counterparts: whether the study of literature is 'academic' enough to compete with disciplines such as history and the sciences; how this study can be made more objective and 'examinable'; and whether attempts to make it more objective risk jeopardising the pleasure to be gained from reading. These debates hint at the existence not just of the 'disciplinary libido' mentioned by Marjorie Garber, but also of a kind of 'disciplinary anxiety': an uncertainty about the kind of knowledge to which literary criticism should lay claim, the usefulness of such knowledge, and the relationship between academic literary criticism and the wider practice of reading in society. Such an anxiety has been particularly apparent in the debates that have surrounded the reform of English Literature at A-level: whether they recognise it or not, teachers involved in these debates are actually revisiting a very old set of arguments. It also extends to the future of literary scholarship itself. When academics such as Harold Bloom and John Carey try – in texts aimed at a general audience – to deny the value of academic special-isation, and when forums such as reading groups and the Internet encourage readers to act as their own critics, the need for the specialist literary knowledge produced in university departments of English seems to be undermined.[15] While academics in other fields have managed to capture the imagination of a general readership, literary criticism seems to have had no such success. The professionalisation of English studies and the development of literary criticism are marked instead by a continuing tension surrounding the relationship between amateur and professional, between academic practice and the needs and values of the wider public, which centres, ultimately, on the question of whether academic literary criticism is actually needed – and, if not, whether it should continue to survive in its current institutional form.

Part I
Institutions

1
Histories of English: The Critical Background

The attempt to write a disciplinary history of English literature is nothing new. Since the early 1980s, the rapid growth of academic literary theory has given many critics the impetus to 'rewrite' English as a subject, claiming to expose the social and political assumptions on which the study of literature is based. Chris Baldick has described such rewritings as central to the deconstruction of the 'lazy' ideologies on which attitudes to English are often based, 'in particular the assumption that the existing institutions and values of society are natural and eternal rather than artificial and temporary'.[1] However, while there is general agreement on the importance of unpicking the subject's complex past, it is clear that this process has itself met with problems, not the least of which is the difficulty of writing a neutral history.

This is particularly the case with the Marxist accounts that have dominated attempts to explicate the rise of English. The majority of these accounts follow the same essential paradigm. Typically, the study of English literature is depicted as an ideologically motivated attempt at bringing about social cohesion, offering an alternative means of security after the decline of religion commonly identified with the mid-nineteenth century, and a way of addressing the 'crises' brought about by Chartism in the 1840s and the General Strike of 1929. These interpretations depict the 'intellectuals' and the 'ruling classes' as instituting English for the purpose of indoctrinating the 'masses', using texts – and interpretations – that were designed to promote harmony between social groups, deference to one's superiors and belief in the greatness of the British Empire.[2] Such accounts frequently acknowledge a debt to Raymond Williams's influential work on the connections between culture and the problems of social class, and are also influenced by theories of the mass market, which see art as a 'fetish' – something that has both a market value, linking the rise of literature to the emergence of consumer capitalism, and a wide range of symbolic values, in its capacity to say something about its owner and reveal a special kind of 'truth'.[3] The student of literature, in such a reading, is a bewildered figure: lured by the promise of gaining a particular (and ostensibly valuable) 'understanding' of the world at large, but in reality brainwashed by the forces of cultural hegemony.[4]

Such accounts have dominated attempts to trace the emergence of English. They received probably their most famous public airing in Terry Eagleton's hugely influential *Literary Theory: An Introduction* (1983), and have been developed, along similar lines and using a remarkably similar vocabulary, by critics such as Brian Doyle and Peter Widdowson. For Terry Eagleton, the study of literature began as an 'ideological enterprise' that would 'rehearse the masses in the habits of pluralistic thought and feeling', reminding them of their place in a wider human enterprise and thus being 'admirably well-fitted to carry through the ideological task which religion left off'.[5] In the same vein, Peter Widdowson describes the formation of the canon as a process that was 'deeply ideologically inscribed', with the teaching of literature being 'an ideologically-driven initiative to "humanise" and "civilise" potentially disruptive elements in a developing class-stratified society'.[6] Brian Doyle argues that the concept of a 'literary' education is fundamentally just one more commodity within a capitalist, class-based society, aimed at 'those wishing to develop the kinds of taste required to participate in polite society'. The rise of English studies, therefore, is a process motivated by social rather than intellectual ends, with the discipline being promoted as 'uniquely suited to a mission of national cultivation'.[7] The reader is left in no doubt as to the writers' own philosophy: whether it is an 'ideological enterprise' or an 'ideological task', 'ideologically driven' or 'deeply ideo-logically inscribed', the interchangeable descriptions remind us that English is a subject founded on a particular set of beliefs, and that these beliefs should be the subject of deep suspicion.

The work of these three critics is interesting in that it shares a common focus, and therefore has a tendency towards a common interpretation of historical material. Its Marxist foundations mean that it implements a model of causality that stresses the use of English as an instrument of power, and therefore produces a particular kind of disciplinary history. However, the extent to which this can be termed an *institutional* history is questionable. What is most significant about the work of these critics is its inclination to focus on what I shall call the 'metadiscourses' of the subject – the public arguments put forward to justify the inclusion of English in the curricula of various institutions – rather than on the forms that the study of English actually took. Moreover, much of this analysis centres not on the universities, but on the development of English in the working men's colleges, Mechanics' Institutes and extension lecture circuits – institutions where a clear social agenda was at work, and where the rhetoric surrounding English is strikingly amenable to Marxist approaches. Doyle, for example, sees the establishment of academic English as part of a wider social movement developing between the 1880s and the 1920s, identified with events such as the publication of the Newbolt Report and the founding of the English Association, which sought to renew 'cultural leadership' by disseminating a sense of tradition, culture and national pride. Doyle comments: 'In this process any shadows of socialist organisation were to be dispersed by the radiance of a common culture and heritage.'[8]

A central figure in this cultural project is that of Matthew Arnold. Eagleton describes him as a 'key figure' in the construction of English as the subject best equipped to 'provide the social "cement", affective values and basic mythologies by which a socially turbulent class society can be welded together',[9] while Widdowson uses his desire to promote 'the best which has been thought and said in the world'[10] as the starting-point for a discussion of the 'ideological imperatives and vested interests' that have given the study of literature its current status.[11] Yet Franklin Court has argued against 'the historical overemphasis' on Arnold as the 'straw-man', a figure who, 'if one is to play by the rules', must be seen as 'primarily responsible for the influence of the humanist myth out of which English literary study evolved'.[12] Such readings, so Court maintains, ignore Arnold's work on education and place undue emphasis on the rhetoric of 'high culture' contained within his social and literary criticism. Court points out that Arnold actually doubted whether the study of English literature should be given academic autonomy: Arnold felt that the trend towards institutional specialisation threatened the 'fullness of engagement'[13] that the model academy should seek to promote. As we shall see in Chapter 5, such doubts were to be echoed in the misgivings of such centrally 'institutional' figures as I. A. Richards and T. S. Eliot – commentators who (like Arnold) are often given a key role within the development of English studies, but whose view of criticism often stood at odds with the needs of academic professionalisation.

The 'problematic indifference to the historical process'[14] that this elevation of Arnold involves is also apparent in its failure to address the processes of professionalisation and specialisation in more detail. For Arnold, criticism represented a form of knowledge that could not be quantified in conventional academic terms. In contrast, the earliest degree courses in English defined valid literary 'knowledge' in terms of factual information that was easy to teach and examine. If, as Court argues, Arnold's opposition to academic specialisation has not been fully acknowledged, then this is perhaps because the gap between Arnold's ideals and the historical process of discipline-formation is an uneasy one. What this gap highlights is, in effect, the difference between two distinct methods of writing disciplinary history: one based on rhetoric, the other on a more documentary approach to institutions and syllabuses.

The failure of some theoreticians to recognise the distinction between the elevation of the critical spirit on the one hand, and the development of academic English on the other, is part of a continuing tendency to generalise about the emerging discipline of English and the forces that enabled it to take up its place in the universities. The most crucial of these generalisations is the ease with which the different types of educational institution existing in England in the mid- to late nineteenth century are collapsed into a notionally unified system, fuelled by the same motivations and operating along similar lines. By the start of this period, education in England took place at a number of different levels, in a number of different types of institution, that can be divided broadly into the schools (including the elementary schools, grammar schools and public schools); the adult education movement; and the universities, both ancient and modern.[15] Each type of institution would have had its own agendas and concerns with regard to what can broadly be termed 'the teaching of English', encompassing a range of activities that included the teaching of functional literacy skills, the so-called 'poor man's Classics' of the institutes for adult education and the philological study that then dominated English at Oxford. However, Marxist accounts often collapse all these separate categories into one all-consuming yet fictional 'institution' that has no existence beyond the realms of rhetoric. Peter Widdowson's reference to 'the institutionalisation of "Literature" in *the academy*'[16] [my emphasis] is one such example. The term 'the academy' functions here as a metaphorical term, with a symbolic resonance that secures its place within a Marxist discourse predicated on a model of base and superstructure. However, as a historical term, it has no meaning: there has never been such a thing as 'the academy', a single, all-powerful institution, within the English educational system. The use of this term as shorthand for such an institution can therefore carry no currency. The institutionalisation of literature was not a simple, unified process, but a piecemeal development that happened for different reasons, and at different stages, in the different educational establishments that existed in England at this time.

A similar process is at work in Brian Doyle's analysis, in which the rise of English studies in the higher education system is described as the result of a 'national' process of institutionalisation. In *English and Englishness* (1989), Doyle argues that one of the most notable features of the discipline's history is its rise from a position of inferiority to one of cultural and educational prominence: that through an 'unlikely course of events', the 'low status symbolic materials' of functional literacy were 'transformed into a high status discipline which came to occupy a central place within the national curriculum'.[17] Yet like Widdowson, Doyle uses a number of terms whose validity needs to be questioned. First, and most obvious, is his reference to the 'national curriculum' – a term that, like Widdowson's 'academy', has no real meaning in relation to the educational systems in place in the late nineteenth century. Secondly, there is the sleight of hand with which functional literacy is elided with the study of English literature, with Doyle's preferred term 'transformed' implying, obviously, a change in the nature of English rather than a gradual multiplication of its forms. Within the terms of Doyle's analysis, this 'transformation' does indeed seem extraordinary: however, in order to accept this, one also has to view both 'English' and the education system as being single, unified institutions. What seems to be absent is a recognition of the different discourses that were at work in each of the different types of institution where English was taught. The ideal of social reform – which plays a key role in Doyle's understanding of the discipline's rise to prominence – was not universally acknowledged or acted upon.

Of similar concern is the way in which primary evidence has been used by these commentators to support interpretations that are not sustained by a more careful consideration of the sources. Josephine M. Guy and Ian Small have drawn attention to Brian Doyle's partial reading of A. C. Bradley's inaugural lecture as Professor of Poetry at Oxford, arguing that Doyle fails to acknowledge Bradley's insistence that the study of literature needed to be defined in epistemological terms rather than justified through moral or political arguments.[18] Meanwhile, in Terry Eagleton's *Literary Theory: An Introduction*, the words of George Gordon, an early Merton Professor of English Literature at Oxford, are used to support an interpretation that is quite significantly flawed. According to Eagleton, Gordon claimed in his inaugural lecture that

> England is sick, and [...] English literature must save it. The Churches (as I understand) having failed, and social remedies being slow, English literature now has a triple function: still, I suppose, to delight and instruct us, but also, and above all, to save our souls and heal the State.[19]

Eagleton comments: 'Gordon's words were spoken in our own century, but they find a resonance everywhere in Victorian England.'[20] However, a more detailed study of Gordon's lecture shows that he had considerable misgivings about the quasi-religious function attributed to English, and was using his lecture for a very specific (and topical) purpose: to examine and refute the missionary role claimed for English by the recently published Newbolt Report, *The Teaching of English in England* (1921). The Report, so Gordon maintained, required 'so rich and incongruous an assemblage of qualities' from English that it threatened the subject's academic integrity, making recommendations about the nature of the canon and the abandonment of medieval and early English literature that Gordon felt were unsustainable. His summary of Newbolt's argument, quoted here more fully, makes for very different reading than Eagleton's brief quotation suggests:

> [Newbolt's case] is briefly this: that England is sick, and that English literature must save it. The Churches (as I understand) having failed, and social remedies being slow, English literature now has a triple function: still, I suppose, to delight and instruct us, but also, and above all, to save our souls and heal the State. For this end everything must be hastened; there must be short cuts and quick returns; *Beowulf* must go if Burke may not be 'mastered'. Literature, to these reformers, is everywhere a sacrament, a holy remedy, and apparently almost the only sacrament now left. We are warned, with splendid disregard of human history, that the nation of which a considerable number rejects this literature, or, as it is called, 'this means of grace', 'must assuredly be heading for disaster' [...] I doubt if Matthew Arnold himself, with whose feathers this Report is plumed, would have undertaken to reassign, in an English literature of sacrament and panacea, the very different places which must henceforth be occupied in public estimation by Chaucer and Shakespeare, Dryden and Johnson, Fielding and Lamb.[21]

Crucially, Gordon is not espousing Newbolt's arguments but rejecting them: his scepticism undermines Eagleton's attempt to make him a champion of Arnoldian humanism. Perhaps significantly, Eagleton's quotation is taken not from the actual text of Gordon's lecture, but from Chris Baldick's quotation of it in the 1981 DPhil thesis on which his book *The Social Mission of English Criticism* is based. Baldick, however, gives a more accurate sense of the context of Gordon's words, drawing attention to the 'biting scorn' with which Gordon expressed the words in his original quotation.[22] Eagleton's selective use of evidence depicts Gordon as being in full support of a proposal to which he was actually profoundly opposed.

It is clear, then, that these political readings of the origins of disciplinary English are highly problematic. Yet they have also exerted an extraordinary amount of power, and have in fact achieved the status of orthodoxy. In many critical studies, the belief that literary study was motivated by political aims is taken as axiomatic, and is subjected to very little questioning. Thus in Bill Ashcroft, Gareth Griffiths and Helen Tiffin's *The Empire Writes Back: Theory and Practice in Post-colonial Literatures* (1989), part of the 'New Accents' series and a key text in disseminating post-colonial theory to an undergraduate audience, the study of English is described in terms that ignore the subject's troubled intellectual history, focusing instead on ideology. The discipline of English, so Ashcroft, Griffiths and Tiffin argue,

> has always been a densely political and cultural phenomenon, a practice in which language and literature have both been called into the service of a profound and embracing nationalism. The development of English as a privileged academic subject in nineteenth-century Britain – finally confirmed by its inclusion in the syllabuses of Oxford and Cambridge, and re-affirmed in the 1921 Newbolt Report – came about as part of an attempt to replace the Classics at the heart of the intellectual enterprise of nineteenth-century humanistic studies. From the beginning, proponents of English as a discipline linked its methodology to that of the Classics, with its emphasis on scholarship, philology, and historical study – the fixing of texts in historical time and the perpetual search for the determinants of a single, unified, and agreed meaning.[23]

In focusing on the 'political and cultural' dimension of disciplinary English, this explanation (like Doyle's) fails to acknowledge the intellectual factors that also played a role in the establishment of the new academic discipline. Its implicit equation of the need for 'a single, unified, and agreed meaning' with the desire to eliminate dissent and impose authority is driven by its assumption that the origins of academic English lie in the promotion of nationalism, ignoring the very real intellectual and institutional factors that made such meanings attractive. Yet the sheer ubiquity of such assumptions, rehearsed in critical texts throughout the 1980s and 1990s, means that they have now gained the status of fact: the 'ideological' roots of the subject of English have passed without question into popular academic mythology.

A more reliable account of the ways in which English came to be established as a professional academic discipline might be provided by another kind of disciplinary history, one which offers a more detailed study of institutional processes rather than seeking to impose a simple political reading. However, there has been a significant lack of such studies. D. J. Palmer's *The Rise of English Studies* (1965) provides a straight-forward narrative history, documenting the development of English from the study of rhetoric and *belles-lettres* to its institutionalisation in the extension lecture circuits and, later, the Honour School of English Language and Literature at Oxford. However, in focusing on Oxford, Palmer's account inevitably excludes the arguments that moulded the subject at other universities. John Gross's *The Rise and Fall of the Man of Letters* (1969) offers biographical sketches of many prominent early academics and literary critics, but is anecdotal rather than documentary, and pays little attention to the institutional contexts within which these figures worked. Finally, Chris Baldick's *The Social Mission of English Criticism 1848–1932* (1983) argues powerfully for a historical study of the rise of English, yet also falls into some of the same traps as the Marxist accounts. Baldick focuses on five major critics (Arnold, Eliot, Richards and the Leavises) and analyses their attempts to claim a wider relevance for English, seeking an engagement with society in which the literary critic was a central figure. However, in concentrating on the criticism produced by a particular set of personalities, Baldick does not pay sufficient attention to the more complex series of social and institutional factors that lay behind their critical 'mission' – namely, the declining social influence of the Victorian 'sage', and the emergence of a class of professional academics who were increasingly withdrawn from public life, possessing a different kind of social and intellectual authority. As a result, little reference is made to the relationship between the professionalisation of literary criticism and the social ideals of Baldick's chosen critics.

An additional problem with Baldick's work is a tendency to assume a causal relationship between certain events without supplying adequate proof that this relationship actually existed. One important part of his argument is that the academic institutionalisation of literary studies was secured by three factors: the needs of the British Empire (examinations in English literature and culture played an increasingly import-ant role in the admissions procedure of the Civil Service); the movements for adult education; and the need to make specific provision for the education of women. According to Baldick, these 'three principal factors [...] ensured literary study, in particular of English literature, a permanent place in higher education', and 'moulded the theory and practice of English teaching'.[24] However, his account does not actually succeed in demonstrating this. Instead, what it does show is that these three factors were actually held in relatively low regard by many educationalists, suggesting that they alone were not enough to gain English Literature its disciplinary status. Writing of the effects of the adult education movement, Baldick offers much evidence to show that certain educationalists did feel very strongly about the value of literature, believing that it provided a necessary, 'harmonising' balance to technical and scientific studies. He quotes, for example, J. W. Hales's claim that 'in schools whose pupils are not destined to proceed [. . .] to a University, or to a life of studious leisure and opportunity, English should, I think, be made the prominent linguistic and literary study'.[25] He then goes on to paraphrase F. D. Maurice's belief that through the adult education movement, 'class may be united to class, not by necessity only, but by generous duties and common sympathies', and to quote the ideas of T. B. Macaulay and Thomas Hughes about the similarity between training teachers and training soldiers, with both being sent out to accomplish a rigorous process of 'drilling' others.[26] However, these examples simply illustrate a particular philosophy: they do not succeed in showing how the adult education movement managed to secure for English 'a permanent place in higher education', nor how it helped to influence the 'theory and practice of [. . .] teaching'. Indeed, some of Baldick's evidence actually undermines his own argument. This is most apparent when he cites an attack by the conservative faction at Oxford on the critic John Churton Collins, a vociferous supporter of the academic study of literature. This attack, published in the *Oxford Magazine* of 4 May 1887, takes the form of a satirical drama, in which the extension lecturer, 'Mr. Random Tearem', declares: 'The eyes of civilised Europe are fixed upon me, and to a lesser extent upon the Hebdomadal Council. A literary education is imperatively demanded for the apostles and exponents of literature in Girton and the Colonies, in the Provinces and at Newnham, in our public schools and at Lady Margaret Hall.'[27] The tone of this extract contradicts Baldick's claim for the importance of the Civil Service, the adult education movement and the women's colleges, as these institutions are explicitly depicted as marginal to 'real' academic life. While literature may have had an important role within such institutions, this was not enough to guarantee it a higher disciplinary status.

To point out the contradictions and problems inherent in the accounts of Eagleton, Doyle, Widdowson and Baldick is not to state that social rhetoric and political aims did not play their role in the development of

English studies. Yet what it does highlight is the need to take into account not just the general context within which this development took place, but also a more specific set of arguments about discipline-formation and the place of academic specialisation within intellectual life, enabling critics to recontextualise those aspects of the history of English that need to be seen in the light of educational and institutional factors rather than political doctrines or aims. The profound changes that academic life underwent during the nineteenth century need to be recognised if the rise of English and the specific forms that it took when it entered the universities are to be fully understood. In looking at this context, it becomes clear that many aspects of the emergence of English as an academic subject – aspects explained by Marxist critics as 'ideological', as elements of a repressive bourgeois hegemony – can be seen in an entirely different light, as the result of factors concerned more with the processes of professionalisation and specialisation than with the 'mission of national cultivation'[28] identified by Doyle.

An important introduction to such issues is offered by T. W. Heyck's 1982 study *The Transformation of Intellectual Life in Victorian England*, and it is worth, at this point, explaining the main direction of Heyck's work as it underlies many of the ideas about English and its place in academic life that I will discuss later. Broadly speaking, Heyck traces the process by which the term 'intellectual', as both adjective and noun, accrued new and different meanings during the course of the nineteenth century: the idea that society contained a distinct group of people classified as 'intellectuals' and marked out by their work within particular spheres of activity was alien in the early part of the century, but widely accepted by its end. Heyck sees this development as brought about by changes in the way in which knowledge and the professors of knowledge were viewed, and in the ways in which intellectual 'work' in Victorian society was carried out. The increasing specialisation and professionalisation of knowledge that took place in the nineteenth century was marked by the gradual disappearance of the early Victorian 'man of letters' or 'sage', a figure who was replaced, over the course of the century, by professional academics. This new class of 'intellectuals' had careers that took place in a different domain, publishing for an audience of fellow specialists rather than for the general public. Their careers were governed by professional codes and structures and were marked by the accumulation of knowledge, over the course of a lifetime, on a specialist field, as opposed to the broad sweep of the generalists. Men of letters had no particular qualifications, and no professional career structure. For the emergent academic class of the later part of the century, the situation was very different.[29]

At this point it is useful to have some idea of what the concept of a 'profession' actually meant in the early- to mid-nineteenth century, in order to articulate the ways in which the organisation of knowledge (especially in the universities) developed along 'professional' lines. In Georgian England, three occupations – the clergy, law and medicine – were recognised as professions. These were joined, by the end of the century, by careers such as architecture, engineering and the Civil Service. Several definitions of the attributes of a profession have been put forward. Bernard Barber, for instance, has defined a 'profession' as having four main features: a high degree of systematic knowledge about a particular subject, an orientation towards the interests of the community rather than the individual, a code of ethics that helps to regulate professional conduct, and a system of rewards that lie within the structure of the profession rather than being made up exclusively of financial gain. Everett Hughes claims that the esoteric nature of the services provided by the professions and the dependence of this upon knowledge gained through years of study are also important.[30] Ideas about the sort of work carried out by the professions, and the knowledge that this involved, have historically been important when deciding whether a particular career was to be considered a 'profession' or not. For example, as Sheldon Rothblatt records in his analysis of the academic community's attitudes towards businessmen, much academic snobbery, and the refusal to countenance business as a possible career for undergraduates, stemmed from the sense that business was definitely not a profession, lacking that category's financial disinterest.[31]

The social status of the professions and their members was also important. The professions both were and were not part of the middle class: they shared some of the attributes of the middle classes, but in many ways sought to rise above them, aspiring to form a 'new gentry' that was inspired by the ideal of public service. Heyck states that 'The three professions became the means by which someone in nineteenth-century England could associate himself with high status and authority. By education and training, a man might lift himself above the commercial and industrial middle class, and so achieve the dignity and win the deference owed to the landed class.'[32] For the new academics, this high social status was undoubtedly important. Their predecessors, the men of letters, had to contend with the ideals and needs of their reading public, made up almost exclusively of the growing middle classes. In aspiring to professional status, the academics of the latter half of the century could at once assert the superiority and exclusivity of their knowledge and detach themselves from the dictates of middle-class opinions.

In doing this, they set themselves apart from the need to cater for the reading public and enabled themselves to focus on a different set of priorities. The aspiration to professional status therefore affected both the organisation and structure of academic life, and the ideas about the sort of intellectual activity that it involved, giving shape to the new and reformed universities of the late nineteenth century.

Part of this new conception of academic life was bound up with a changing view of the nature of the subject to be mastered. Heyck traces the processes by which academics in two fields, science and history, established new definitions of their subjects as areas of specialist knowledge, a command of which – within an academic framework, rather than the general sphere of the man of letters – was a worthy enough achievement to enable a person to be considered a 'professional'. In the sciences, which expanded rapidly in the nineteenth century, this included a number of factors: ideas about progression through specialisation (the sciences were fast becoming so wide-ranging that generalisation was impractical), precise methods of research, a belief that the accumulation of knowledge should not be limited by the demands of the market, and a concomitant desire to pursue knowledge for its own sake. The growing self-consciousness among men of science, fuelled by the opportunity to exchange ideas and publish research offered by the rise of scientific organisations such as the Royal Society and the Royal Institution, led to a desire to acquire a place within other institutions that could confer status and autonomy on scientific subjects; in other words, the universities. Honours courses in the natural sciences were introduced at both Oxford and Cambridge in the mid-nineteenth century, and the sciences formed an important part of the curriculum at all the new provincial university colleges.

Consequently, beliefs about the theory and practice of scientific research, particularly practical ideas about research methodology and the importance of precision and impartiality, came to act as a paradigm for other areas of intellectual activity, providing 'a model for the acquisition and cultural function of knowledge'.[33] History, for instance, became institutionalised – and professionalised – along scientific lines.[34] At the beginning of the century, it was almost an offshoot of literature, a preserve of the man of letters that was described by Macaulay as 'a compound of poetry and philosophy' that could 'impress general truths on the mind by a vivid representation of particular characters and incidents'.[35] However, the changes undergone by the discipline of history during the nineteenth century were so far-reaching that by 1902, J. B. Bury (then Regius Professor of Modern History at Cambridge) could announce – in as clear a refutation as possible of Macaulay's views – that though history 'may supply material for literary art or philosophical speculation, she is herself simply a science, no less and no more'.[36] This statement articulates a different concept of history – and of its relationship with its audience – that illustrates the effects of the twin processes of professionalisation and specialisation.

According to Stefan Collini, these processes were at the root of modern anxieties about the withdrawal of knowledge from the sphere of the non-specialist reading public, leading to 'a heightened sense that a wide range of intellectual, scientific, and literary topics were starting to become the preserve of people [. . .] whose authority was more than personal, deriving ultimately from the socially endorsed authority of the institutions of the "higher learning"'.[37] Nevertheless, Collini stops short of endorsing Heyck's model of a wholesale transition of knowledge from the generalist to the professional. Indeed, his statement that 'few topics were seen as wholly the preserve of university teachers'[38] is particularly relevant to literary criticism. Heyck's paradigm, for instance, seems to imply that as English entered university syllabuses, a consensus was reached as to how the practice of literary criticism could be codified and formalised along professional lines, in much the same way as professional historians were adopting 'scientific' norms of both epistemology and methodology. However, this paradigm does not do justice to the many tensions and inconsistencies – in both philosophy and practice – that characterise the development of academic English. It is difficult to define a 'professional' methodology of literary criticism that was practised and taught by academics employed in the universities, although these academics often borrowed the methodologies of other disciplines in an attempt to lend validity to their own. Equally, it is also difficult to identify a point at which the 'amateur' methods of the men of letters became defunct. The institutional basis of the terms 'amateur' and 'professional' creates its own problems: the so-called 'professional' methods characterised by objectivity and the sourcing of evidence were sometimes employed by critics working outside the universities while, conversely, the 'amateur' methods of the men of letters, relying on a different kind of intellectual authority, were often drawn on by professional academics. While Heyck's work provides much useful information about the intellectual climate of nineteenth-century England, and about other academic disciplines, its function in relation to English is more that of an abstraction: a set of principles against which the professionalisation of literary criticism can be measured, rather than an authentic account of this process.

What I hope to offer is an analysis of the development of English that combines Heyck's framework of professionalisation with a more sustained account of the institutional forms of literary study than has been offered to date. This analysis will contend that the subject's rise to professional status was complicated by a number of factors, such as the clash between humanist ideals and the demand for rigour, and the resistance of academic norms that formed part of the backlash against the intellectual and social changes brought about by the spread of professionalisation. These factors mean that the professionalisation of English, and more specifically of literary criticism, were marked not by the smooth continuum implied by Heyck's analysis of academic history, but by a much more complex set of processes. While the problem of creating an academic version of English seemed to be solved initially by grounding its knowledge in practices borrowed from other areas of study, it seems that there was also, among some academics and at some institutions, a growing awareness that there was more to English than such a process would allow. However, the missing component – literary criticism – was much harder to codify and define. The techniques that it involved, the knowledge it produced and the value of this knowledge were, instead, the subject of much dissent and inconsistency. What made this dissent so fierce was the fact that what was being contested was the nature of the authority that underwrote the critical process, and whether this belonged to the 'amateur' or the 'professional': what was at stake was nothing less than the ownership of literary knowledge.

2
English in the Universities

It is easy to see why the paradigms of disciplinary development outlined in Chapter 1 have played such an important role in accounts of the 'rise of English'. Offering on the one hand an overarching vision of the 'social mission' of English studies, and on the other an abstraction extrapolated from other disciplines, they are attractive in their simplicity: their accounts of the subject's development are neat, persuasive and easy to grasp. Nevertheless, this neatness can also be deceptive; and it is significant that many of the flaws contained in these paradigms stem from their tendency to remain at a distance from the day-to-day business of 'doing English'. What these accounts do not engage with is precisely what is needed in order to bring the subject's early years to life: the vexed and complex questions of what students were actually taught, who they were taught by and what they were expected to learn.

Relatively few disciplinary historians have tried to use this kind of evidence. D. J. Palmer's *The Rise of English Studies* (1965) offers what is probably the most comprehensive account of how English came to be established as a university subject, but its main focus is on how English achieved this status at Oxford, meaning that it does not explore the different ways in which English Literature was envisioned, taught and experienced elsewhere. Personal memoirs and biographical approaches have made a useful contribution to this field, but display varying degrees of tendentiousness. Stephen Potter's *The Muse in Chains* (1937), an account of Potter's own experiences as a student in the English School at Oxford, is coloured by its author's scorn at what he disparagingly refers to as 'Ing. Lit.': for Potter, the institutional study of literature was to be deplored, not welcomed.[1] E. M. W. Tillyard's *The Muse Unchained* (1958), a response to Potter from the very different perspective of English at Cambridge, remains limited to one institution and pays little attention to wider developments in the study of English at other universities. Meanwhile, Jo McMurtry, in *English Language, English Literature* (1985), explores the subject's academic history in a manner that is emphatically liberal-humanist, aiming to allow her readers to 'communicat[e] with a part of [them]selves' rather than offering 'columns of figures stating how many students enrolled in what courses, in what institutions, during what years'.[2] And crucially, while all four of these texts offer much that is of interest, none acknowledges the broader institutional and intellectual contexts within which the professionalisation of literary studies took place.

What I hope to provide in this book is an analysis of the subject's development that restores a sense of these broader contexts, comparing the forms English took in different institutions and relating these forms to wider debates about the nature and purpose of literary criticism. In doing this, I will focus on five English universities, selected to represent both the ancient universities and the nineteenth-century foundations that were seen as the natural home of the 'poor man's Classics': Oxford, Cambridge, Manchester, Nottingham and King's College, London. Such an endeavour is itself, of course, fraught with problems. A complete picture of the experience of studying English at any place and time (of the way in which English is 'actualised' by both teachers and learners) is gained only through an awareness of the interactions between staff, students and texts, and the philosophies that govern them – an awareness that not even the most detailed of archival sources can provide. My attempt to grasp the richness of the subject's past will therefore draw on a range of different sources, including primary data such as lecture lists, syllabuses and examination papers, and the secondary evidence provided by personal memoirs and biographies, bearing in mind that the personal nature of such evidence may lead to distortions. While Heyck's general framework of the professionalisation of academic life (an abstract account of institutional developments) is crucial in providing a context for my interpretation of archival material, the nature of English was also shaped by the individual contributions and philosophies of its early professors and lecturers – some trailblazing, some idiosyncratic and some profoundly mistrustful of the very subject that they were helping to establish. These contributions may have taken place in institutional settings, and been influenced by institutional concerns, but they were undoubtedly infused with the same kind of personal authority that had underwritten the work of the men of letters. It may be significant that F. R. Leavis, I. A. Richards and Sir Arthur Quiller-Couch, the best-remembered of those early academics, were possibly those who were most adept at using their personal authority to further their critical philosophies.

This approach becomes more problematic where the nineteenth-century civic foundations are involved. Those who taught English at London and the regional institutions are largely shadowy figures whose work has generated much less critical and biographical interest. This dearth of secondary material means that the business of fleshing out the philosophies and opinions that would have shaped English at these colleges is much more a matter of conjecture. Nevertheless, what the archival material does suggest is that the course taken by English literature at the regional universities – using King's, Nottingham and Manchester as a representative sample – was markedly different to its counterparts at Oxford and Cambridge. Moreover, these differences represent aspects of the subject's development that cannot be elided into the familiar narrative that sees 'the rise of English studies' in terms of a straightforward ideological project passing directly from the 'poor man's Classics' through John Churton Collins to F. R. Leavis. In my account, the discipline of English will appear as more fragmented – and more dependent on local practices and concerns – than it does in the 'grand narratives' discussed in Chapter 1.

While this account will focus on the differences between my chosen institutions, this does not mean that similarities did not exist. In each of the early English degrees I shall consider, there are a number of common strands. One is the appearance of a recognisable canon of authors and genres, representing not only a core body of knowledge that students were expected to master but also a certain kind of difficulty that in turn represented a particular kind of value. Another, particularly in the earliest stages of the subject's development, is a reliance on bodies of knowledge borrowed from other disciplines, providing English with an intellectual validity that helped to rescue it from the accusations of 'nebulousness' that formed a major part of the opposition to the study of English literature. However, in several important respects the new university colleges differed radically from Oxford and Cambridge. One of these differences lies in the system of tuition: while teaching at the new institutions was lecture-based, the tutorial system at Oxford and Cambridge allowed for a more discursive and individual approach that demanded different skills and different kinds of knowledge. In addition, English was only one part of the Bachelor of Arts programmes at the new colleges, which offered a general, broadly based programme of studies. Oxford and Cambridge, with their increasing focus on English as an independent subject, offer a different kind of scope to study the process by which it became a specialist academic discipline – and the problems that formed an inevitable part of this.

English at the new universities

Histories of the development of English have paid relatively little attention to London and the regional institutions. The new universities, when mentioned at all, tend to be cast as special agents in the subject's 'social mission', spreading the benefits of a literary education to the provinces and the working classes, and encouraging the study of literature as a counterbalance to the technical and vocational subjects in which these institutions often specialised. It is true that these new institutions – including the colleges at Manchester (founded in 1851), Leeds (1874), Sheffield (1879), Birmingham (1880), Liverpool and Nottingham (both 1881), and the London colleges, University (1826) and King's (1831) – all made some kind of provision for the study of English literature, often well before the subject was admitted into syllabuses at Oxford and Cambridge. It is also true that this provision was frequently under-pinned by an Arnoldian conception of literary culture as an antidote to the perceived philistinism of the middle classes and the demands of industrial and economic expansion. Literature was regularly depicted as a 'humane, moralizing subject which could harmonize an otherwise anarchic profusion of "dry facts" '[3]: Alan Bacon has argued that the study of literature at King's College was a vital part of the college's anti-utilitarian stance.[4] Yet accounts which focus on this rhetoric often fail to attend to the problems that occurred when supporters of English tried to convert these ideals into practice. For example, Bacon's analysis of the origins of English at King's emphasises the role of the Reverend Hugh James Rose in securing literature its place in the college's curriculum, quoting Rose's elevation of literature's capacity to 'correct the taste [...] strengthen the judgement [...and] instruct us in the wisdom of men better and wiser than ourselves'.[5] Yet Rose's conception of literary study was dominated by its moral and spiritual power: he failed to define it in epistemological terms. It was precisely this failure that was seized on by Edward Copleston, who later became part of a 'ruling triumvirate'[6] at King's, when he objected to the importance Rose placed on the study of English: for Copleston, 'the enjoyment of English literature' was merely a 'recreation', as the skills it drew on were 'not of [a] lengthened or systematic kind'.[7]

As Bacon later acknowledges, Copleston's arguments 'hinted at what became one of the major objections to the academic study in later debates [...namely], that as a subject [English] was not sufficiently rigorous'.[8] Yet what Bacon does not explain fully is how English *did* finally achieve its place within the syllabus at King's. In Bacon's account, F. D. Maurice, who became Professor of English Literature and Modern History at King's in 1840, is credited with creating 'a subject recognizably akin to modern English studies',[9] with King's therefore being cast by Bacon in the role of 'pioneer'. Yet there was still a significant gap between Maurice's ideals and the form that English at King's eventually took. Like Rose, Maurice had great faith in the power of literature to connect its readers with 'what is fixed and enduring' by 'emancipat[ing] us from that which is capricious and changeable, from the notions and habits which are peculiar to our own age'.[10] However, such claims sit uneasily alongside a curriculum that was, for many decades, dominated by factual knowledge – and therefore open to the kind of 'cramming' that in turn undermined the college's anti-utilitarian, anti-functionalist agenda. At King's, the practical demands of teaching and learning appear to have meant that the ideal of spiritual renewal was a difficult goal to pursue: the study of literature was shaped instead by more mundane institutional concerns.

The study of English

The three nineteenth-century foundations analysed here have very different origins. King's College, London, which was founded in 1831, was established as an Anglican alternative to the secular University College, founded five years earlier. It prepared students for a range of internally validated qualifications and, later, for University of London degrees, as well as entry to Oxford, Cambridge and the professions. University College, Nottingham, was founded in 1881 and granted its charter in 1903: it also entered students for University of London degrees, and offered a range of vocational courses designed to serve the region's mining and manufacturing industries. Owens College in Manchester was founded in 1851 and later became the nucleus of the Victoria University of Manchester, a federal institution whose other constituent colleges, at Liverpool and Leeds, formed the basis of their respective cities' universities when they were granted independence in 1903. All offered courses in English from their earliest foundations, although this was as part of a wider programme of studies rather than as an independent subject.

Any attempt to study the development of English at the new university colleges is complicated by the incompleteness of the surviving evidence as to what their early degree courses would have included. The records that do exist are concerned largely with course content rather than with philosophies of teaching and learning, and this means that conclusions about pedagogical and methodological approaches – and therefore about the kinds of intellectual authority that underpinned the early forms of English at these institutions – are, at best, tentative. It is clear, nevertheless, that English would have formed only a small part of the BA course at each institution. The University of London BA, taken by students at King's and Nottingham, offered English as an option alongside Latin, Greek, Mathematics, Logic, History, Political Economy and various modern languages, with students having to offer four subjects at Intermediate and Pass levels.[11] English could also be studied on its own for Honours, which involved a further year's study after completion of the Pass course. The University of Manchester BA allowed for a little more specialisation, with students being allowed to opt for courses that were broadly historical, classical, philosophical or literary and linguistic in character, but within these groups students still had to follow a relatively broad curriculum. The literary and linguistic course, for example, covered not only English language and literature, but also ancient and modern history, Latin, French, German and mathematics.[12]

The English Literature component of these courses helped to establish a model of the subject that still dominates many degree courses in English Literature today. In this model, the literary canon was divided into a number of broad historical periods, with the syllabus for each year typically consisting of a period of literary history and the study of a number of canonical authors.[13] At King's and Nottingham, students were also examined on Anglo-Saxon, while their counterparts at Manchester studied the history of criticism.[14] In 1892–3, undergraduates at King's would have studied Anglo-Saxon, the history of English literature from 1815 to 1830, Wordsworth's 'White Doe of Rylstone' and Scott's 'Essays on Chivalry and Romance'.[15] Honours students at Manchester in 1910 were examined on the outlines of English literature (a survey course running from Anglo-Saxon to the Romantics), English literature from 1558 to 1630, Shakespeare, and the history of literary criticism, as well as sitting a number of special papers.[16] Assessment was generally by examination, although Manchester undergraduates had to submit a dissertation on an approved topic: exams typically lasted three hours and invited students to answer between five and seven questions.[17]

This historical approach helped to map the scope of literary study, defining a body of knowledge that gave English Literature its disciplinary shape. Significantly, this body of knowledge extended beyond the purely textual. Examination papers indicate that students had to gain a great deal of historical and biographical knowledge: students were invited to outline 'the impressions which might have been made upon Chaucer by the general aspect of national affairs in the time of his early manhood', and to explain Shakespeare's allusions to current affairs.[18] Many of the most factual questions were set by the University of London: 'What is known of Shakspeare's life? Carefully distinguish the facts from the fictions'; 'Mention some of the chief public events that happened during Shakspere's boyhood'; 'Make a list of Pope's chief works in chronological order, with brief descriptions.'[19] In 1883, students at London were asked to comment on the significance of Baynard's Castle, Pomfret, Chertsey, Stony Stratford and Crosby Place to Shakespeare's history plays; in 1885, they were asked to discuss Langland's relation to the views of Wycliffe.[20] Questions were also set on the influence of various authors on their successors, on metre and rhetoric and on the definition of various technical terms.[21] The ability to condense one's knowledge was also important: one common instruction was to 'write notes' on a number of topics such as 'the Interlude, the Heroic Play, the Opera, and the burlesque or satiric drama before 1800'.[22] And if such formulae seem to encourage the simple 'downloading' of facts, this impression can only be strengthened further by questions that asked students to quote and summarise, inviting them to give an outline of any one of the *Canterbury Tales* or to 'quote any passage' from 'Christabel'.[23]

There are a number of factors that help to explain this emphasis on factual knowledge. One is the limited amount of time students would have had to spend on English. It seems that most students would have attended classes in English for about two hours each week, and that these classes were effectively lectures (the fact that by 1910 Manchester's Honours students were also expected to attend weekly seminars so that 'subjects arising out of the English studies of the year [could be] reported on and discussed' indicates that such discussion would not have formed part of regular classroom activities).[24] If tuition time was limited, and if students had a range of subjects to master, then the straightforward knowledge of facts would have lent itself neatly to the demands of both teaching and assessment. The knowledge demanded by the questions cited above would have been relatively simple to disseminate at lectures, or to learn from the literary histories that formed the basis of students' recommended reading.[25] They would also have been quick and easy to examine. It may even be the case that those questions that did seem to invite a more personal, discursive response – 'Describe and discuss Caliban', 'Show exactly why Pope fails comparatively as a writer of prose', 'To what extent is the great length of *Hamlet* necessary?'[26] – could be answered by means of a set interpretation that had been learned in advance. In the absence of any Examiners' Reports, it is difficult to judge whether what was sought was a genuinely individual response, or a regurgitation of judgements handed down in classes.

It is likely that wider arguments concerning the value of certain types of knowledge also played their part. The emphasis of verifiable, factual knowledge helped English to ward off the accusations of subjectivity and 'gossipiness' that were often mounted by its detractors. E. A. Freeman, Regius Professor of History at the University of Oxford, commented in 1887 that the study of literature was 'all very well in its own way, perhaps amusing, perhaps even instructive, but [...] not quite of that solid character which we were used to look for in any branch of a University course'. Instead, Freeman went on, the university 'must have subjects in which it is possible to examine'.[27] Literary history and biography were eminently examinable subjects, especially in the rather crude forms in which the early degree courses often interpreted them: questions asking students to put lists of texts in chronological order allowed no room for the kind of vagueness that English was frequently accused of showing. For English to achieve parity with other academic disciplines, it would have to demonstrate its amenability to testing; and such methods certainly rendered this possible.

The intellectual value of this kind of knowledge must be distinguished from the moral purpose that is seen by Eagleton as the central force behind the entry of English Literature into higher education syllabuses. As stated earlier, Eagleton's interpretation of the origins of English concentrates on the importance of the traditional canon in relation to the moral functions of literary study, emphasising its perceived role in engendering 'solidarity between the social classes, the cultivation of "larger sympathies", the instillation of national pride and the transmission of "moral" values'.[28] However, the factual nature of these early programmes of study, coupled with the absence of any kind of moral rhetoric in official university documents (as distinct from that which is present in the 'metadiscourses' offered by figures such as John Churton Collins and F. D. Maurice), suggests that the canon and the knowledge associated with it were important for markedly different reasons.

It is useful at this point to consider the analysis of canon-formation carried out by John Guillory. Guillory argues that the wider 'capital' represented by the canon is more important than the narrower sense in which the canon is usually analysed, in which the ideological content of those texts included and excluded by the traditional canon is brought under scrutiny. For Guillory, points of change in the education system are crucial to understanding the kinds of value that are being promoted. One such point is represented by the evolution of the vernacular canon in the eighteenth century, an event that saw educationalists trying to negotiate the gap between what Raymond Williams has termed 'residual' and 'emergent' cultural formations: in this case, the classical learning of the traditional elite and the desire for an alternative vernacular education shown by the new middle classes. Guillory states that this negotiation was achieved through the use of poems which preserved a sense of the traditional learning (and hence the 'cultural capital') of the elite – such as Gray's *Elegy*, whose normalising of classical and Renaissance sources lent it an 'immediate but sophisticated accessibility'.[29]

Guillory's analysis focuses on a much earlier period than the one considered here, but raises ideas that are relevant to the development of English in the universities. The writers who featured most heavily in university syllabuses were poets and essayists, with a familiar canon whose mainstays included Chaucer, Milton, Spenser, Pope, Dryden, Addison, Gibbon and Johnson. More specifically, most of the poets studied were writers whose work drew on classical, Biblical and folkloric sources, meaning that students could be examined on both the poets' own work, and their knowledge of the texts from which they borrowed. Meanwhile, questions on essayists frequently tested a knowledge of history and philosophical thought. This presented students with an additional body of knowledge and an extra level of 'difficulty': the texts in question could not be read on a transparent, personal level but needed to be seen against the background of their sources and the ideas on which they drew.

On a simpler level, there is also a sense in which poetry as a genre possesses a kind of difficulty that sets it apart from prose: metre and versification offer themselves as a definite field for analysis in a way that the more diffuse-seeming language of prose does not. As Guillory goes on to explain in his analysis of the New Criticism, such difficulties possess a kind of 'cultural capital' 'by virtue of imparting to cultural objects a certain kind of *rarity*; the very difficulty of apprehending them'.[30] While the sustained analytical skills of close reading had not yet gained the emphasis that would be placed on them in the 1930s and later, the existence of questions on metre and poetic diction in exams at both London and Manchester[31] suggests that the ability to analyse the language of poetry was part of the package of skills that students of literature were expected to acquire.

Such factors help to explain the nature of both the particular body of knowledge that was central to the earliest English degrees, and the practices used to study it, which employed the methods and techniques of other disciplines and practices (history, Classics, text-editing) to produce further kinds of knowledge that could be learned and assessed. Nevertheless, such methods were not exhaustive. Some elements of the new degrees drew on forms of knowledge not produced by the methods outlined above – namely, the judgements implied by questions such as 'Compare or contrast Beatrice and Benedick as wits and humorists' and 'What do you consider the real importance of Spenser in English literature?'.[32] However, the evidence that is available suggests that the development of individual judgement was not considered a priority, and that the judgements students were expected to discuss were actually made by others, transmitted to students through lectures and reading and reproduced by them in examinations. If this was indeed the case, then the effect of this is that the subject's methodology is reduced to little more than rote-learning, with the process of making judgements being placed implicitly beyond the student's grasp.

This commodification of knowledge was, in fact, part of the general character of university life in the nineteenth century, and a factor that eventually played its part in the reform of the tutorial system at Oxford and Cambridge. Heyck sees the ancient universities' focus on examinations as reflecting the wider ideals of industry and seriousness that were current in the nineteenth century, providing the student body with a measure of discipline and emphasising the value of hard work and productivity.[33] On the other hand, this emphasis on examinations was also blamed for narrowing the syllabus and encouraging students to 'cram', rather than to acquire a genuine understanding of their subjects. In 1878, Alfred Barry, a former Fellow of Trinity College, Cambridge, warned that a truly liberal education should value the 'general culture of the human character', rather than simply the ability to pass exams.[34] At Oxford and Cambridge, such concerns led individual colleges to develop new methods of tuition that included individual supervisions and the adoption of the dialogic or 'catechetical' style of teaching.[35] But at the new universities, the focus on factual knowledge appears to have persisted. The practical expediency of such an approach may have been crucial in securing its continuing importance, with the transfer of facts being the only realistic means of instruction and assessment available to lecturers with limited amounts of time.

Another explanation may lie in the nature of the new institutions and their student constituencies. Institutional and departmental aims and charters reflect the new colleges' intention of providing technical and vocational education and educating students for entry into the professions, and it is likely that many of their students would have been motivated by the same aims, enrolling for vocational reasons rather than pursuing knowledge for its own sake. King's College and Manchester both intended to prepare students for entrance to professional careers. The Department of General Literature and Science at King's stated that its purpose was 'to prepare Students (1) for the Universities, Holy Orders, the Bar, and other professions, (2) for the Indian Civil Service, (3) for the examinations for admission to Woolwich and Sandhurst, (4) for Direct Commissions, and (5) for appointments in the Civil Service of Her Majesty's Government at home, and in the Colonies'.[36] The Arts course offered by Owens College before its incorporation into the Victoria University of Manchester was 'suitable to persons preparing for the learned professions, to those who contemplate offering themselves as candidates for the Civil Appointments of Her Majesty's Government, and to persons whose aims in education are general rather than specific'.[37] The aims of University College, Nottingham, were rather more abstract, and included the intention to 'establish classes at which the working men of Nottingham might have advantages offered to them for becoming instructed in those subjects which are most important to them as workmen, as fathers of families, and as sharers in the political power of the country'.[38] Arguably, the desire of Owens College to provide for a 'general' education and of Nottingham to enable working men to share in the country's political power do encompass the transmission of cultural heritage that is often associated with the study of literature in the civic universities. Nevertheless, all three institutions also placed a strong emphasis on utility; and this may have presented a problem for disciplines which (like English) did not lead directly to any recognisable end or profession. English had to avoid charges of uselessness, as well as of frivolity. In order to escape these charges, it would have been extremely important for students of English to be able to demonstrate that in the course of their studies, they had also acquired a body of transferable skills that would prepare them for the demands of certain careers. If the new English graduates could learn facts, paraphrase and summarise, and quote accurately, they would certainly fulfil this need, justifying their decision to spend part of their degree on a subject that had little else to demonstrate in the way of practical utility.

The new universities, then, appear to have been the home of a version of literary study that emphasised factual knowledge rather than the process of judgement and analysis implied by the activity of 'literary criticism'. As a result, the role they played in the development of academic English needs careful assessment. They undoubtedly helped to raise the profile of English literature as an area of study and educated future generations of teachers (a role which, as we shall see, was given much emphasis by John Churton Collins in his campaign on behalf of English at Oxford). They also helped to define the basic shape of English by consolidating its canon and establishing the chronologically based form of its typical degree course, drawing on the conceptual framework offered by literary history. However, their contribution to the development of literary criticism seems to have been much smaller. At the new institutions, criticism appears to have been neither explicitly theorised nor particularly welcomed.

Oxford and Cambridge: The development of criticism

Unlike London and the regional institutions, Oxford has played a central role in accounts of 'the rise of English'. It is easy to see why this is the case. For one thing, its story has the attraction of controversy, in the form of the lengthy battle against the university authorities that was led by the lecturer and critic John Churton Collins. In addition, Oxford's initial rejection of English on the grounds of its perceived lack of rigour, followed by its adoption of a version of the subject that rested on the 'difficulty' provided by existing disciplines, has a neatness that lends its support to the linear model of disciplinary development offered by Heyck. One result of this is that the events at Oxford in the second half of the nineteenth century have come to assume an almost mythical importance that obviates the need to describe the foundation of English at other institutions. Another is the perception that once Oxford had gained its Honours course in English, it then stood aside to let Cambridge get on with the difficult work of making the developments in literary criticism that Oxford's English Faculty never quite managed. This has the effect of casting Oxford in the role of a rather primitive precursor, an institution whose failure to develop an adequate methodology for the critical study of literature meant that English remained torn between the philologists and the belletrists. Eagleton's comparison of Cambridge's 'rationally demonstrable' criticism with Oxford's 'mystically ineffable' style neatly epitomises this view, exposing the perceived differences between the intellectual cultures of the two institutions.[39] It is certainly true that the perceived innovators of early twentieth-century literary criticism – Leavis, Empson, Richards – were all Cambridge men, while the 'big names' of the Oxford English

Faculty, J. R. R. Tolkien and C. S. Lewis, are remembered more for their fiction than their work as literary critics and university teachers. However, this does not mean that Oxford lacked any kind of critical philosophy. In fact, if academic disciplines are to be judged by factors such as their objectivity and systematisation, it could be said that the 'Oxford English' of the 1920s was more strictly codified than its counterpart at Cambridge – which, in turn, possessed more 'mystical ineffability' (to paraphrase Eagleton) than Oxford.

The English courses at Oxford and Cambridge actually had very similar beginnings. In their early days, both were dominated by philology, a discipline that had no difficulty in proving its academic credentials: philology drew on specialist knowledge and specialist practices, and was a subject one mastered through a prolonged period of systematic study. Oxford's Honour School of English Language and Literature, established in 1894, was heavily weighted towards this study of early forms of English. It contained papers on Old and Middle English texts and translations, Shakespeare, Chaucer and *Piers Plowman*, the history of the English Language and of English Literature to 1800, and two special topics, as well as a Critical paper. And although Cambridge only gained an independent English Tripos in 1917, it had, since 1890, allowed students to specialise in English as part of the Medieval and Modern Languages Tripos. This course consisted of two parts: English language and literature from Anglo-Saxon to the present; and English language and literature from Anglo-Saxon to the Middle English period, along with Anglo-French or Icelandic, and Gothic. Only two papers dealt with authors after 1500, and one of these was exclusively on Shakespeare.

The evolution of English at both universities can be seen in terms of a gradual movement away from these philological beginnings. However, English developed along markedly different lines at each university, in response to localised cultural and academic factors and the work of those responsible for the subject and its teaching. These early developments determined the course of the later divisions between the two institutions, and the differing critical philosophies they espoused.

John Churton Collins and the campaign for English

The campaign to have English literature established as an academic subject at Oxford was dominated by John Churton Collins, a Balliol Classics graduate who worked as an extension lecturer and tutor for the Civil Service examinations before his appointment as Professor of English Literature at the University of Birmingham in 1904. In the

1880s and 1890s Collins mounted a number of attacks on Oxford and Cambridge for their refusal to teach English literature as a separate subject, including a series of very public broadsides in the Press and a questionnaire circulated in 1886 to eminent figures such as the Archbishop of Canterbury, leading headmasters and politicians and distinguished writers and scientists. As a result, he is one of a group of proselytisers whose Arnoldian rhetoric about the moral value of literature is often drawn upon in Marxist interpretations of the subject's history – precisely because the force of this rhetoric lends itself to readings which privilege the subject's supposed ideals over the forms it took in practice. What is most significant about Collins is the fact that his vision of English could not be translated into any actual programmes of study – which, in turn, reflects the increasing importance of academic specialisation, and the criteria that fields of knowledge had to demonstrate in order to achieve disciplinary status.

In many respects Collins's vision seems plausible enough. His main argument was that the enormous popularity of English literature on the extension lecture circuits made it essential for Oxford and Cambridge to include it in their syllabuses, so that a new generation of teachers could be educated in preparation for the future. He was also vehemently opposed to the dryness of philology, and to the narrow, factual approach that had been adopted by the University of London exams, believing that literature's humanising potential had been 'pervert[ed...] into material for unprofitable teaching'.[40] He was keen to find a way in which the study of English literature could be made more rigorous, while avoiding the sterility of a fact-laden curriculum. His own educational background meant that it seemed natural to him to do this by drawing on the model offered by Classics, in which literature was seen as inextricable from the study of culture as a whole, giving the student an insight into the 'sentiment, ethic and thought' of a society.[41] This model was marked by an insistence on analytical skill: for Collins, a curriculum that focused on knowledge alone was useless, encouraging the narrowness of 'cramming'. In theory, Collins's ideal programme of study would be both scholarly and humane, retaining the potential of literary study to civilize and enlighten. As a result, his claims for the subject were grandiose. On the one hand, it was to be 'as susceptible of serious, methodical, and profitable treatment as history itself'.[42] Yet it was also to be 'a powerful instrument of popular education' that could

> contribute to the formation of sound conclusions on social and political questions; to right feeling and right thinking in all that

appertains to morality and religion; to largeness, to sanity, to elevation, to refinement in judgement, taste and sentiment, to all, in short, which constitutes in the proper sense of the term the education of the British citizen.[43]

Nevertheless, this dualistic conception of English – as both a serious academic discipline and an instrument of spiritual and moral enlightenment – only served to weaken it. Collins was ambitious in his plans for English, but was ultimately unable to convert his ideals into a practical programme of study that would justify giving English disciplinary status. There are a number of reasons for this. One is a sense of confusion over the importance of literary texts themselves. In seeking to professionalise literary study by borrowing the methodology of Classics, Collins paradoxically demoted the text to the status of historical document, valued primarily for its capacity to offer insights into the past. However, he also wanted the text to be much more than this, a 'masterpiece' (a recurring term in Collins's essays) that carried with it a significantly different kind of value. The second problem, which stems directly from this ambivalence about the identity of the text, is a blurring of the arguments Collins used to justify the place of English in the university. Many of his statements about the importance of literary study rest not on its intellectual credentials, but on its capacity to influence and mould character and beliefs. It is important to note, for example, that Collins's dualistic conception of English – defining the subject as both a 'serious' and 'methodical' intellectual discipline, and an 'instrument' of 'right feeling and right thinking' – contains a shift from an *academic* proposition to a *humanist* statement about the moral benefit of literary study. The fervent tone of Collins's credo – virtually a manifesto for the 'poor man's Classics' – indicates that while Collins duly acknowledged the place of the new scholarly practices in the academic study of literature, he was much more concerned with the subject's power to shape character and provide moral guidance. His definition of literature as an 'instrument' is particularly telling, for it indicates that he saw literary study as being about much more than academic knowledge.

Consequently, this set of arguments undermined any claims Collins wished to advance about the specialist nature of the study of literature. If literature was to enter university syllabuses, it had to do so on the same grounds as other newly professionalised disciplines: it had to demonstrate that it was marked by objective methods of enquiry and a concern for the accumulation of knowledge for its own sake, and possess a recognisable structure that would map the student's progress from novice to expert through a succession of lessons, examinations and qualifications. In insisting on another version of literary study – one marked by a concern for what A. C. Bradley would later term the 'ulterior value' of morality and spirituality[44] – Collins also insisted on defining English in terms of a kind of knowledge that could not possibly be considered professional or specialised.

The importance of particular kinds of academic rigour in relation to the proposals for English is evident in another, related set of debates taking place in late nineteenth-century Oxford: those concerning the establishment of the Merton Professorship of English Language and Literature in 1885. Collins was an unsuccessful candidate for this post, and the reasons for his lack of success are apparent in the arguments that circulated about the exact nature of the incumbent's duties. The University Statutes pertaining to the Merton Professorship are unspecific, stating only that the role of the professor was to 'lecture and give instruction on the history and criticism of English Language and Literature, and on the works of approved English authors'.[45] This vagueness allowed room for a great deal of argument as to what kind of person should be appointed. A very public debate in the pages of the *Academy* (a weekly review founded by the Oxford don Charles Appleton in 1869 to 'serve as an authoritative intellectual organ to which serious readers could turn for reliable judgments on matters of high culture'[46]) saw the issue polarised between advocates of philology on the one hand, and supporters of literature on the other. One applicant, the Oxford medievalist Henry Sweet (now remembered mainly as the author of the *Anglo-Saxon Primer*), claimed that if a 'literary' man were to be appointed, 'the general opinion seems to be that we shall get a man who will add to the social attractions of Oxford, and pose as a kind of high priest of literary refinement and general culture, but will be otherwise sterile, neither adding to knowledge himself nor training others to do so'.[47] The author Andrew Lang, on the other hand, argued that the 'literary' man did have a valid claim to the post, and 'should [...] not be regarded as a mere trifler'.[48] Nevertheless, it is a mark of the strength of the counter-arguments that the first appointment to the Merton Professorship was the philologist Arthur Sampson Napier, then a lecturer at the University of Göttingen. Sweet's disappointment that his own application had been turned down was mitigated by the knowledge that 'the mythic claims of the light literaries' had also been rejected.[49]

It is worth pausing to consider the nature of Sweet's objections to literary study in more detail, since the nature of these objections helps to illuminate the readiness with which the struggle for literature at Oxford can be assimilated within Heyck's paradigm of disciplinary development. These objections were threefold. First, there was the belief that the study of literature was not a specialised academic pursuit, but a social grace – an 'accomplishment' that was genteel and generalist, but lacking in intellectual calibre. Second, linked to this, was the accusation of sterility, the belief that the study of literature was not designed to produce the kinds of knowledge that could be considered 'useful'. Finally, there was Sweet's belief that in failing to add to knowledge himself, the professor of literature also failed to train others to do so – and therefore lacked any kind of academic and pedagogical purpose.

With the benefit of Heyck's paradigm in mind, it is easy to explain why Sweet failed to find any intellectual validity in the study of literature, as it clearly did not fulfil the essential criteria for disciplinary status: it possessed neither a methodology nor a clearly defined body of knowledge, and was unable to demonstrate any kind of social utility. Sweet's dismissive image of 'the high priest of literary refinement' represents a vision of literary study as based on a solipsistic aestheticism, a view that was common currency in some late nineteenth-century academic circles and which – perhaps significantly – some critics and men of letters did little to contradict.[50] It explains why the degree course in English Language and Literature that was eventually established at Oxford took the form that it did – and why, well into the twentieth century, there were continuing anxieties about the value of the knowledge that it represented.

In spite of the weight of the opposition to English, and the derision heaped on Collins for his continuing espousal of literature's case, it was not long before Oxford finally gained its English degree. Collins's campaign had drawn the attention of public figures such as John Morley and Lord Goschen, then Chancellor of the Exchequer and President of the London Extension Society, who wrote to Oxford's Vice-Chancellor on 15 January 1887 demanding that English be given the same academic status as other subjects.[51] At the same time, discussions were taking place in Oxford about the foundation of an Honour School of Modern Languages and Literature in which English was to be one option.[52] In 1891 this was followed by a petition signed by 108 members of the university's Congregation, supporting the foundation of an independent Honour School of English Language and Literature.[53] Significantly, the case this petition made was pragmatic rather than intellectual, and echoed a central tenet of Collins's arguments, pointing to the 'increasing stress' on English elsewhere in the education system. The subject's rapid growth had led to 'an increasing demand for teachers or lecturers competent to handle the subject efficiently [...] It would [therefore] seem to be the plain duty of an English university to give English Studies a recognised place in its ordinary curriculum'.[54]

These arguments formed part of a wider debate about the role of the ancient universities in relation to the nation as a whole, borne out of complaints about academic torpor, the inadequacies of the tutorial system and the failure of the universities to prepare students for careers in the professions. They also, inevitably, lend credence to accounts such as Eagleton's, which depict the establishment of Oxford's English degree in terms of the subjugation of the ivory tower to the 'poor man's Classics'. However, it is significant that it was another three years before the petitioners' wish was granted – and then only in a heavily revised form. The original Statute detailing the structure and requirements of the English School, submitted to the University for approval on 1 May 1894, went through a series of amendments before it was finally passed, with the most notable additions being the recommendations that students should be required to show a knowledge of history, and of Classical languages and literature, to support their study of English.[55] These were joined later by the stipulation that the English School would only admit candidates who had either passed the First Public Examination of another Honour School, or obtained Honours in another subject. In practice, this was to mean that the English School would recruit mainly from those who had passed the First Public Examination (Honour Moderations) in Classics.[56]

The importance of Classics: The literary tradition

These suspicions about the academic validity of the study of English literature were also apparent at Cambridge, where once again they crystal-lised around the inauguration of a professorship, the King Edward VII Professorship of English Literature. This Professorship was established in 1910 as the result of a donation from the newspaper magnate Sir Harold Harmsworth (later Viscount Rothermere), and its holder was intended – according to Harmsworth's stipulation – 'to deliver courses on English Literature from the age of Chaucer onwards, and otherwise to promote, so far as may be in his power, the study in the University of the subject of English Literature'. Harmsworth also specified that he wanted the Professor to 'treat this subject on literary and critical rather than linguistic and philological lines' – a recognition, perhaps, of the fact that the University's existing English courses (part of the Medieval and Modern Languages Tripos) were heavily language-based.[57]

The university's Congregation was eager to accept Harmsworth's offer, and the Vice-Chancellor even acknowledged that Cambridge's provision for the study of English Literature had, until then, been inadequate.[58] But some dons were more sceptical. Their reluctance may have been fuelled by snobbery about the Chair's benefactor: Harmsworth was associated with the rash of 'mass culture' that was already despised among academic circles, and many felt that the offer was simply beneath the university's dignity, even 'positively harmful'.[59] It was also tinged with a familiar suspicion about the validity of studying literature, an activity that (as we saw in the Introduction) was reduced by one Cambridge don to the level of basic literacy – a skill best gained in the nursery.[60] Perhaps because of this dissent, the first appointment to the Chair was a cautious one, just as it had been at Oxford. A. W. Verrall was a noted Greek scholar and fellow of Trinity College, who may, according to Tillyard, have been offered the English chair as a form of consolation after failing in his attempt to become Professor of Greek.[61] While Verrall was keen to draw parallels between Classical and modern literature, he was not given the chance to make any lasting impression on the study of English at Cambridge: he died, after only 16 months in the post, on 18 June 1912, aged 61.

Nevertheless, the link between English and Classics would be important to the future direction of Cambridge English. In the years that followed Verrall's death, Cambridge English underwent a series of reforms that led to its eventual separation from the Medieval and Modern Languages Tripos, and to the creation of an independent English Tripos in 1917. These reforms saw a gradual shift away from Germanic philology, and towards a greater integration of English literature with its Greek and Roman background.[62] This link was intended to be fostered by the Tripos system itself. Students had to sit two separate parts of a Tripos in order to gain a BA, but these did not have to be from the same subject, and in fact many students chose to combine elements of different courses. The English Tripos that was created in 1917 consisted of two parts: Section A, 'English Literature, Modern and Medieval', and Section B, 'Early Literature and History'. The former was made up of papers on Shakespeare; Literature, Life and Thought from 1066 to 1350 and from 1350 to 1603; a special period of literature (usually the Romantics); a special subject, such as Tragedy; the history of literary criticism; and the history of English literature from 1603. The latter was essentially a revised version of the course that had been offered under Medieval and Modern Languages, consisting of papers on the history, life and literature of

the Teutonic and Celtic peoples, early Norse, and the history, literature and antiquities of England before 1066. While these two sections
would, in theory, allow students to take a whole degree in English, it
was not expected that they would necessarily do so. The assumption,
instead, was that they would progress to Section A after taking part of
the Tripos in Classics – hinting at a view of English as part of a broad,
humane education, rather than the philological study it had been in
the past.

Both Oxford and Cambridge, then, leaned towards the model of
literary study provided by Classics as an alternative to that which was
offered by philology. At Cambridge, this movement from philology to
Classics seems to have been relatively straightforward, with compulsory
philology being absent from Section A of the Tripos and the importance
of Middle English being diminished. Cambridge's version of philology
was, in any case, markedly different from its Oxford counterpart:
H. M. Chadwick, the Elrington and Bosworth Professor of Anglo-Saxon
at Cambridge, had acquired a dislike of philology as an undergraduate
and was keen to develop a syllabus that replaced the study of sound
changes and dialects with a broader view of Anglo-Saxon and other
early cultures, effectively creating a Germanic version of classical
study.[63] At Oxford, however, the shift towards Classics was a much
more complicated process. While a knowledge of Classics was a
prerequisite for the study of literature, it must be remembered that
Collins's vision of an English syllabus underpinned by Classical ideals
had received little sympathy within Oxford and that the earliest form
of the Honour School was weighted towards philological study.
Palmer sees this as a sign of the independence of Oxford English from
a 'poor man's Classics' view of the subject, with the emphasis on
Anglo-Saxon and philological knowledge being an attempt to distance
the Honour School from the arguments about the moral function of
literature that had shaped the rise of English in other educational
contexts. Palmer interprets the foundation of the Honour School at
Oxford as part of a series of attempts to reform the university curriculum in the face of accusations of academic laxity: he describes the
Oxford reformers as trying to emulate German academic methods in
their insistence on 'the concept of a university as an institution for
the pursuit of advanced knowledge in all fields'.[64] We have seen how
the Germanic discipline of philology lent itself to the systematic study
of verifiable knowledge that was prioritised within the newly professionalised academic disciplines, and it is not surprising that these
factors, together with the presence of a large body of staff who already

specialised in philology and the Germanic languages, influenced the scope and nature of Oxford's earliest Honours degree in English, with only grudging space given to the study of post-Chaucerian literature.

However, this is not to say that the course at Oxford remained in the grip of philology. Records indicate that there was a growing need to define what the study of literature actually involved – the scope of the canon, the knowledge students were expected to demonstrate and the skills that this would draw upon.[65] This in turn implies a desire to move away from both a version of literary study that was dominated by linguistics, and its methodological opposite, the 'chatter about Shelley' that E. A. Freeman had attacked during the debate over the proposed Honour School of English at Oxford in 1887.[66] The new version of English that was created was one that drew on Classics not (as Eagleton argues) as a model of a humane, civilising education, but rather as part of an emerging concept of literary history – one that was central to the direction that Oxford's English degree continued to take.

This concept of English literature as part of an unfolding tradition, with roots and analogues in other European cultures, was evident in many aspects of Oxford's English course. While it continued to include Old and Middle English (as part of a broad historical survey of literature up to the end of the nineteenth century) the Honour School emphasised that Classics was at its base. The original Statutes' stipulations about the English School's historical and Classical content have already been noted; and it is significant that even when English gained its own First Public Examination in 1927, thus ending the requirement that students must have passed the First Public Examination of another Honour School, this exam consisted of Old English, a period of English social and political history, Classical texts and translations from two or three modern European languages – meaning that students could not begin to study modern English literature until the second year of a three-year course.[67] When the structure of this exam was changed 11 years later, to papers on Old English, Aristotle's *Poetics* and a study of either Virgil or Homer, the rationale offered was that the study of Classical literature would ensure 'a right knowledge of Greek or Latin for literary students [...] The general idea underlying our scheme is that some study of the Classics is the best basis for the Honour School of English Language and Literature.'[68] In 1922, meanwhile, the University's Vice-Chancellor had expressed concern over the future of Hellenic studies and recommended that students in the Schools of English and Modern Languages should only be awarded first-class Honours if they could 'successfully offer some study of relevant Classical originals in connexion with their advanced study of Modern Literature'. Such students, it was claimed,

> would be well-equipped for the highest critical work hereafter, as they alone could trace back our modern European literature to its fountain-head. [...This knowledge] would more than compensate for any special portion of our modern literature being left unstudied or more lightly studied, because it would give these students a much fuller and finer equipment for higher and more critical studies in the future. [...] This ought to be the highest object of our Honour training, not the mere accumulation of half-knowledge.[69]

This reference to 'half-knowledge' sets up a hierarchical vision of the value of certain kinds of learning that can be related to wider developments in the field of literary history, and the emergence of a recognised canon. The period papers – each dealing with about a century of English literature – that made up the bulk of Oxford's English course were, from 1917, entitled 'the History of English Literature', as if literary history, rather than literature itself, was the main object of study.[70] Such an approach linked the unfolding of English literary history to its Classical origins, seeing canonical authors as key points within the development of the literary tradition. In turn, certain authors came to be prioritised within Oxford's conception of what academic English should be. The curricular reforms of 1917 included a recommendation that students should 'study the greater authors rather than the minor ones', and the study of some specific authors was made compulsory in a further set of reforms in 1931, with the period papers from 1550 to 1850 focusing on Bacon, Donne, Browne, Dryden, Pope, Johnson, Wordsworth and Coleridge.

Examiners' reports throughout this period also attest to these priorities. In 1916 the examiners for the Final Honour School lamented students' neglect of 'the greater poets and still more the greater prose writers': 'They should be reminded that knowledge of Crashaw or Traherne will not compensate for ignorance of Milton and Bacon.'[71] A year earlier, a candidate for the BLitt was failed partly on the grounds of his overestimation of the works of Aphra Behn, the examiners reporting somewhat incredulously that the candidate 'seriously speaks of her as "worthy to be ranked with the greatest dramatists of her day", and asserts that she has "a rightful claim to a high and honourable place in our glorious literature". We think that this shows a complete lack of literary perspective.'[72] It appears that what students were expected to develop was not the ability to make independent judgements, but a concrete body of knowledge about a pre-defined literary tradition. In 1916, the examiners bemoaned the fact that 'owing to ignorance of fundamental facts [students] confused and mis-stated the relations of great writers to each other and to their times'. As a result, the examiners claimed, 'their critical or aesthetic estimates of the writings of particular authors, while showing some feeling for literature and some acquaintance with the terminology of criticism, frequently revealed the absence of exact knowledge of their lives and works'.[73]

What is most significant about this comment is the manner in which literary criticism *per se* is downgraded in favour of an understanding of historical contexts and relationships, with students appearing to have been given most credit for their ability to absorb received opinions about the significance of particular authors to the literary tradition. In view of this, the First Public Examination's insistence on a knowledge of Old English, Homer and Virgil seems not so much an attempt to increase the subject's academic credentials as an entirely suitable prolegomenon. It seems that during the Honour School's first few decades, little attempt was made to theorise what literary criticism might actually involve, beyond the agreement that it must acknowledge historical contexts and the development of the canon. There clearly seems to have been some reluctance to allow students to voice their own judgements, as the comments about Behn, Crashaw and Traherne indicate. They were certainly not expected (or invited) to contest the values and judgements that defined the particular literary tradition they studied. Yet beyond this, the attempts that were made to isolate the skills involved in literary criticism fell short of describing the critical process itself. Early Examiners' Reports, for instance, focus almost exclusively on students' philological knowledge, perhaps reflecting the specialisms of the examiners themselves, with only the most cursory of glances towards the Literature papers.[74] While there was a growing dissatisfaction in the 1920s with students' tendency to consider the early periods of literature from a wholly philological perspective (hinting at a faith in the idea of 'literary' criticism as a valuable skill in itself) there was little attempt to define what literary criticism might actually involve. The only sustained definition present in the Examiners' Reports focuses on the need for a more detailed knowledge of texts, with a report of 1925 commenting that 'candidates wrote "round" the subject, often cleverly enough, but without naming the titles of any books, or if books were named, without intimating any definite knowledge of their content'.[75]

It may be, quite simply, that the early teachers of English at Oxford did not possess a concept of literary *criticism* that we would recognise today. Instead, what they seem to have been dealing with was literary *knowledge*. This knowledge was validated by its emphasis on a canon of authors whose role in passing on a tradition that could be traced to its Classical origins was clear evidence of their worth as objects of study. Critical judgements, therefore, were already implicit in their canonical status. As a result, Oxford was not explicitly teaching the process of making judgements, nor was it enabling undergraduates to contest the judgements handed down to them. This, instead, was what was focused on at Cambridge – thus producing a very different kind of English degree.

Literary judgements: The Tripos at Cambridge

The early years of English at Cambridge are dominated by the figure of Sir Arthur Quiller-Couch. Appointed to the King Edward VII Professorship after the death of Verrall, he seems, in some respects, an odd choice. He had spent only five years in academia (four of them as an undergraduate at Oxford) at the time of his appointment, and his career certainly has more in common with the Victorian man of letters than with the newly professionalised academic of the early twentieth century. His vast output includes editions of Shakespeare's comedies for the *New Cambridge Shakespeare* series, volumes of letters and three series of *Studies in Literature*, as well as the compilation of anthologies such as the *Oxford Book of English Verse*. He was also a novelist, freelance journalist and assistant editor, from 1890, of the Liberal weekly paper *The Speaker*. His knighthood, in 1910, was for his services to local government, and E. M. W. Tillyard suggests that his appointment at Cambridge was a similar kind of reward. One of his proudest achievements was his appointment as Commodore of the Fowey Yacht Club – a fact that did not cease to amuse F. R. Leavis, who remembered Quiller-Couch with affection.[76]

Opinion is divided as to the precise extent of Quiller-Couch's influence over the English Tripos. While many accounts place him at the social and emotional centre of Cambridge English – Ian MacKillop refers to him as its 'master of ceremonies'[77] – it is also acknowledged that he disliked the administrative spadework of curricular reform, and left the bulk of this to H. M. Chadwick, Cambridge's professor of Anglo-Saxon.[78] In the early years of the English Tripos Cambridge's English staff consisted only of Quiller-Couch, Chadwick and the medievalist G. G. Coulton; they were accompanied by a shifting network of tutors and supervisors who were employed by individual colleges but did not hold university posts. In such circumstances it would have been natural for Quiller-Couch to play a role that was very public, drawing on the personal authority he had consolidated in his earlier career as a writer. It is easy to see why he is often presented as an amateur, a genial sentimentalist who, in John Gross's words, 'seldom did much more than ramble cheerfully round the subject, shedding a vague glow of enthusiasm'.[79] However, he used this eclecticism to his advantage, developing the persona of an amused observer who knew much more than was initially apparent. Quiller-Couch's lectures also suggest that he was aware of the problems encountered by the emerging discipline of English. He was anxious to preserve a sense of the 'specialness' of literature, and to demonstrate that it could not be reduced to the impersonality of a science or a mere checklist of facts for rote-learning. What Quiller-Couch valued, rather than the accumulation of received knowledge, were the qualities of 'understanding' and 'appreciation'. Such skills were treated with suspicion at Oxford, where J. R. R. Tolkien was to remark that if 'the primary end of English as a scholastic and academic discipline is to teach "appreciation" [. . .] it might as well be asserted that the direct end of Scripture lessons is Conversion'.[80] However, they were to become the bedrock of Cambridge's course, placing increased emphasis on the student's own experience of the text.

What distinguished Cambridge's early English degree from Oxford's was a different conception of the kinds of knowledge and skills that a degree course should value and validate, emphasising individual judgement over the received order of the canon. Tillyard describes the new Tripos as pervaded by a spirit of liberalism that meant that 'the barriers were down: there was to be no academic distinction between a good short story written yesterday and a Petrarchian sonnet in the age of Elizabeth; and the learner had the right to sport in every glade and green pasture'.[81] This is borne out by the nature of the questions students were expected to answer in examinations, demanding reasoned argument and a certain amount of playful lateral thinking. Ian MacKillop has described Cambridge's English Literature exams as 'garrulous' in tone, seeing this as epitomising Quiller-Couch's idiosyncratic approach.[82] If this implies a lack of rigour, then MacKillop is rather unfair: the exams certainly demand an amount of intellectual ability, but often not in a form that would be easy to quantify, according to any recognisable disciplinary criteria. The first candidates for the English Tripos were invited to consider 'With the substitution of which of the three characters Rosalind, Celia and Miranda for Desdemona as the wife of Othello would the play have been least likely to culminate in a tragedy?'.[83] A few days later, in the exam on the English Literature from 1785 to 1840, they were asked

'What were the idealistic Utopias of Wordsworth, Shelley, and Blake respectively? Which of these Utopias would you prefer to inhabit, and for what reasons?.'[84] If such questions carry overtones of fireside gossip, it was gossip with an edge. Key verbs in the Cambridge exam papers include 'examine', 'estimate', 'contrast', 'criticize' and 'discuss', all with their suggestions of rational debate, and their explicit invitation of students' own judgements.[85]

At the heart of Quiller-Couch's professorial lectures and writings is an attempt to define the kind of knowledge that such a course would encourage. His response to the objections voiced by Mayo and others was to raise the status of the skills he saw as being fundamental to a true understanding of literature, creating an opposition between the artificial rote-learning of factual information and the less tangible qualities of a more personal appreciation. Students were told that the School of English 'should train men of your age in understanding, rather than test them in memorised information; should teach you less to hoard facts than to deal with them, to sift out what you accumulate and even to accumulate with economy'.[86] An emphasis was placed on the capacity to judge, with the reading of Shakespeare being seen as essential in enabling students to learn 'what the first-rate truly is, and to discern what marks it above the second-, third- and fourth-rate'.[87] They were advised to skip lectures if they felt that their time could be spent more profitably in independent study, and to read literary histories in order to gain 'a general sense' of the relationships between authors and texts rather than to acquire the less important factual details of names and dates.[88] What Quiller-Couch wanted was to facilitate students' first-hand experiences of texts rather than encouraging them to rely on 'massed information which at best can be but derivative and second-hand'.[89] Significantly, this involved a rejection of what were becoming accepted elements of academic practice: the amassing of facts and details, and a knowledge of the work of experts in one's chosen field. In his own tripartite formulation, explained at length in the first lectures in the collection *On the Art of Reading*, 'What Knows' and 'What Does' – the essence of academic and professional life – were to be subordinated to 'What Is', 'the spiritual element in man' that represented a longing for universal harmony surpassing all worldly ambitions.[90] This was clearly a departure from the norms of academic life that were establishing themselves at Cambridge and elsewhere.

Underlying Quiller-Couch's definition of the study of English is a more general concept of what the ideal education should be, resting on an etymological exploration of the word 'education' that in turn challenges the notion that 'knowledge' (as defined and validated by Quiller-Couch) can ever be a professional domain. This sense of the word is articulated in *On the Art of Reading*, in which reading is described as a force that is able to encourage 'that spark, common to the king, the sage, the poorest child – to fan, to draw up to a flame, to "educate" *What Is* – to recognise that it is divine, yet frail, tender'.[91] Education, so Quiller-Couch implies, should be concerned less with the acquisition of a body of knowledge than with 'a leading-out, a drawing-forth' of what is already latent within the individual.[92] This is supported by the use of metaphors of natural growth and the body – of 'incorporating' literary masterpieces within the self – that express how literature should be bound up with individual selfhood and the concept of 'What Is'. Quiller-Couch redefined the notion that intellectual authority was located within a professional system: for him, knowledge was only valued inasmuch as it contributed to the perfection of the soul, and was not to be treated as an external acquisition, a mere scholarly accomplishment.

Of course, a logical consequence of this argument is that as well as questioning the idea that knowledge can be professionalised, it also makes the concrete agents of this professionalisation – universities and professors – redundant. This is a paradox that Quiller-Couch never really managed to resolve. On the one hand, he was convinced of the need for tutors of English, and did much to promote their importance, instructing students to treat their tutors as elder brothers and to seek their advice and companionship.[93] In so doing he was acting in the spirit of the reforms that had altered college life in the Cambridge of the late nineteenth century, promoting the college (and the tutor) as important figures in the life of the undergraduate and the agents of his moral and spiritual welfare.[94] However, this suggests that the tutor's primary role was pastoral rather than pedagogical, concerned with the student's personal and spiritual development rather than with passing on and regulating a clearly defined body of knowledge. For all his insistence on the power of the English Tripos to 'train' and 'teach', Quiller-Couch returned again and again to a model of literary knowledge that valued above all, that which was not teachable, which was innate rather than learned. On several occasions, for example, he conflates education with 'breeding'. His vision of the ideal Cambridge English graduate, described in his inaugural lecture, is of a man who 'will be remarkable less for anything he can produce from his wallet and exhibit for knowledge than for being something, and that something a man of unmistakable breeding, whose judgement can be trusted to choose the better and reject the worse'.[95] When informing students of what their degree would involve, he stated that his intention was to 'train *capacity*, to breed men of a certain intellectual quality rather than to give them, or to expect from them, reams of memorised facts and dates'.[96] In both cases, the shift from education (or training) to breeding is a subtle one, but the emphasis is clearly switched from knowledge gained through learning to a talent that is either there or not there – and if not, cannot be acquired artificially.

The effect of Quiller-Couch's insistence upon innate forms of knowledge and skill is to endow literary study with a certain mystique. This contrasts with the increasing professionalisation of other areas of academic life in that it resists any kind of need to make the skills and knowledge that were central to English objective or easily verifiable. It also insists on a 'specialness' particular to English, marking it out as different from those disciplines whose defining qualities were easy to enumerate. This often leads to a kind of discourse that seems highly reactionary, linking Quiller-Couch to the persona of the Victorian sage. His lectures often have an oracular, sermonic tone that confers a spiritual authority on his words, suggesting that he is communicating truths of an eternal and intuitive kind and thereby heightening the mystique of his role. He also adopts an assumed vagueness that allows him to dispense with facts, hinting again at a superior kind of knowledge. Lectures that purport to deal with the nuts and bolts of elementary education or preparing for exams often digress into prolonged reminiscences and paraphrases: audiences are apostrophised and texts quoted at length, but rarely are straightforward answers given. Moreover, when Quiller-Couch tries to defend the English Tripos against charges of triviality, he does so not by marshalling facts about what students were expected to know and do, but by presenting his audience with an idealised image of what the study of English could provide. Speaking of those critics who scorned the academic study of vernacular literature, he offers a vision of the English School that transforms early twentieth-century Cambridge into classical Greece:

I imagine that, as well-intentioned men, these *a priori* critics would be happy indeed if we and they together could in modern England recreate that spirit of intellectual curiosity, that thirst for truth, that passion for beauty governed by temperance, that energy of experiment in art, politics, poetry and the comely adornments of life, civic, social, domestic and all that efflorescence of the human mind which broke over Hellas in the fifth century B.C., and especially over Athens. [...] If our friends share this hope, let them consider the astonishing fact that all these marvels were achieved by a race which knew its own language and *that language alone*.[97]

The English Tripos at Cambridge therefore seems to have given students much more interpretive freedom than their Oxford counterparts, lacking Oxford's focus on the received critical judgements embedded in the canon and its related version of literary history. Even though the Student Handbook contained lengthy lists of secondary reading – including texts such as A. C. Bradley's *Shakespearean Tragedy* (1904) and C. E. Vaughan's *Types of Tragic Drama* (1908) – it was clear that such reading was of secondary importance, as it was better for the student 'to make himself acquainted at first hand with the leading works of the principal authors in each period than to spend his time on minutiae of literary history and biography or on appreciations by secondary authorities'.[98] While most staff acknowledged the importance of facts over 'vague appreciation', some were sceptical about the value of modern scholarly editions of texts, and particularly about the interpretive assistance (especially in the form of historical and linguistic information) that they offered. Tillyard saw such editions as hiding the 'pure text' and emphasised instead the importance of ideas, linking this to the wider education he hoped students would receive: 'We thought that if a man entered his subject in this way he could learn to deal with the experience of life better than if he had been trained to accumulate the facts of vowel-changes in Middle English dialects or of literary biography.'[99] The scholarly value of such texts was therefore downgraded in favour of a more personal form of understanding.

This gives the impression of a subject that was developing along very different lines from its Oxford equivalent. Moreover, as stated above, this is also a subject that sits uneasily alongside a concept of 'professionalism' as rooted in verifiable knowledge and skills that could be recognised objectively. It does, however, help to explain some of the differences in the content of the two courses. Oxford's insistence on the canon's centrality was countered by Cambridge's more liberal attitude towards the body of texts that constituted 'literature': not only the 'good short story written yesterday', but also other contemporary forms.[100] The 1919 History of English Literature paper at Cambridge includes a question on the Irish literary renaissance of the twentieth century, and invites students to 'Review and estimate the more considerable additions which have been made to English Literature as a result of the war.'[101] In the same year, the Tragedy paper included a question on the condition of malaise in modern theatre;[102] while the following year students were asked to consider the potential of the cinema as a medium for tragic drama.[103] Cambridge's emphasis on judgement over knowledge means that it was entirely logical that students were expected to apply this skill to as wide a range of material as possible. In turn, this flexibility helps to challenge the traditional Marxist view of a fixed canon whose constituent texts were used to promote a certain set of values. Cambridge's course seems strikingly modern in its breadth: the use of contemporary material would require students to see their subject as a living one, changing and developing even as they studied it.

The reasons why such an approach was, and could be, adopted at Cambridge are unclear. Certainly, the university's tutorial system would have fostered the skills of argument and personal judgement that such a programme required; but this does not explain why similar skills were not the focus of teaching and learning at Oxford, where the approach to English seems to have been altogether more cautious. One notable difference, however, seems to have been the role played by Quiller-Couch himself. He seems to have carried out the same kind of 'evangelising' on the subject's behalf as Collins did at Oxford – with the crucial difference being, of course, that while Collins's ideas were rejected by Oxford, Quiller-Couch was able to play a much more active and decisive role at Cambridge. While Oxford's early English degree was defined by its insistence on certain given kinds of knowledge, Cambridge's was marked out by its encouragement of judgement – and with this a set of ideals, about personal development and its place within a university education, that seem in many ways to belong to a much earlier stage in the subject's history.

Tillyard's comments on text-editing offer a useful perspective on these differing philosophies. His objections to the scholarly apparatus of edited texts would not have been accepted at Oxford, where biographical and editorial skills were central to the training of graduate students. By the late 1920s the English Faculty offered classes in bibliography, manuscript work, textual criticism and the history of scholarship to all its graduate students, with this course being described by David Nichol Smith, the Merton Professor of English Literature, as a 'school for editors [. . .] a technical school in which students are instructed in the handling of manuscripts and printed evidence, and in the methods and stages by which our knowledge of our older literature have been accumulated, as well as in the ways and means by which our knowledge may be advanced'.[104] This emphasis on tangible, objective skills can be linked to the mechanisms of professionalisation and specialisation identified by Heyck and Levine: it is evidence of a concern with the ways in which knowledge is acquired and validated. Heyck's use of history as an example of the influence of scientific method on other fields of knowledge, and Levine's more detailed study of the professionalisation of

history, both point to an increasing focus on the verification and interpretation of original sources, the accumulation of bibliographies (central
to the definition of a body of 'required reading' on a particular topic)
and the editing of manuscripts as activities that helped to define the
scope of academic history, distinguishing it from earlier, narrative-driven
forms. The importance of these methods is certainly apparent in
Examiners' Reports on BLitt and DPhil candidates in English Literature.
Students are praised for qualities such as close attention to manuscript
sources,[105] bibliographical skills,[106] close textual study[107] and a wide knowledge of relevant literature,[108] and criticised for a reliance on unsound
editions of texts,[109] 'lack of care in the choice of critical authorities'[110]
and an insufficient knowledge of historical contexts.[111]

However, it seems simplistic to infer (following Heyck and Levine) that
the importing of these skills points to a corresponding rise in the professionalisation of literary criticism. It could, in fact, hint at quite the
opposite, since the wholesale borrowing of historical methodology does
not, in itself, serve to isolate the skills and knowledge that defined literary
criticism. Instead, it threatens to treat literature as just another type of
historical source; for if literature is studied using the same methods and
principles as history, then there is little to justify its existence as an
independent discipline. In fact, the increasing praise of a much less
tangible set of skills may, paradoxically, tell us much more about the
nature of English at Oxford. This praise – of 'independence of judgement',[112] 'critical insight',[113] 'unusually sensitive taste and discernment'[114]
and points that are 'incisively and brilliantly made'[115] – suggests that
while the subject's central skills had not yet been defined in any
systematic way, it was also recognised that there was more to literary
criticism than the objective knowledge offered by textual study and
literary history.

It would be easy to argue that these references were little more than a
throwback to earlier days, to a time when literary criticism was the preserve
of belletrism and gossip. However, the history of Oxford's English
degree suggests that this is not the case. The unease about the intellectual
validity of literary study meant that Oxford's earliest English degree had
been dominated by Old and Middle English texts and an emphasis on
philological knowledge, plus an insistence on history and Classics that
was still enshrined in the First Public Examination. Later, this historical
and Classical background was drawn upon in a more concerted way, as
a means of envisaging and studying the unfolding tradition of English
literature. It is possible that the subjective qualities mentioned in the
Examiners' Reports were not part of a tenacious attempt to cling to aspects

of literary criticism that had been challenged half a century earlier, but were, instead, part of a resurgence: a recognition that the study of literature needed something to distinguish it from its related disciplines, however vaguely this was defined. Seen in this way, such qualities become evidence of literary criticism's complexity, rather than reminders of its 'gossipy' past.

At Cambridge, the reverse was taking place. The personalised style fostered by the English Tripos under Quiller-Couch was beginning to show its limitations: the increasing craving mentioned by Tillyard, for 'something that stuck closer to the text and sought to give reasons for a given literary effect', was the result of a growing dissatisfaction with the impressionism of earlier forms of criticism and the beginning of a movement towards something more objective.[116] One possible alternative would be provided by the Practical Criticism of I. A. Richards, a methodology that sought to remove criticism from a personal context and give it a more scientific basis. Nevertheless, criticism still had some way to go before it would reach this stage. The study of literature may have gained a place within the universities, but the practice of criticism was still not an established part of this study. Indeed, rather than aspiring to academic status, many critics continued to align themselves with the 'amateur' discourse of the men of letters. As a result, literary criticism in the late nineteenth and early twentieth centuries was by no means a unified practice. Instead, as Part II will demonstrate, it drew on a range of methodologies and was underpinned by differing sources of authority, as the knowledge of the amateur was set in opposition to that of the academic.

Part II

Philosophies and Practitioners

3
Critics and Professors

In the last chapter, we saw that a number of models of English were starting to emerge from the earliest degree courses, as staff in the new university departments tried to decide what kind of academic syllabus would be most appropriate to the study of English literature. Wallace Martin has identified three distinct conceptual structures as dominating these early courses – the historical, philological and classical conceptions of literary study[1] – and these structures are clearly supported by the archival research outlined in Chapter 2. The new institutions represented by King's, Nottingham and Manchester were the home of a version of literary study that was dominated by remembered historical facts, while the early course at Oxford had been philological in content. At Cambridge, meanwhile, Quiller-Couch had promoted a version of English that emphasised the continuum between classical and modern civilisations, centring on the power of culture to communicate a humane understanding of life.

More importantly, however, the Cambridge Tripos had also initiated a belief in the centrality of individual judgement and argument that attempted to address the problem of enabling the discipline of English Literature to gain independence from other, related subjects. The conceptual structures outlined above, particularly history and philology, succeeded in making English examinable, but they did not help to make the study of literature an independent academic subject. Philology focused attention on the linguistic properties of Anglo-Saxon and medieval texts, approaching the study of language in a systematic and objective manner. A historical method of organisation gave English a clear chronological shape, and therefore provided a convenient outline for degree courses to follow. However, it often resorted to a reliance on categories of factual knowledge that were not strictly 'literary', treating the text as simply another kind of historical document. A classical philosophy, meanwhile, restored a sense of the 'literariness' of the text but demanded (as at Oxford) that students make a preliminary study of Classics before progressing to English, casting English literature in a subsidiary role. In order for English to be truly independent, it would need to be seen in terms of a self-sufficient body of knowledge with a methodology of its own.

Quiller-Couch's vision of the English Tripos as a vehicle for the encouragement of evaluation and debate, rather than the mere accretion of factual knowledge, was a sign that this new methodology was beginning to emerge; but the nature of this vision – and its timing – raise a number of questions that need to be examined. These questions focus on a broader set of changes (themselves part of the trend towards specialisation) that had taken place in literary criticism during the nineteenth century, and concern the ways in which the activity of criticism was theorised and explained, both for fellow practitioners and for the wider reading public. In the mid-nineteenth century, according to Laurel Brake, the terms 'critic' and 'criticism' functioned in much the same way as the contemporary terms 'reviewer' and 'review', with their connotations of generalist writers, general audiences and subjective judgements.[2] In the second half of the century, the concept of 'criticism' became more specialised, with many critics embarking on attempts to define their role through 'articles in which they grope their way through problems of identity, method and language'.[3] Leslie Stephen, for example, heralded the prospect of a more rigorous critical method in the *Cornhill Magazine* in 1877, stating that

> though criticism cannot boast of being a science, it ought to aim at something like a scientific basis, or at least to proceed in a scientific spirit. The critic, therefore, before abandoning himself to the oratorical impulse, should endeavour to classify the phenomena with which he is dealing as calmly as if he were ticketing a fossil in a museum. The most glowing eulogy, the most bitter denunciation have their proper place; but they belong to the art of persuasion, and form no part of scientific method.[4]

Such definitions suggest that a more rigorous, specialised form of criticism had begun to emerge well before the foundation of the Cambridge Tripos. Furthermore, the popularity of volumes of collected critical essays, such as Leslie Stephen's *Hours in a Library* (1874) and George Saintsbury's *Miscellaneous Essays* (1892), also hints that there was a readership for criticism that treated such essays as more than just occasional writing. Yet if criticism was becoming a more specialised activity, with practitioners who sought to give it an increasingly scientific rationale and methodology, why had it not been included in any of the degree courses that were founded before 1917? If the reasons for its exclusion were so persuasive, why was it that Quiller-Couch was able to give it such a central role in the English course at Cambridge? And was the English Tripos successful in establishing a different kind of conceptual structure for the study of English: did it solve the problems associated with making literary criticism part of an academic discipline?

The next three chapters will attempt to address these questions by setting the development of these early English degrees in the context of wider debates about the function of literature and the nature of the reading process. These debates will include, specifically, the issue of criticism's role in bringing about social and spiritual harmony, developed in detail in the work of Matthew Arnold; the belief in the importance of aesthetic experience that was formulated by Walter Pater; and the insistence on the difficulty of understanding 'high' culture that formed an important element of Modernist philosophy.

My decision to focus on Arnold requires some explanation, given my earlier acknowledgement of the misgivings about Arnold's status within the disciplinary history of English that have been raised by Franklin Court. While I endorse court's view that Arnold has been 'dehistoricised', to some extent, by political interpretations of the subject's history, Arnold is nevertheless a crucial figure: in drawing attention to the role of criticism within society, he raised the profile of both literary criticism and literary critics. Later in the century, Walter Pater performed a similar function, drawing attention to the intellectual rigour involved in the critical process. On a number of other points – as I shall discuss later in this chapter – Arnold and Pater differed radically. Even so, what they shared with each other – and with the Modernists – was a belief that the critical process was essentially unteachable, and this similarity is crucial to the next phase of my discussion. In the next two chapters, I will argue that the central problem facing literary criticism was the fact that the rationalism sought by Leslie Stephen – that of a discipline motivated by a 'scientific spirit' – was by no means universally accepted or practised: that debates about literary criticism in the late nineteenth and early twentieth centuries were problematised by continually-contested perceptions of what criticism was, what it was supposed to achieve and who was best equipped to carry it out. The philosophies of Arnold, Pater and the Modernists stood at odds with the need to define a paradigm for the study of English as a systematic and clearly defined academic discipline. Nevertheless, they also helped to shape an important philosophy of resistance that was embraced by many critics and academics of the late nineteenth and early twentieth centuries. Put simply, this philosophy rested on the paradoxical belief that while criticism was important enough to warrant a place within the universities, it also rested on special qualities that set it apart from other academic disciplines. As a result, it did not need to fulfil the same criteria as other subjects: if it were to be restricted to these criteria alone, a large part of its 'specialness' would be lost.

Literary criticism: The influence of scholarship

These attempts to define the nature of literary knowledge took place in a society where the audience for, and purpose of, literary criticism were undergoing a number of changes. A brief outline of these changes will enable the debates about criticism to be set in context, and illuminate the source of many of the tensions that surrounded them: the changing nature of intellectual authority, brought about by the professionalisation and specialisation of disciplines of knowledge.

Before its entry into the professionalised environment of the universities, literary criticism was the preserve of the generalist writers known as the 'men of letters', who ranged from important public figures such as Bagehot, Mill and Carlyle to a shifting group of writers who scraped an income from the 'hack-work' of reviewing. Typically, the man of letters wrote for an educated readership, and published his work in journals and magazines. The major Victorian periodicals – including the *Edinburgh Review, Macmillan's Magazine*, the *Fortnightly Review*, the *Cornhill Magazine* and the *Athenaeum*[5] – were bought by libraries and reading rooms as well as private individuals, making precise readership numbers difficult to determine: circulation figures of between 7200 (for the *Athenaeum* in 1854) and 20,000 (for the *Cornhill Magazine* in the 1870s) conceal an audience that may have been several times higher. Their audience was, nevertheless, 'a relatively unified group, intelligent, educated, middle-class and serious-minded', keen to be kept informed of a range of topics which included not only literature (itself a much broader category than it is today) but also history, politics, religion and economics.[6]

The paradigm of disciplinary development offered by Heyck sees the decline of these men of letters as a direct result of the processes of professionalisation and specialisation. These processes were, in turn, part of a wider set of changes in nineteenth-century cultural and intellectual life. As the century progressed, a series of educational, technological and economic developments altered the constitution of the reading public, with increasing levels of literacy leading to its growth and fragmentation. These developments were assisted – and capitalised upon – by the invention of cheaper methods of printing and the emergence of publications aimed at the mass market, from popular fiction to Harmsworth's *Daily Mail*. The subsequent division between what can simplistically be termed 'high' and 'low' culture led to the creation of several different 'reading publics', each representing a different section of the market. The men of letters could no longer rely on a stable reading public with a homogeneous set of values, or assume that the topics they had covered in the middle of the century would still be accessible and of interest to all.[7]

In addition, the processes of professionalisation and specialisation meant that disciplines of knowledge – and the intellectual authority associated with them – were being transferred from the public sphere of the knowledgeable generalist to the narrower arena of the academic institution. Consequently, disciplines of knowledge such as history and the social sciences became characterised by a growing focus on particular areas of learning, the adoption of new methodologies and the addressing of a professional peer group made up of other specialists in the field. What was valued, in short, was no longer the knowledge represented by the impressionistic, narrative-based judgements of the men of letters, rooted in the concept of the author as moral authority or 'sage', but the knowledge of the expert, marked out by careful research and the use of certain methods and conventions. On a simple level, these methods were used to ensure objectivity and a lack of bias, but they also included a change in style: many experts also wrote in a manner that was designed to differentiate their work from that of the generalists, ensuring that it was no longer accessible to readers who lacked specialist knowledge.[8]

It is true that literary criticism witnessed a concomitant set of changes, and that by 1880 the 'professional' methods of the academic were beginning to be used in a number of books and articles about literature, even those ostensibly aimed at a generalist audience. Such texts turned away from the judgements implied by the term 'criticism', and focused instead on those areas of literary study that could draw most closely on the examination of primary material: literary history and biography, and text-editing. A review of David Masson's *The Life of John Milton*, published in the *Athenaeum* in March 1880, drew on the new methods of historical enquiry to challenge Masson's characterisation of Milton as a heroic, Blakean outcast, marshalling documentary evidence relating to Milton's arrest and the events of 1660 to support the refutation of Masson's portrait.[9] In the same month, James Spedding's article in the *Cornhill Magazine* on 'The Story of *The Merchant of Venice*' dealt with the question of sources and textual provenance, carrying out a detailed comparative study of Shakespeare's play and Giovanni's *Il Pecorone*, and discussing different editions of Shakespeare's texts, including the Clarendon Press edition and Collier's *Shakespeare's Library*.[10] While the men of letters were often compelled to write from memory, sacrificing accuracy to tight deadlines and narrative interest, the new practitioners of a more 'scientific' form of criticism – a group that included both journalists and professors – were able to prioritise scholarly precision and a more sustained examination of the available evidence.

This shift towards academic practice may have been occasioned by editorial policy. Laurel Brake notes that from the 1870s, the *Athenaeum* began to assign work to reviewers with specialist knowledge of particular fields, rather than to generalists.[11] Nevertheless, the *Athenaeum* also seems to have tried to maintain the eclecticism on which it had long prided itself, appealing to generalist as well as specialist readers. An anonymous review of Rhoda Broughton's *Second Thoughts*, published in the *Athenaeum* three months after the review of Masson's *Life of Milton* quoted above, exemplifies the techniques of the man of letters: its author's description of Broughton's 'impassioned jerkiness and boisterous and ornate familiarity' and depiction of the novel's hero as 'plain, rude, somewhat shrill, uncommonly virtuous and earnest and well informed, a sort of jumble of reminiscences of Jane Eyre's Rochester, the coffee palace movement, and the *Contemporary Review*' bear all the hallmarks of an evaluative essay designed to inform and entertain the well-read generalist.[12]

In the early twentieth century, many of the great Victorian periodicals were affected by closure, mergers or declining sales. The *Gentleman's Magazine* and *Westminster Review* both folded in 1914, and were followed by the *Fortnightly Review* in 1934; the *Athenaeum* merged with the *Nation* in 1921 and was taken over by the *New Statesman* a decade later. The *Nineteenth Century*, a high literary periodical that was heavily influenced by the theological and ethical debate of the Metaphysical Society, closed in 1900. Other periodicals, such as the *Cornhill Magazine*, changed to accommodate the demands of a new kind of audience. Under the editorship of Leslie Stephen – who, as noted above, sought to give criticism a more scientific basis – the magazine had been noted for being 'liberally interfused with literary criticism of a high class'.[13] Its contributors included John Churton Collins, Edmund Gosse, J. W. Hales and Sidney

Colvin, and *Culture and Anarchy, Literature and Dogma* and *Unto this Last* had made their first appearance in its pages. Even so, its circulation had fallen and it was relaunched in July 1883 as a more generalist publication, devoting itself to fiction, poetry and articles on more lightweight topics. Meanwhile, the *Academy*, founded in 1869 by the young Oxford don Charles Appleton as 'an authoritative intellectual organ to which serious readers could turn for reliable judgments on matters of high culture', became lighter in tone after 1874 and dwindled into a state of 'respectability and dullness' after 1910.[14] Some of the more 'academic' journals had even shorter runs: the *Reader*, founded in 1863 and seen by Christopher Kent and John F. Byrne as 'a self-consciously academic literary weekly' that appealed to a 'highly educated, politically liberal, and philosophically radical' audience, lasted for only four years.[15] As literary criticism lost its generalist audience, the next generation of literary periodicals took the form not of academic journals, but of the 'little magazines' of Modernism: publications such as *The English Review* (founded 1908), *Rhythm* (1911) and *The Blue Review* (1913), whose small circulations testify to both the increasing specialisation of literary criticism and the perceived obscurity of Modernist debate.[16]

Specialist academic writing would eventually find a home in the discipline-based journals such as *The Year's Work in English Studies* (founded in 1921) and the *Review of English Studies* (1925), although it is significant to note that these lagged behind their counterparts in other fields by some forty to fifty years: *Nature* was founded in 1869, *Mind* in 1870 and the *English Historical Review* in 1886. Yet the emergence of increasingly 'academic' forms of criticism – in both articles and longer works – was not universally accepted. Many critics felt that its emphasis of research and objectivity threatened the special nature of literature. This opposition had been evident in the polarisation of the 'light literaries' and the pedants of philology in the debate about the Merton Professorship at Oxford, and persisted in the distaste with which scholars were depicted by writers such as Virginia Woolf, typified by the 'ungentlemanly' student who 'mak[es] the neatest abstracts' but nevertheless 'breathes hard, wears a ready-made tie, and has not shaved this fortnight'.[17] Such disapproval was often rooted in snobbery rather than in methodological differences: the expansion of the professions meant that the academic gained his status through a different kind of social configuration than that which rested on the older hierarchy of birth. It also drew on a more specific sense of anxiety about how academic literary criticism was carried out, and for what purpose – as well as who 'owned' criticism and the knowledge that it produced. Even after literary criticism became a part of institutional syllabuses, its place there was questioned by a number of writers, both inside and outside the universities, who felt that its benefits could not be reduced to a regulated process of scholarship and research. Stephen Potter, author of *The Muse in Chains*, characterised 'Ing. Lit' as 'the study of the externals of English Literature, from plots to punctuation, in which the educative function of literature, its unique power of expressing, with every degree of directness, absolute difference in men, and the subtle processes by which these differences are achieved, is lost sight of'.[18] Stanley Leathes, who helped to reshape the Civil Service examinations in English in the early twentieth century, felt nonetheless that 'there is danger in submitting the delicate flowers of English literature to the methods of the lecture room, the schedules and tests of the examination room. If in any conditions English literature is being spontaneously studied, it is best to leave those conditions alone.'[19]

Leathes's elevation of 'amateur' values over those of the 'professional' rested on a belief that the kinds of knowledge possessed by the amateur were more genuine than those gained through academic study, which threatened to stifle literature's humanising power. Other critics shared these feelings, and expressed them in a series of meditations on the value of a scientific approach to literary criticism. In an article published in the *Quarterly Review* in 1886, John Churton Collins attacked Edmund Gosse for his failure to adhere to standards of scholarly accuracy in his book *From Shakespeare to Pope*, enumerating a range of mistakes such as errors of chronology, the misidentification of various authors and the designation of certain prose works as poems. For Collins, such errors were 'not mere slips of the pen', but the result of ignorance, a sign of the disregard in which serious literary study was held by both Oxford and Cambridge. Nevertheless, while Collins was convinced that the study of literature was 'worthy of minute, of patient, of systematic study', he was also cautious about taking such an approach to extremes, railing against the 'repulsive' annotation of 'some historical allusion [...] some problem in antiquities, or [...] wholly superfluous parallel passages'. His critique of the Clarendon Press editions of the English Classics turned on his belief that its method of annotation was 'not [...] calculated either to enlarge a youth's mind or to refine his taste; it is still less calculated to awaken rational curiosity, or to inspire a love of literature for its own sake; but, regarded as a mode of discipline, it may possibly, in some cases, be of service in forming and confirming habits of accuracy'.[20] Ironically, Collins's scepticism about the validity of a scholarly approach was shared by Gosse himself, who used the extended metaphor of a chemical reaction to show the unsuitability of quasi-scientific forms of criticism:

Within the last quarter of a century, systems by which to test the authenticity and the chronology of the plays have been produced with great confidence, metrical formulas which are to act as reagents and to identify the component parts of a given passage with scientific exactitude. Of these 'verse-texts' and 'pause-texts' no account can here be given. That the results of their employment have been curious and valuable shall not be denied; but there is already manifest in the gravest criticism a reaction against excess of confidence in them. At one time it was supposed that the 'end-stopt' criterium, for instance, might be dropped, like a chemical substance, on the page of Shakespeare, and would there immediately and finally determine minute quantities of Peele or Kyd, that a fragment of Fletcher would turn purple under it, or a greenish tinge betray a layer of Rowley. It is not thus that poetry is composed; and this ultra-scientific theory showed a grotesque ignorance of the human pliability of art.[21]

For Gosse, the special nature of art meant that science was too gross and unsophisticated a method to be applied to its study, blurring the more subtle knowledge that could be gained through a sensitive exploration of the literary text's human dimensions. Meanwhile, W. P. Ker, who was Professor of Literature at Cardiff from 1883 to 1889 and subsequently Quain Professor at University College, London, articulated his own belief in the special status of literature through his feeling that the literary critic should maintain 'a certain dignity' that was not commensurate with a move towards a more scientific methodology. A concern for the minutiae of scholarly conventions was seen by Ker as a distasteful intrusion:

Books of Science are often very ugly. They have a trick of scattering symbols over their pages. Our philosophers, who ought to know better, have caught this ugly trick. Locke, Berkeley and Hume had more self-respect than to patch themselves with algebra – like Mr. W. S. Jevons and Mr. F. H. Bradley and others. Modern psychologists again will consort with medical students and bring away nasty things out of the dissecting rooms. The older generation had many friends in the faculty of medicine, but they were treated like men of the world; there was no prurient curiosity about the *arcana* of the profession.[22]

Ker even complained about the systems of referencing – 'the classification, the naming, the scientific apparatus' – that had 'spoilt' Alexander Bain's 'Emotional Qualities of Style', claiming rather haughtily that 'No work can stand high as literature that allows itself to jumble up large type and small type on the same page. The Germans do it, but we know what the Germans are.'[23]

These reactions against scientific methodology should not, however, be taken as signs of a wholesale move towards a reactionary bellettrism. If the professional authority represented by literary scholarship was viewed as unfavourable (even by some members of the profession itself), it at least made critics aware of a need to defend and define their own methods, often in the form of a search for some kind of accommodation with the demands of objective accuracy. The writer George Saintsbury's mistrust of 'the merely dilettante and "tasting" critic' hinted at a desire for a more rigorous form of critical practice which acknowledged the value of the new scholarship in enabling the critic to 'hunt the fugitive by a closer trail than usual through the chambers of her flight'.[24] Saintsbury regretted that philology had 'claim[ed] the term "scholarship" exclusively for itself', as this led to an opposition between philology and literary study that left the latter to a 'looser æsthetics', and to those who 'consider themselves entitled to neglect scholarship in any proper sense with a similarly scornful indifference'. While he felt that literature could 'never be scientific', what he sought was a return to a form of critical enquiry which drew on the 'sufficiently minute' yet 'still clung to the literary side proper', retaining a sense of the perceived 'difference' of literature that set it apart from other fields of knowledge.[25]

Matthew Arnold and Walter Pater

The distinction between the differing philosophies of literary study that was becoming apparent in both general critical discourse and the early English degrees has been described by Wallace Martin in terms of the opposition between 'scholarship', a concern with the accumulation and analysis of knowledge along scientific lines; and 'criticism', a more evaluative approach that drew on an older, humanist conception of literature. For Martin, exponents of these methods were, effectively, 'representatives of different conceptions of knowledge': while scholars aligned themselves with 'canons of truth current in the natural sciences', critics inclined towards 'alternative models of understanding' that privileged moral and aesthetic conceptions of 'truth' and an imaginative engagement with the text.[26] The status given to literature by this latter group owed much to the work of Matthew Arnold and Walter Pater, whose critical philosophies can be traced in the debates about academic English that were advanced by a number of its early professors. Arnold and Pater differed in a number of important respects – Arnold advocated a belief in the power of criticism to act as a disinterested force able to restore social harmony, while Pater emphasised the essential autonomy of the aesthetic experience – yet crucially, what they shared was the belief that criticism depended on skills that could neither be taught, nor reduced to the narrowness of an academic specialism.

The fact that both Arnold and Pater occupied academic posts makes this belief in the 'unteachability' of criticism particularly significant. Both held Fellowships at Oxford colleges (Arnold at Oriel and Pater at Brasenose), although, as Stefan Collini points out, 'such Fellowships were in those days prizes, not the first steps in an academic career'.[27] Arnold was appointed Inspector of Schools in 1851 and was also Professor of Poetry at Oxford from 1857 to 1867, a post he used as a forum for his lectures on literary and social criticism. Yet in neither of these posts was he actually required to teach literary criticism: moreover, his lectures on literary criticism emphasised criticism's general functions rather than making a plea for increased academic specialisation. Such specialisation was also rejected by Pater, whose work presents what Ian Small has described as a deliberate challenge to the norms of scholarship that were becoming established at Oxford and elsewhere: 'the authority for the type of criticism he was practising resided in the sensibility of the critic, and not in any body of specialist fact or theory'.[28]

Arnold's version of criticism stemmed directly from his sense of its social urgency. His defence of the critical spirit – a force that in his work is metaphorised, variously, as 'sweetness and light', a 'fresh and free play' of the mind and the Hellenic spirit of 'see[ing] things as they really are'[29] – was fuelled by his anxiety over years of self-interest in industry, economics and politics, and by increasing tensions between the established Church and representatives of dissenting factions. The unrest that followed the second Reform Bill of 1866 heightened his sense of the need to counteract the philosophy of 'doing as one likes' and put in its place a sense of the overarching value of social harmony and the kinds of activity that could bring it into being. This meant that criticism, for Arnold, could never be a narrowly academic exercise. It is true that he saw it as needing to be underpinned by a 'scientific passion' for 'pure knowledge' – only thus could it maintain its rigour and avoid the relativism that had, in Arnold's eyes, caused so much damage throughout public life – but this drive for knowledge should not be allowed to take precedence over what Arnold saw as criticism's most important function, the promotion of 'the moral and social passion for doing good'.[30] In short, criticism was too important to be confined to the universities: it would only be able to carry out its duties if it belonged to the general sphere of public life.

Arnold's defence of criticism was also an attempt to address some of the objections voiced by its detractors. Many of these objections circulated around the belief that criticism was a self-indulgent symptom of a decadent society, a parasite that was inherently inferior to the acts of creation on which it relied.[31] Arnold's belief that culture could not be reduced to a mere 'smattering of Greek and Latin' and that both criticism and culture needed to be held up as a vision to remind people that 'the perfection of human nature is sweetness and light' formed an important part of this defence. He was also keen to refute Frederic Harrison's association of criticism with pettiness, indolence and a philosophy of 'small fault-finding, love of selfish ease, and indecision in action', relevant only to 'a critic of new books or a professor of *belles-lettres*'.[32] Nevertheless, Arnold was reluctant to describe the act of criticism in specific terms, and this reluctance means that in his writing criticism remains a vague concept, comprehensible only to a closed circle of individuals. While Arnold states, repeatedly, that criticism consists of 'the free play of the mind', he never gives a detailed account of what this process might involve, and therefore fails to set out a precise methodology for the accomplishment of his vision. Instead, the strategy he adopts is one of assuming that the skilled critic will simply recognise what he is referring to without needing it to be defined, almost as if he is protecting what Baldick has described as an 'intellectual trade secret'.[33] When Arnold states, evasively, that 'the grand style is the last matter in the world for verbal definition to deal with adequately [...] One must feel it in order to know what it is', he effectively creates a closed community of potential critics who share his sense of appreciation and his capacity to single out 'the best which has been thought and said'.[34] And crucially, such a community is defined not in terms of its professional skills and qualifications, but by its possession of a particular sensibility. The qualities that enable the individual to be a critic appear to be gained as if by birth, rather than being developed through the organised and systematic structures that were being put in place to regulate other disciplines of knowledge.

Pater's vision of the ideal critic took a different form, but ultimately he shared both Arnold's sense of urgency and his belief that criticism was an activity that could not be taught. For Pater, this urgency stemmed from his awareness of the increasing commodification of culture and the threat this posed to the 'cloistral refuge' represented by fine art.[35] In *The Renaissance*, Pater presents aesthetic objects as offering a form of experience that was both rich and varied, standing in marked contrast to the vulgarity of the world at large: such objects included 'the picture, the landscape, the engaging personality in life or in a book, *La Gioconda*, the hills of Carrara, Pico of Mirandola [...] a herb, a wine, a gem'. The critical process was important in enabling the individual to determine the precise nature of the impressions presented by these objects, and to discriminate ever more closely between the different kinds of experience that life offered them: in Pater's philosophy, 'our education becomes complete in proportion, as our susceptibility to these impressions increases in depth and variety'.[36]

One important strand of Pater's critical thought is the intellectual rigour involved in this discriminatory process, with the critic needing to possess a certain alertness to the demands of the aesthetic object. When reading, the critic needed to be aware of the 'challenge for minute consideration' presented by the author's command of language, recognising that 'it is worth the reader's while to be attentive [...] the writer is dealing scrupulously with his instrument, and therefore, indirectly, with the reader himself also'.[37] Such activity could be enjoyable, as it offered a 'pleasurable stimulus' to 'really strenuous minds', but this pleasure clearly differed from the more immediate satisfaction offered by popular culture, involving an appreciation of

> self-restraint, a skilful economy of means, *ascêsis* [...] that frugal economy of style which makes the most of a word in the exaction from every sentence of a precise relief, in the just spacing out of a word to thought in the logically filled space connected always with the delightful sense of a difficulty overcome.[38]

'High' culture demanded that the critic must make a certain effort in order to do justice to the artist: indeed, part of its value stemmed from this very difficulty.

Given his opposition to the norms of academic practice, it is significant that Pater often borrowed the language of academic discourse to articulate his sense of the rigour involved in aesthetic perception, referring to the 'science' involved in the writer's control of language and the 'scholarly attentiveness of mind' required by the critic.[39] Nevertheless, this appreciation ultimately belonged to a personal world that lay beyond the bounds of academic analysis. Aesthetic judgements were related not to the verifiable facts prioritised by the 'scientific rule' of the new academic disciplines, but to a kind of truth that Pater characterised as 'fact [...] connected with soul',[40] requiring for their appreciation 'a certain kind of temperament [. . .] the power of being deeply moved by the presence of beautiful objects', rather than 'a certain abstract definition of beauty for the intellect'.[41] This emphasis on 'soul-fact' is apparent in the vagueness of Pater's critical vocabulary, a lexicon that Adam Phillips has described as being 'evocative by being unspecific': 'His indefinite words, "sweet," "peculiar," "strange," "delicate," are resonant as blanks that can evoke powerful personal associations in the reader.'[42] This evocative sense is perhaps most apparent in the Conclusion to *The Renaissance*, in which the fleeting, idiosyncratic nature of aesthetic experience is described in a manner that recreates the sense of trying to pin down an impression that is ultimately elusive:

> Experience, already reduced to a group of impressions, is ringed round for each one of us by that thick wall of personality through which no real voice has ever pierced on its way to us, or from us to that which we can only conjecture to be without. Every one of those impressions is the impression of the individual in his isolation, each mind keeping as a solitary prisoner its own dream of a world [. . .] Analysis goes a step further still, and tells us that those impressions of the individual mind to which, for each one of us, experience dwindles down, are in perpetual flight; that each of them is limited by time, and that as time is infinitely divisible, each of them is infinitely divisible also; all that is actual in it being a single moment, gone while we try to apprehend it, of which it may ever be more truly said that it has ceased to be than that it is. To such a tremulous wisp constantly reforming itself on the stream, to a single sharp impression, with a sense in it, a relic more or less fleeting, of such moments gone by, what is real in our life fines itself down. It is with the movement, the passage and dissolution of impressions, images, sensations, that analysis leaves off – that continual vanishing away, that strange perpetual weaving and unweaving of ourselves.[43]

By using such techniques, Pater not only emphasises the value of the aesthetic in terms that can be related to the reader's own experience, but also foregrounds an 'inwardness of response' that separates the aesthetic from the structured objectivity of academic analysis. And Pater's description of this experience shares the same suggestive vagueness as Arnold's account of the 'Grand Style': he invites his readers to identify with the experience he presents to them while also refusing to define this experience in concrete terms. While Pater demands a great deal of rigour from the critic himself, he also places criticism in a private world beyond theorisation and analysis, described in terms that would make it recognisable only to those who were already aware of its value.

Arnold and Pater's denial that criticism could (or should) be taught and examined in conventional academic ways lent support to a number of critics who were trying to resist institutional attempts to define literary knowledge in objective, factual terms. The fact that these critics worked both inside and outside the universities means that any attempt to see the institutionalisation of English in terms of a Heyckian paradigm of professionalisation and specialisation must be treated with caution. Rather than undergoing a straightforward assimilation into academic structures, criticism was the subject of ongoing debates as to what it involved, who was to carry it out and what kind of knowledge it was to produce: it continued to be practised outside the universities, and was underpinned by differing concepts of intellectual authority. These questions were complicated further by the notion of audience. Academics in other disciplines (such as law, medicine or the sciences) produced knowledge that was used on behalf of the general public, but not by members of the public themselves: instead, it was used by other academics and professionals, who acted as a medium through which knowledge was diffused and put to work. Academics in these fields were therefore writing for their professional peer group, rather than the public at large. Yet the audience for literary criticism was unclear. The critics of the mid-nineteenth century had written for the general public, to promote and explicate texts to a wider audience. The decline of the generalist periodicals and the changes in periodical criticism discussed earlier in this chapter indicate that this audience was diminishing. Nevertheless, the continuing adherence to sources of personal authority suggests that this broader audience was still an important presence in critics' minds. If criticism was justified in Arnoldian terms, with reference to its social, moral and spiritual role, then its utility would depend on its readership – and to reach a general audience, criticism would, of course, need to be non-specialist.

This heterogeneity of audiences and approaches serves to problematise the clear outlines of Heyck's paradigm of professionalisation. The new techniques developed in history and the social sciences were sometimes drawn upon by critics working outside the universities, while the evaluative methods of the men of letters were also used by some of the new professors and lecturers. As a result, any notional gap between the 'professionals' working within university departments and the 'amateurs' who continued to operate outside academia is difficult to detect in practice. An alternative set of terms – based on the abstract concept of authority, rather than the concrete fact of institutional employment – is supplied by Ian Small's distinction between 'personal' and 'professional' forms of authority. Small argues that as intellectual authority was progressively removed from the hands of the individual and relocated in the institutional structures of the new academic disciplines, critics operating both inside and outside these institutions tried to sustain a belief in the existence of a more personal form of authority, making use of rhetorical techniques (such as the use of paradox and dialogue, an ambivalence in the handling of sources and a foregrounding of the authorial persona) which reasserted the individual's claim to prominence. We have already seen, for instance, how Pater (an Oxford don) emphasised the importance of 'fact [...] connected with soul' over the objective facts prioritised by the sciences, and how his insistence on accurate distinctions and fine discriminations was balanced by a reliance on impressionism and vagueness: while Phillips sees this in terms of a lack of rigour and 'an absurd and characteristic disregard for [his] subjects',[44] Small is careful to define it as a conscious rejection of the 'paraphernalia and devices' of contemporary scholarly practices, and 'an attempt to relocate the authority for the assessment and appreciation of a work of art within the individual'.[45]

The concept of personal authority, which continued to influence critics well into the twentieth century, produced literary criticism of a markedly different kind to that which was underwritten by the developing professional norms of the universities, distinguished by the type of knowledge that it privileged, the judgements it made and even the nature of its rhetoric. Significantly, this type of criticism was produced by a wide range of critics, both inside and outside the universities. The impression produced by this movement towards personal authority is of an attempt to remove criticism from the increasingly objective, scholarly direction in which it was being taken by activities such as text-editing and literary history, and to restore the importance of the personal relationship between text and reader, meaning that criticism was still available to the general audiences discussed above. In turn, of course, this movement problematised attempts to locate criticism exclusively within the universities: many of criticism's advocates – and even, ironically, many of the new professors of English – produced accounts of criticism that rendered it practically unteachable.

The remainder of this chapter will take the form of an exploration of how personal and professional sources of authority were drawn on by a range of critics in the late nineteenth and early twentieth centuries. It will consider, first of all, the philosophies of criticism advanced by some of English's earliest professors, before moving on to the fields of literary history and the criticism of Shakespeare – two areas in which the authority that underpinned literary judgements was particularly heavily contested. What this exploration will reveal is that criticism was often used to comment on and undermine the methods and procedures that literary scholarship was putting into place: what this ultimately indicates is that the professionalisation of criticism and the institutionalisation of English were two very different processes.

The new professors and professional criticism

The careers of many of the early professors of English blur the boundaries between the terms 'amateur' and 'professional'. The literary historian W. J. Courthope was a civil servant and assistant editor of the *National Review* before becoming Professor of Poetry at Oxford (although this was an honorary post rather than one that carried 'professional' academic status); George Saintsbury worked as a schoolmaster and journalist until his election to the post of Professor of Rhetoric and English Literature at Edinburgh; and Edmund Gosse had a varied career as translator, biographer and transcriber at the British Museum before being elected Clark Lecturer at Cambridge. Indeed, the structure of professorial stipends (which, at some institutions, were calculated on an hourly basis) meant that some of the new class of academics were forced to continue their journalistic writing in order to make a living. Professors and men of letters often engaged in the same kinds of intellectual activity, such as text-editing, biography and literary history, and publishing enterprises such as Macmillan's 'English Men of Letters' series, whose first editor was the politician and man of letters John Morley, brought together representatives of both spheres in producing critical biographies intended to appeal to both the student and the general public. Given the varied nature of their careers, it is hardly surprising that many of these professors continued to draw on the personal authority that had underpinned their work as men of letters, and that they adopted strategies – such as the creation of a certain kind of authorial persona, and the addressing of a wide and non-specialist audience – that gave their writing a distinctly generalist tone.

A number of the subject's early professors were also engaged in more direct challenges to the authority of the institution, of the kind outlined earlier in this chapter. W. P. Ker's suspicion about the application of scholarly methods of research, analysis and presentation is also apparent in the work of Sir Walter Raleigh, who became Oxford's first solely literary professor – the Merton Professor of English Literature – in 1904. Raleigh devoted much of his career to challenging the norms of academic analysis that were being established in other disciplines, and was also sceptical about the claims made on behalf of literature by writers such as Arnold and Churton Collins. Chris Baldick describes him as being contemptuous of the institutionalised study of literature and prizing 'what he took to be the real human presence of an author over against the boring technicalities of literary works themselves', with his cynical attitude arising from 'a very clear-headed understanding of the ridiculousness of literary culture's ambitions for bringing about social change'.[46] Certainly, Raleigh was dubious about the value of the 'systems, rules, standards, and principles' of academic analysis, and felt that the claims made on behalf of textual scholarship were misleading, describing its results as 'command[ing] no general assent, and depend[ing], for the most part, on a chain of ingenious hypotheses'.[47] His successor, George Gordon, echoed these sentiments, hoping to rescue literary study from the 'nightmare of organized boredom'[48] represented by German scholarship. For Gordon, English was too important a subject to concern itself with the minutiae of academic life. Its preoccupation with scholarship was an 'unlovely adolescence' that would soon (so Gordon hoped) give way to the subject's 'manhood', a time 'when a maturer scholarship shall make amends to life, when, even in literary treatises, a smile shall play about the lips of truth, and learning, having digested (preferably in concealment) the accumulations of a century, shall be once more polite'.[49] This 'politeness', recalling both Arnold's 'disinterestedness' and Ker's emphasis on the need to preserve 'a certain dignity', offered to return criticism to a position of social removal that challenges ideologically motivated readings of disciplinary history: Gordon's attack on the Newbolt Report and 'the growth of a religious jargon about literature and literary genius'[50] was motivated by his doubts about the moral and social benefits of literature, and his feeling that for many working people, the pressures of everyday life were so great that literature was at worst irrelevant, and at best a luxury that was easily dispensed with.

Gordon's dismissal of the Arnoldian concept of the civilising power of literature can be seen as embodying one of two opposing strands of thought about the nature of criticism that were voiced by its early professors, deriving from the philosophies of Arnold and Pater. These two views can be interpreted as emphasising, respectively, a 'public' conception of literature (as both a civilising force, and a way of keeping alive 'the best which has been thought and said') and an opposing, 'private' conception, in which the reading of literature becomes a solipsistic act that need justify itself only to the individual. Despite their underlying differences, both philosophies shared a sense of anxiety about the value of literary scholarship, and it is significant that their proponents often drew on similar arguments and rhetorical techniques, offering a covert challenge to the objective methods of academia. Two of these proponents were W. P. Ker and A. C. Bradley, and a detailed consideration of their critical philosophies will show how these Arnoldian and Paterian tendencies were borne out in practice.

Ker's critical stance was Arnoldian in nature. His vision of literary criticism as 'executor to a dead genius'[51] recalls Arnold's emphasis of 'the best which has been thought and said' and also defines it as a generalist activity aimed at a non-specialist readership, in contrast to the increasingly specialised nature of other kinds of academic writing. The mistrust that he displayed for scientific methods of presentation and research was accompanied by the sense that scientific writing could be excused its uncouthness, as it would be read only by other scientists: literary criticism, with its more general audience, was called on to provide a kind of guidance that surpassed mere scholarly knowledge, and should therefore strive to maintain its dignity. Such a dignity gave Ker's ideal critic a mystique that was closer to that of the Victorian sage than to the newly professionalised academic.

This mystique was heightened by the nature of the task that the critic had to fulfil. In outlining this task, Ker gave a clear indication as to his view of the role of scholarly methods in literary study: they were to be little more than tools, and not the ends in themselves that some academics believed them to be. The distinction between generalist and academic criticism that Ker drew in his inaugural lecture seemed initially to favour the latter, which was described as 'infinitely more interesting' and praised for its incorporation of the advances made in other disciplines. However, Ker was also anxious to define disciplines of knowledge in a manner that played down the importance of academic specialism, and saw them instead in terms of the humanist understanding they could offer.[52] In a passage that recalls Arnold's emphasis on the need to yoke 'scientific passion' with 'the moral and social passion for doing good', Ker states that while literary criticism, history and the natural sciences all drew on 'methods of observation' and a 'regard for the minutest particulars bearing on their study', such methods were only valuable for their potential to offer a 'sense of the vastness of the world, and the power of time to work changes'. Such a sense, significantly, could be provided by a range of different writers – by scientists such as Darwin, and also by 'historians [...] poets and romancers', a list that becomes increasingly non-specialist as it progresses.[53] Ker therefore diminished the importance of the structured and systematic accumulation of knowledge associated with academic specialism, and asserted instead a more abstract objective – the enlargement of a student's appreciation of the world – which could be produced by many 'widely different subject matters'. Developments in academic methodology were not seen as a means of adding to the specialist knowledge associated with the new disciplines, but as a way of validating a vision of the world that could ultimately be produced, so Ker claimed, by any discipline. In essence, the specialist knowledge that distinguished one subject from another was denied by Ker in favour of a kind of insight that belonged to the world of the generalist, one which promised to civilise and enlighten those who entered into it.

Ker's philosophy of criticism did also display some traces of Pater's influence, most notably in his statement that the most important skill required by the critic – the 'essential valuable part of modern criticism' – was the capacity to empathise with the world of the author. This empathy involved the ability to 'reckon every author as one individual, with his own particular story to tell, his own individual manner, his own value', and stemmed from the view that the critic's task was 'not to judge abstractedly, but to see concretely',[54] echoing Pater's statement that the critic needed to define beauty 'in the most concrete terms possible' rather than possessing 'a correct abstract definition of beauty for the intellect'.[55] However, Ker's insistence on the critic's role in communicating a sense of this genius to a wider audience – a very Arnoldian role – means that his concept of criticism differs significantly from that of Bradley, as the latter pleaded – like Pater – for the reading of poetry to be a unique, autonomous act.

Bradley, who held professorships in literature at Liverpool and Glasgow before his election as Professor of Poetry at Oxford in 1901, was vehement in his opposition to attempts to make literature into a key to philosophy or morality, seeing its *'poetic* value' as '[its] intrinsic worth alone'.[56] He defined the act of reading as a process of entering into the text on its own terms, and stated that this process offered a satisfaction that needed to be judged 'entirely from within' rather than against any external standards.

> Poetry may have also an ulterior value as a means to culture or religion, because it conveys instruction, or softens the passions, or furthers a good cause; because it brings the poet money or fame or a good conscience. So much the better: let it be valued for these reasons too. But its ulterior worth neither is nor can directly determine its public

worth as a satisfying imaginative experience; and this is to be judged entirely from within [...] its nature is not to be a part, nor yet a copy, of the real world (as we commonly understand that phrase), but to be a world by itself, independent, complete, autonomous; and to possess it fully you must enter that world, conform to its laws, and ignore for the time the beliefs, aims, and particular conditions which belong to you in that other world of reality.[57]

Furthermore, the personal nature of this experience meant that poetry could not be explained to a third party, but had to be experienced at first hand by a sensitive reader who could appreciate the text's mysterious and complex qualities.

Pure poetry is not the decoration of a preconceived and clearly defined matter: it springs from the creative impulse of a vague imaginative mass pressing for development and definition. If the poet already knew exactly what he meant to say, why should he write the poem? [...] Only its completion can reveal, even to him, exactly what he wanted. When he began and while he was at work, he did not possess his meaning; it possessed him. It was not a fully formed soul asking for a body: it was an inchoate soul in the inchoate body of perhaps two or three vague ideas and a few scattered phrases. The growing of this body into its full stature and perfect shape was the same thing as the gradual self-definition of the meaning. And this is the reason why such poems strike us as creations, not manufactures, and have the magical effect which mere decoration cannot produce. This is also the reason why, if we insist on asking for the meaning of such a poem, we can only be answered 'It means itself.'[58]

Such a view of poetry clearly insists on the self-sufficiency of the experience of reading, and ironically threatens to undermine one important role of the critic (that of explicator) by defining this experience as something that cannot be communicated to another person. It also, importantly, makes use of allusive, metaphorical terms that refer the audience to a personal world in which the individual is paramount, while at the same time emphasising the primacy of the 'unique expression' contained within the text. Like Pater, Bradley makes use of an impressionistic prose style that oscillates between vagueness and the illusion of precision: the sense is that the skilled reader will recognise what he is referring to without needing it to be explained. The 'atmosphere of infinite suggestion' that surrounds the text is something that must be entered into by the individual reader in order for its full value to be appreciated:

> The poet speaks to us of one thing where seems to lurk the secret of all. He said what he meant, but his meaning seems to beckon away beyond itself, or rather to expand into something boundless which is only focussed in it; something also which, we feel, would satisfy not only the imagination, but the whole of us; that something within us, and without, which everywhere
>
> makes us seem
To patch up fragments of a dream,
Part of which comes true, and part
Beats and trembles in the heart.[59]

In formulating this Paterian definition, Bradley also draws on a technique that was used by Arnold and would be adopted later by Quiller-Couch. Arnold's insistence that his readers should recognise the qualities of the 'Grand Style' without needing it to be explained, Quiller-Couch's appeal to his audience's awareness of the golden age of Athenian culture and Bradley's call to the individual's own emotional experience of reading all operate on the same level: namely, that of implying that the phenomenon in question should not need to be defined explicitly, but should simply be recognised and appreciated by those who are adequate to it. As a result, the explicit, objective grounds on which scholarly enquiry is built are rejected in favour of a form of expression that appeals to subjectivity, a secret that can only be understood by a suitably sensitive minority.

These particular professors, then, were not arguing in favour of an academic version of literary criticism, but theorising an experience of reading that belonged to both private and generalist worlds, and depended on the possession of the kind of temperament that would give the reader access to the personal 'truths' contained in the text. Their views emphasised the aesthetic nature of literature and saw it as having a value that stood apart from the objective facts revealed by literary scholarship. Crucially, they frequently expressed their sense of this value through a mysticised, impressionistic rhetoric that seemed to test out their own readers' possession of this temperament, elevating personal over professional authority by speaking not to an academic peer group but to a circle of fellow sages. As a result, their philosophies exemplify the uneasy relationship between literary criticism and academic institutions, and the difficulty of separating the 'amateur' from the 'professional': while they were employed by the universities, they were promoting and producing versions of criticism that attached little importance to the methods of scholarship that were being developed in other disciplines of knowledge.

Literary history: Scholarship and narrative

The personal forms of authority to which these professors clung stand at an ironic distance from the courses outlined in Chapter 2, in which the factual bodies of knowledge associated with the text's language, sources and historical background offered themselves as a ready solution to the problem of how literary knowledge could be taught and examined. As we have seen, such knowledge soon became central to the emerging discipline of English, a discipline that was very different from the way it was envisaged in the rhetoric of early supporters such as Hugh James Rose (at King's) and John Churton Collins (at Oxford). This factual knowledge was codified and elaborated upon in a range of publications, many of which were written by staff of the new English departments and aimed at a student audience. Two genres that underwent a particular expansion at this time were literary history and literary biography. Both genres helped to contribute to the body of knowledge drawn upon by the new English degrees. They also had the potential to draw on the methods and practices that were being established in history proper, such as an emphasis on documentary sources and the systematic collection and referencing of evidence. As a result, their authors were able to claim for themselves the professional authority that was associated with a command of specialist knowledge and methodology. Such a command was clearly valued by many writers and editors of literary biography. One series of biographical studies, the 'Great Writers Series' established by Eric S. Robertson in 1887, drew attention to its adoption of scholarly methods in listing its main features as 'a chronicle of the chief events in a famous author's life [. . .] a critical history of that author's works [. . .] a full bibliography of these works; and [. . .] an analytical Table of Contents, that will summarize the biography on a new plan'.[60] Edmund Gosse's 1882 study of Thomas Gray, his contribution to the 'English Men of Letters' series published by Macmillan, paid meticulous attention to the details of Gray's career at Cambridge and the composition and publication of his poems, including dates and financial particulars: Gosse also included a Prefatory Note in which he listed his sources, acknowledged the various holders of Gray's manuscripts and reviewed the available editions of his works.[61]

Similar conventions of referencing and bibliography are also apparent in the work of the literary historian W. J. Courthope. In *A History of English Poetry* (1895), Courthope paid meticulous attention to the sourcing of texts and the quoting of other authorities, using footnotes and specifying dates and editions. Courthope was also careful to explain aspects of his terminology, such as his classification of pre-Renaissance texts as 'Early English Literature'; to supply translations of passages quoted in the original; and to clarify his elucidation of metrical patterns.[62] Such techniques reflect a growing concern for objectivity and the verifiability of evidence, and indicate that Courthope was keen for his methods to be transparent: his Preface records his intention to draw on the methods being established in the social sciences, and to ensure that scholarly accuracy was allowed to take precedence over the 'personal sympathy and intuition' of contemporary aesthetics.[63]

Courthope's treatment of the works and authors included in his text reflects a similar emphasis on analysis over narrative. His decision to trace particular movements within the literary tradition rather than analysing authors in isolation leads him to carry out a detailed examination of topics such as the metrical patterns of the *chansons de geste*, the tradition of the *scop* in Anglo-Saxon heroic verse, the influence of Pagan mythology on early English literature, and connections between allegory and drama. When canonical writers do appear, they are dealt with in terms of facts rather than in the laudatory, anecdotal judgements present in the work of the men of letters. Chaucer's career, for example, is recounted in meticulous detail, with attention given to the publishing history of his works and the provenance of some of the translations credited to him: of the *Romaunt de la Rose*, for instance, we are told that 'Chaucer himself says that he translated it in his youth; but there is no external evidence to show that the translation included by Stowe in his works was made by him, while the omission of the piece from Shirley's MS. and from Thynne's edition raises a presumption against its authenticity.'[64]

While Courthope's only academic role was that of the honorary post of Professor of Poetry at Oxford, his scrupulous recording and dating of factual events, along with the attention paid to sources and references, exemplifies the professional authority that stems from a command of a specialist subject area and the methodology that accompanies this. Nevertheless, while many literary histories and biographies drew on similar kinds of evidence and similar techniques, others continued to emphasise the markedly different forms of authority that belonged to the generalist. This generalist orientation was arguably part of the nature of both genres, as their authors frequently presented them as introductory studies aimed at a broad readership rather than writing for an audience of fellow experts. Indeed, many early literary biographers and historians belonged to the group of academics whose early careers had been in journalism or schoolteaching, and who therefore viewed the general public as their natural audience. If literary history offered itself as a way of outlining the new discipline of English, it could also be used to introduce this discipline to an audience new to literature. Literary biography, meanwhile, helped to establish a body of knowledge about a canonical author: it also drew on a concept of individual agency that was central to popular notions of the writer as autonomous creator, and allowed for an imaginative identification with the subject that was central to many generalist critics' vision of the ideal act of reading. The literary biographies that made up the 'English Men of Letters' series were sold in 1907 at a price of two shillings per volume, within the reach of a broad range of readers: their generalist reach is reflected in the fact that they were reviewed in journals and newspapers as wide ranging as the *Westminster Gazette*, the *Athenaeum*, *The Times*, the *Daily Graphic*, the *Globe* and the *Morning Post*, rather than in specialist publications. Many of these reviews praised the authors of this series for qualities that would help them to appeal to such an audience, such as their 'tolerant sympathy', 'sanity and virility of temper' and their 'safer, kindlier, [and] more sympathetic keeping' of their subjects.[65] Such reviews indicate that what was prized was a sober and balanced account of an author's life that combined clarity of expression with an imaginative capacity to 'illuminate' the subject, rather than any overt evidence of scholarly methods.

A similarly generalist slant is apparent in Edmund Gosse's Preface to *A Short History of Modern English Literature* (1897), in which he states his aim to give his audience, 'whether familiar with the books or not [...] a feeling of the evolution of English literature in the primary sense of the term, the disentanglement of the skein, the slow and regular unwinding, down succeeding generations, of the threads of literary expression'.[66] Meanwhile, in *A History of Nineteenth Century Literature 1780–1900* (1896), George Saintsbury, Gosse's contemporary, adopts the genial role of the knowledgeable amateur, distinguished from his readers by the breadth of his reading rather than by his command of professional methodologies. Nonetheless, Gosse and Saintsbury differed in the methods they adopted and the narrative paradigms on which they drew, and it is worth exploring these differences in detail, as they (together with Courthope) demonstrate that the genre of literary history was not characterised by any unifying set of principles. Instead, it remained a form that was susceptible to individual differences and intentions, and to variations in the nature of the intellectual authority upon which its authors chose to draw.

Saintsbury's work, for example, takes the form of a straightforward historical survey that provides biographical details of authors along with information about their major works and the style in which they were written. Unlike Courthope, whose references to the historical and political background of literature enabled him to draw on the methodology of another academic field, Saintsbury defined his task as being to 'preserve a perfectly independent, and, as far as possible, a rationally uniform judgement, taking account of none but literary characteristics, but taking account of all characteristics that are literary'.[67] The desire to focus on 'literary' qualities alone means that Saintsbury does not set such information within any historical or social context; nor does he give any detailed information about other aspects of the various authors' lives. In fact, his treatment of his chosen authors often eschews verifiable evidence altogether, resting on a mythologised version of their lives rather than on the kind of detailed research evident in Courthope's history. Saintsbury's discussion of Blake is representative of this approach. We are informed, for example, that it 'has never been doubted' that 'Blake was not entirely sane'; that 'though he had the finest gift of literary expression, he chose often to babble and still oftener to rant at large'; and that much of his work was marred by the effects of his instability:

> After the *Songs* Blake did not care to put forth anything bearing the ordinary form of poetry. We possess indeed other poetical work of his, recovered in scraps and fragments from MSS.; and some of it is beautiful. But it is as a rule more chaotic than the *Sketches* themselves; it is sometimes defaced [...] by personality and coarseness; and it is constantly puddled with the jargon of Blake's mystical philosophy, which [...] spreads itself unhampered by any form whatever over the Prophetic Books.[68]

Saintsbury's critical vocabulary has a judgemental, almost gossipy tone (shown here in terms such as 'chaotic', 'beautiful', 'defaced' and 'puddled', and continued further in his description of Blake as 'distinctly *non compos* on the critical, though admirably gifted on the creative side of his brain') that is continued elsewhere: Wordsworth is 'absolutely destitute of humour'; the merit of Browning's lyrics lies in their 'charm', 'beauty', 'variety' and 'vigour', despite their 'outrageous rhymes'; the work of Wilkie Collins shows an 'aberration of taste and sentiment'.[69] This manner of expression conveys a kind of authority that rests not on Saintsbury's superiority as a scholar (his text does not share the historical and editorial knowledge evident in Courthope's literary history) but on the breadth of his knowledge and his assumption of a superior taste, as conjured by the evaluative tone of his critical method. As such, it recalls the personal authority of the old 'man of letters' rather than the professional authority of the academic.

This dependence upon personal authority is also apparent in Gosse's literary history, although his narrative method is markedly different to that of Saintsbury. Gosse's decision to 'show the movement of English literature [...] to give the reader [...] a feeling of the evolution of English literature in the primary sense of the term, the disentanglement of the skein, the slow and regular unwinding, down succeeding generations, of the threads of literary expression' drew on an evolutionary, Whig paradigm that replaced Saintsbury's evaluative vocabulary with metaphors of disentanglement, growth and ascent.[70] This is particularly apparent in Gosse's analysis of Shakespeare, in whom 'an heroic epoch culminates; he is the commanding peak of a vast group of mountains [...] More than any other of the greatest poets of the world, he rises, by insensible degrees, on the shoulders and the hands of a crowd of precursors'. The allusive, Romantic imagery continues in an extended metaphor that is almost self-parodic: we are told that by the time he wrote *Hamlet*, Shakespeare had 'reached the very summits of his genius';[71] and of the other major tragedies, we are informed that *King Lear* is a 'colossal peak [...] with *Othello* on our right hand and *Macbeth* on our left, the sublime masses of Elizabethan mountain country rolling on every side of us, yet plainly dominated by the extraordinary cluster of *aiguilles* on which we have planted ourselves. This triple summit of the later tragedies of Shakespeare forms the Mount Everest of the poetry of the world.'[72] While the evolutionary model Gosse seems to be proposing is not a consistent one (he refers to the 'evil taint' of Donne's poetry and the 'decline' represented by the period from 1620 to 1660), it nevertheless means that the reader is constantly kept aware of the presence of Gosse himself.[73] As with Saintsbury's highly personal tone, it appears that Gosse used this narrative method to remind his readers of his own status, in a manner associated more with the 'men of letters' than with the professional academic.

These three texts suggest, then, that the methods being developed in history proper were not being transferred to literary studies with any degree of consistency. Instead, their adoption seems to have been more a matter of personal preference. The differing techniques of personal and professional authority produced different interpretations of literary history. Gosse and Saintsbury were writing primarily as literary critics, explaining the development of the canon in terms of the 'greatness' of its constituent authors. Courthope, meanwhile, offered a factual examination of the circumstances in which individual authors worked, which would have lent itself more readily to the demands of the new university syllabuses. The existence of these variations in practice is in itself a sign that the objectivity sought by Courthope was not a universally desirable form of literary knowledge, even for critics working within the universities. Even though Gosse and Saintsbury both held academic posts, the manner in which they themselves chose to 'possess' the canon differed radically from the scholarship practised by Courthope: their ownership of literature took the form of an assertion of personal sympathy, resulting in a type of knowledge that was both mysticised and incontestable.

The analysis of Shakespeare

The literary histories of Courthope, Gosse and Saintsbury, written in the closing years of the nineteenth century, exemplify two markedly different approaches to the genre that draw on the opposing techniques of scholarship and criticism. Such differences are also apparent in early twentieth-century studies of Shakespeare, which can be used to illustrate the ambivalent attitudes of certain early professors of English towards recent developments in academic methodology. This ambivalence, in turn, highlights a gap between the rhetoric and practice of Shakespeare study. Shakespeare was a central element of all the early degree courses in English literature, and while the precise form of this study differed in each institution, many early professors (as outlined in Chapter 2) drew on literary history and bibliography to give their questions an objectivity that would make them easy to examine. Students taking University of London exams in the 1880s, for example, were expected to tackle questions on the dates of composition of Shakespeare's plays, the textual history of *Richard III* and Shakespeare's reliance on Plutarch.[74] Some critics saw this emphasis on scholarship as misplaced. Walter Raleigh claimed that a 'rapid, alert reading of one of the great plays brings us nearer to the heart of Shakespeare then all the faithful and laudable business of the antiquary and the commentator', seeing such 'business' as offering nothing more than 'laborious descriptions of the facts to be explained'.[75] Nevertheless, both Raleigh and his Oxford contemporary A. C. Bradley displayed attitudes towards professional scholarship that were much more complex than this initial rejection suggests. Both were professors, writing and speaking to audiences that included their own academic peer group as well as their students: both would have been fully aware of the developments in contemporary scholarship and of the status that professional authority was beginning to occupy in intellectual life. It is significant, then, that while both drew on certain aspects of literary scholarship in order to claim such authority, they also sought to distance themselves from the methods it employed and the types of knowledge that it prioritised, foregrounding a personal sympathy that offered itself as the only route to a 'true' understanding of Shakespeare and his characters.

In Bradley's case, this sympathy appears as a natural extension of the philosophy of personal engagement outlined in his inaugural lecture as Professor of Poetry. *Shakespearean Tragedy*, published in 1904 and based on lectures and classes delivered during his professorships at Liverpool, Glasgow and Oxford, involves a psychological exploration of Shakespeare's characters, depending on a concept of human agency that in turn requires a detailed examination of each character's 'fundamental tragic trait'.[76] This method was famously criticised by L. C. Knights in 'How Many Children had Lady Macbeth?' as producing 'irrelevant moral and realistic canons', carrying out a 'sentimentalizing' of Shakespeare's heroes that detracted from 'the *whole* dramatic pattern of each play': for Knights, such treatment reflected the naïve belief that characters had an existence independent of their dramatic roles. Yet while Knights saw Bradley as the 'most illustrious example'[77] of this form of criticism, Bradley was drawing on a long tradition of humanist scholarship. He alludes frequently, for example, to the work of Edward Dowden, who used Shakespeare's plays as the key to an exploration of the playwright's own growth and maturity, and believed that his depiction of 'the mysteries of human experience' allowed his audience an uncomplicated access to his 'living mind': 'We are in company with a man; and a sense of real human sympathy and fellowship rises within us [...] We are conscious of his strength communicating itself to us.'[78] Bradley was less lyrical than Dowden about the benefits of Shakespeare's company, but shared his view of the reading process as a struggle to comprehend the mind of the author as displayed through his characters, stating that true lovers of Shakespeare 'want to realise fully and exactly the inner movements which produced these words and no other, these deeds and no other, at each particular moment'.[79] He also continued to iterate his belief in the importance of an untutored sympathy with the author, establishing an opposition between criticism and scholarship which neatly exemplifies the ways in which they were seen by many of his contemporaries. Such an opposition held that the study of literary history and textual sources was 'useful and even in various degrees necessary', but that

> an overt pursuit of them is not necessary [. . .] nor is any one of them so indispensable to our object as that close familiarity with the plays, that native strength and justice of perception, and that habit of reading with an eager mind, which make many an unscholarly lover of Shakespeare a far better critic than many a Shakespeare scholar.[80]

Nevertheless, it is significant that even while Bradley asserted the importance of an intuitive approach to literature, he also drew on techniques that would help to give his work the appearance of a more scholarly kind of text. The first two lectures on which *Shakespearean Tragedy* was based took the form of an investigation of the moral and philosophical world of Shakespeare's tragedies, and of the patterns Bradley identifies in their underlying structure. In describing these patterns, Bradley emphasises the need to make careful distinctions and logical deductions. For instance, after discussing the role of chance, insanity and the supernatural, he concludes that

> thus it appears that these three elements in the 'action' are subordinates, while the dominant factor consists in deeds which issue from character. So that, by way of summary, we may now alter our first statement, 'A tragedy is a story of exceptional calamity leading to the death of a man in high estate,' and we may say instead [. . .] that the story is one of human actions producing exceptional calamity and ending in the death of such a man.[81]

Bradley's conjunctions give his argument an orderliness that helps to convey this authoritative tone: there is a sense that his definitions are both systematic and carefully reasoned, and therefore incontrovertible. This sense of order continues when Bradley's discussion of 'the constant alteration of rises and falls in [. . .] tension or in the emotional pitch of the work'[82] leads him to adopt an alphabetical form of notation in order to simplify his argument:

> Let us for the sake of brevity call the two sides in the conflict A and B [. . .] through a considerable part of the play, perhaps the first half, the cause of A is, on the whole, advancing; and through the remaining part it is retiring, while that of B advances in turn [. . .] And since we always more or less decidedly prefer A to B or B to A, the result of this

oscillating movement is a constant alternation of hope and fear, or rather a mixed state predominantly hopeful and a mixed state predominantly apprehensive.[83]

For all Bradley's claims about the 'unscholarly lover' of Shakespeare, the use of such techniques gives him an authority that would not be afforded by a more superficial empathy with the text: he is asserting a kind of knowledge that is gained only through depth of study and analysis. Moreover, his use of quasi-algebraic notation to simplify the different elements of this structure also gives his work an impersonality that balances the emotions ('hope and fear') that these elements represent, and mimics the appearance of a more scientific kind of writing. This appearance is heightened by his use of an alphanumerical system to demarcate separate points in his argument, giving the sense not of a personal meditation rooted in feelings, but of a carefully structured analysis of facts (derived from traditions of philosophical logic) in which different strands of thought have been meticulously distinguished from one another. It seems that Bradley was aware of the intellectual authority that such techniques could convey, and that he was keen to draw on this authority – and the sense of professionalism and objectivity that went with it.

Yet such claims must be seen in the context of the personal authority upon which Bradley's work also rests. For all its surface appearance of logic and precision, and its attempt to imitate the new scholarly methods of the social sciences, *Shakespearean Tragedy* is a work of imagination: the technique Knights so roundly criticised – that of treating characters as real people, and carrying out explorations of their notional psychological state – is apparent throughout, and consequently these characters appear as having 'inner lives' that can be reached through the medium of Shakespeare's text. This emphasis of the characters' realism actually serves to diminish any sense of Shakespeare's role in their creation and manipulation, as what is foregrounded is an impressionistic sense of how each character responds to, and is affected by, the events that unfold around them. Hamlet, for example, 'cannot prevent himself from probing and lacerating the wound in his soul':[84] he is described in terms of his intellectual power; his 'pathological condition' of melancholy; and his speculative genius, a 'necessity in his soul' that 'dr[ove] him to penetrate below the surface and to question what others took for granted'.[85] The audience is constantly invited to identify with characters, to examine their traits and to consider themselves in their position, exploring their psychology in a way that sees them as autonomous agents rather than created figures within a wider dramatic conception. Such an exploration draws much of its weight from the imagination of both Bradley and his audience. When he asks his students to consider the situation of Ophelia, he emphasises his own powers of sympathy in his impressionistic re-creation of Ophelia's state of mind:

> Consider for a moment how matters looked to *her*. She knows nothing about the Ghost and its disclosures. She has undergone for some time the pain of repelling her lover and appearing to have turned against him. She sees him, or hears of him, sinking daily into deeper gloom, and so transformed from what he was that he is considered to be out of his mind [...] She is frightened, then; frightened, if you will, like a child.[86]

Such descriptions draw attention not to Bradley's intellectual powers, but to a more personal understanding and an ability to empathise with the human dilemmas in which characters find themselves. As a result, his work can be linked to an Arnoldian tradition of generalist criticism in which an understanding of the text was seen as a route to an enriched awareness of the human condition. The endings of Bradley's lectures, for example, typically emphasise the spiritual gains of reading Shakespeare's tragedies. *Hamlet* 'brings home to us at once the sense of the soul's infinity, and the sense of the doom which not only circumscribes that infinity but appears to be its offspring': it affects us because of its capacity to make us recognise that 'in all that happens or is done we seem to apprehend some vaster power'.[87] Similarly, *King Lear*'s blend of 'pity and terror' with 'law and beauty' enables us to feel 'a consciousness of greatness in pain, and of solemnity in the mystery we cannot fathom', a reminder of the ineffability of poetry that Bradley tried to capture in his Inaugural Lecture.[88] For all his cautiousness about the 'ulterior motives' of literary study, Bradley is convinced of the power of the sense of awe and mystery that accompanies Shakespeare's tragedies: his iteration of this theme places his work firmly in the tradition of the Victorian sage.

In view of this, it is significant that Bradley reserves his discussion of more 'scholarly' textual matters for the Notes appended to his text, where he deals with questions of editorship (he recommends several emendations to the stage directions in Rowe's edition of *Hamlet*) and dating. These notes do show evidence of a knowledge of contemporary research: Bradley's summary of the various metrical tests used in establishing the order of the plays involves references to the work of the

German scholars König and Hertzberg and a discussion of the relative merits of methods known as the Speech-ending test, the Overflow test and the Light-and-Weak ending test.[89] Bradley acknowledges that such topics will be 'of interest only to scholars'[90] and separates them from the main body of his text, where footnotes are used mainly to develop and clarify points in the argument rather than to give references, and where the interpretations discussed tend to be drawn from a wider group of men of letters (Schlegel, Goethe, Coleridge) rather than from Bradley's academic peer group. It is significant that Bradley chose to give *Shakespearean Tragedy* this more scholarly dimension, however grudging it might appear: he appears to be making a concession to the changing nature of academic practice while also seeking to distance himself from these changes. But his logical rhetoric and references to contemporary research do not conceal the fact that his interpretation of Shakespeare is founded on a much more personal set of skills: for Bradley, the 'justice of perception' involved in a close study of character was clearly more important than any evidence of scholarship.

Walter Raleigh, in contrast, had serious misgivings about the merits of a psychological exploration of Shakespeare's characters, and distanced himself from critics who 'must finish his sketches for him, telling us more about his characters than ever he knew'.[91] His criticism of such an approach encompasses Bradley's work and anticipates the direction that would be taken in the future by some of Cambridge's Tripos questions. For Raleigh, speculation about character and motivation had 'no meaning for criticism':

> We seem to know them all, and to be able to predict how each of them will act in trials to which [they] cannot be exposed. What if Desdemona had been Lear's daughter, and Cordelia Othello's wife? Would not the sensitive affection of the one and the proud sincerity of the other have given us a different result?[92]

Yet despite this disagreement, Raleigh shared Bradley's emphasis on the need for a personal engagement with the text, and saw such an engagment as taking precedence over the artificial 'canons of judgment' offered by criticism.[93] Indeed, Raleigh's own criticism can be seen as an attempt to demonstrate the power of the 'real reader', a person who saw the text as a living force rather than an object for academic study. Stephen Potter described Raleigh as having the power to 'send his audiences away tingling with a sense of the unique value of the particular writer he had been expounding, eager to find out more on their own account'.[94]

Raleigh's book *Shakespeare* (1907), part of Macmillan's 'English Men of Letters' series, demonstrates how he achieved this, with a characteristic technique being the building of impressionistic descriptions of the playwright's greatness and breadth of experience. Like Bradley, Raleigh saw this greatness as a key to an enriched understanding of life; one which could not be gained through the 'prosaic enthusiasm and learned triviality'[95] of scholarly enquiry. Shakespeare, for example,

> keeps us out of doors, and we find the width of his wisdom fatiguing, the freedom of his movements bewildering. He is at home in the world; and we complain that the place is too large for us, the visitation of the winds too rough and unceremonious [...] But Shakespeare's apology for his own life is more than sufficient. We know something of what he felt and thought, for he has told us. If we ask what he did, his answer admits of no human retort – he wrote his plays.[96]

The 'indispensable preliminary' for understanding Shakespeare was, then, 'not knowledge of his history, not even knowledge of his works, but knowledge of his theme, a wide acquaintance with human life and human passion as they are reflected in a sensitive and independent mind'.[97] Such statements attest to the emphatically humanist nature of Raleigh's study: his aim was to take his readers 'nearer to the heart of Shakespeare than all the faithful and laudable business of the antiquary and the commentator',[98] in order that the playwright's unique understanding of life may be communicated to a wider audience.

However, this generalist philosophy was not without its specialist foundations. For all Raleigh's caution about the benefits of scholarship, he was clearly in possession of a 'scholarly' body of knowledge about Shakespeare's sources, influences and historical background: he writes, for instance, of the dramatic tradition that preceded Shakespeare; his use of contemporary songs, ballads and proverbs; and the differing treatment he gave to sources such as Holinshed, Plutarch and the Bible. His discussion of Shakespeare's cultural background makes use of contemporary archival sources and the accounts of witnesses: his description of Shakespeare's early years in London draws on a considerable depth of historical research.[99] Nevertheless, Raleigh is careful not to betray too much of his scholarship. It is significant that while his text belonged to the same series as Gosse's study of Gray (and, indeed, was written 25 years later), it differs from Gosse's work in that it contains no biography or list of sources, and has no system of referencing quotations or citations, despite its discussion of textual variants and the work of other writers. Raleigh's scholarship acts as a means to an end rather than an end in itself, allowing him to anchor his impressionistic descriptions in significant details. His description of the world of Elizabethan theatre and the popular dramatic tradition within which Shakespeare worked begins by referring to contemporary pamphlets (*The Serving-Man's Comfort* of 1598); actors such as Will Summer, Richard Tarlton and Will Kempe; choirs such as the Children of Paul's and the Children of the Chapel Royal; and the emergence of the University Wits: these factual details culminate in the broad descriptive sweep with which Raleigh depicts

> the wild Bohemian life of actors and dramatists [...] a time when nothing was fixed or settled, when every month brought forth some new thing, and popularity was the only road to success. There was fierce rivalry among the companies of actors to catch the public ear. Tragedy acknowledged one man for master; and a new school of actors was growing up to meet the demand for poetic declamation. Comedy, the older foundation, was unchanged, and remained in the hands of the professional jesters [...] Force, stridency, loud jesting and braggart declamation carried the day, and left no room for the daintiness of the literary conscience.[100]

Such passages are rooted in fact, but nevertheless have an oracular tone that glosses over the fact that what is being displayed is the imaginative power of the man of letters – a form of writing used to improvisation and speculation – rather than the research of the scholar. Raleigh's concept of reading was similar to Bradley's in that it prioritised imagination, sympathy and a capacity for the instinctive perception of the author's greatness, underpinned by the humanist knowledge of the critic. In comparison, the knowledge produced by scholarship was seen as both laborious and inferior.

The sheer range of critical practices and philosophies outlined in this chapter points to the lack of agreement about what constituted literary criticism at the end of the nineteenth century. Moreover, the fact that many of the early professors of English still espoused the practices used by the generalist critics of the mid-nineteenth century indicates that these varied critical practices cannot be mapped onto a simple binary division between 'amateur' and 'professional'. While literary scholars, keen to advance the subject's claim to disciplinary status, were willing to draw on history and philology as paradigms for academic English, critics both inside and outside the universities were insisting that literature could not be reduced to the accumulation of facts – that it possessed special qualities that set it apart from other newly professionalised disciplines.

The philosophies expressed by these critics can be distinguished along the lines of the differing models of critical practice espoused by Arnold and Pater: the former emphasising literature's role as an agent of social change; the latter concerned with the private relationship between text and reader. While these two models rest on opposing notions of the uses to which criticism could be put, what links them is their resistance to the kind of specialism that the early literary scholarship sought to encourage. For both, the immediate audience and purpose of criticism were envisaged not as a community of experts and the pursuit of academic knowledge, but in broader and more general terms: in Arnold's model as a non-specialist community of 'aliens', led by 'the love of human perfection'[101] and the desire to spread the benefits of culture throughout humanity; and in Pater's as a sensitive, attentive reader who stands outside the notion of 'community' altogether, dedicated to a precise understanding of his or her inward response to art. These views, and the ways in which they were adapted and promoted, defined criticism in ways that made it neither teachable nor examinable. While scholarship was leading to the codification of literary knowledge along historical and linguistic lines, criticism was concerned with an understanding that was much more personal and consequently much less tangible.

However, as with 'amateur' and 'professional', the idea of a straight-forward distinction between 'scholarship' and 'criticism' needs to be approached with caution. As we have seen, both Bradley and Raleigh adopted some elements of scholarship while also appearing to reject it, recognising the professional authority that it was able to give to their work. And by the early twentieth century, elements of a more critical approach were becoming apparent in the degree courses which had previously emphasised the objective knowledge associated with scholarship: in 1910, the Victoria University of Manchester asked students to comment on Shakespeare's characterisation, and on his treatment of concepts such as jealousy and the 'tragic fault', in a manner that seems to draw directly on Bradley's psychological treatment of his characters.[102] As a result, the relationships between professors and institutions, and criticism and scholarship, appear to have been highly complex. As academic critics became more aware of the professional authority that scholarship was able to confer on their work, some of them sought an accommodation with scholarly methods that is apparent in their adoption of certain techniques of referencing and bibliography, as well as in the language they use and the concepts on which they draw. Conversely, there are signs that institutions previously concerned with scholarship were beginning to recognise the alternative kinds of knowledge that were made available by criticism. As noted at the end of Chapter 2, Oxford's Faculty of English was beginning to acknowledge, by the 1920s, that literary study drew on skills that were not encompassed by the objectivity of philology or textual study. These skills had not yet been formalised, but they would be given a more enthusiastic welcome in Quiller-Couch's Cambridge.

Outside the universities, many critics had a more straightforward approach to the complexities of criticism and scholarship, using their writing to reclaim literature from academic methods and institutions, and replace it in the hands of the non-academic reader. Yet this latter figure could not be identified with the general reading public of the Victorian periodicals. While some scholars had aimed to infuse literature with a rigour that would secure its place in the universities, the critics associated with Modernism sought to give it a different kind of difficulty: one that could be grasped not through education, but through the possession of what Pater had deemed 'a certain kind of temperament'.[103] Such definitions, which will form the basis of Chapter 4, took criticism out of the hands of the academic professionals, and gave it to a different kind of elite.

4
Criticism and the Modernists: Woolf, Murry, Orage

The resistance to literary scholarship, in the form of a set of critical philosophies that emphasised the relationship between text and reader over the codes and practices of academic study, was to become a recurring theme in the arguments about academic English that took place over the next few decades. Significantly, this debate about different forms of literary knowledge took place not just within the universities, but also in other cultural arenas. Laurel Brake's work on nineteenth-century periodicals has uncovered the extent of theorising about criticism that took place even in apparently 'generalist' publications such as the *Cornhill Magazine*, with the 'problems of identity, method and language' experienced by the men of letters being seen as symptoms of the chaos brought about by the fragmentation of criticism into its various journalistic and scholarly forms.[1] Just as the early supporters of literary study had to defend the subject's claims to academic status, it seemed that those who worked outside the universities had to justify their right to include it in non-specialist debate, arguing that its wider relevance meant that it should not be allowed to become the possession of a purely academic domain. Specialists may have succeeded in claiming some aspects of English as theirs, but the continuing presence of literature in general debate meant that they could not 'own' the subject entirely.

The extent of these critical divisions is shown by the fact that the arguments Brake summarises – about the purpose of criticism, its claim to objectivity and the skills it involved – were also dominant themes in the critical writing of Virginia Woolf, John Middleton Murry and A. R. Orage, some thirty to forty years after the foundation of the Honour School of English at Oxford. The careers of these writers exemplify the continuing difficulty of drawing a clear distinction between 'amateur' and 'professional': they all made a substantial part of their living from their work as literary critics, yet only John Middleton Murry, who gave a series of lectures at Oxford at the invitation of Sir Walter Raleigh, came close to any kind of professional involvement with the universities. They were also working at a time when the influence of the great Victorian periodicals was in decline and when non-academic literary debate was becoming restricted either to the increasingly specialist 'little magazines' of Modernism or to the book reviews published in daily and weekly newspapers, a forum that carried the taint of commercialism and popular appeal.[2] It is significant, then, that their criticism not only displays varying degrees of ambivalence (even, at times, hostility) towards professional scholarship, but also draws on the values and rhetoric of the 'amateur', appealing – in a number of different ways – to the personal authority of the 'man of letters'. This opposition, as we shall see, often rested on a view of academic literary study as being much more unified and coherent than was actually the case, but this rhetorical simplification was useful in helping to strengthen the argument against scholarly practice: the suggestion was that the academic study of literature was reductive and stifling in its desire to mimic the precision of the sciences, with its attention being focused on matters that did not reveal the true 'essence' of the text. Moreover, its empiricism meant that it did not require any kind of instinctive engagement with literature, relying on knowledge that could be taught and learned – and which was therefore, by extension, available to the 'masses' – rather than apprehended through what Orage described as 'some power of the mind to which it is difficult to give an exact name'.[3] This may, in turn, have led to an anxiety about the 'ownership' of literary knowledge. If everyone could be taught to be a critic, then the role of the non-academic critic was put in jeopardy. As a result, such writers sought to define their work in terms of qualities that were not acknowledged by either the objectivity of scholarship or the bluntness of the mass market.

All three of these writers can also be linked to the cultural movement of Modernism, with Woolf's stylistic innovation and Murry and Orage's promotion of the early work of T. S. Eliot, D. H. Lawrence and Ezra Pound securing them an important place in Modernist literary history.[4] Nevertheless, the sense of upheaval commonly associated with Modernism – the 'abrupt break with all tradition' identified by Herbert Read in 1933[5] – means that it is easy to overlook the connections between some aspects of Modernism and what preceded it, focusing on dislocation rather than causality. Woolf, Murry and Orage may indeed have played an important role in early twentieth-century literary culture, but their invocation of an older kind of critical authority means that they can also be seen in terms of a tradition whose association with Modernism may otherwise seem tenuous.

This disjunction from 'classic' models of Modernism can be demonstrated through a reading of John Carey's analysis of Modernism in his highly contentious *The Intellectuals and the Masses*. In this text Carey portrays Modernism in terms of a hostile reaction to 'mass' culture and the rise in literacy brought about by late nineteenth-century educational reforms. Carey describes these changes as precipitating a moment of crisis for the 'intellectuals', and identifies this crisis as the source of a 'fault line' which divided Western culture: 'A gulf was opening, on one side of which the intellectual saw the vulgar, trivial working millions, wallowing in newsprint, and on the other side himself and his companions, functionless and ignored, reading Virginia Woolf and the *Criterion*.'[6] The intellectuals' response was to cultivate a kind of art that was too difficult for the masses to understand, with its 'irrationality and obscurity' leading to an exclusivity that Carey sees as 'the principle around which modernist literature and culture fashioned themselves'.[7]

There is no doubt that Woolf, Murry and Orage were all concerned, in varying ways, with popular culture's debasing of art, and with the threat posed by commercialism and the desire for profit. Indeed, Murry, writing in 1930 on 'Northcliffe as Symbol', defined the ideal businessman as one who 'accepts no moral responsibility whatsoever' for art, allowing 'principle [... to] yield to circulation' and giving the age a 'sinister quality'.[8] However, it is also important to acknowledge that what these critics advocated was often not a particular view of art, but rather a particular view of *reading* – a shift, in other words, from object to method. Woolf's interest in the 'rubbish-reading' that lay outside the traditional canon and Orage's insistence that while Vorticism may have been possible it was not 'right',[9] contradict Carey's model of Modernist culture in that they do not claim that the 'value' of art is dependent on its stylistic difficulty. Instead, what they do emphasise is the difficulty of the act of reading itself: what separates the 'real' reader from the newly literate masses is not so much the kind of texts they read as the depth of perception that the former could bring to these texts.[10] This focus on the act of reading means that the work of all three can be traced back to the influences of Arnold and Pater, and to the philosophies of criticism outlined in the last chapter.

Consequently, this chapter seeks to detach these three critics from a version of Modernism that rests on disruption, and to trace instead the ways in which they were influenced by the same forces that shaped the work of more 'academic' critics such as Bradley and Ker. For if Woolf,

Murry and Orage were attempting, in their various ways, to revive a sense of the personal authority that underwrote the work of the nineteenth-century critics, they also shared with some of their academic counterparts the problem of how this could be carried out in a cultural climate radically different to that which had been enjoyed by their predecessors, marked by the growing fragmentation and stratification of the reading public. Yet in doing this, their methods and intentions differed. While Woolf was developing a form of criticism that focused on the individual sensibility, a different kind of impulse was present in Murry's search for a precise vocabulary in which to express his theory of style, prompted perhaps by his closer accommodation with the universities and his addressing of a mixed audience of students and lay readers. Different again was Orage's desire to create an arena for the debate of literature, politics and philosophy in his weekly journal *The New Age*, described by Wallace Martin as an attempt to 'mediate between specialized fields of knowledge and public understanding'[11] in the spirit of the great mid-Victorian periodicals. If Woolf's emphasis on the individual act of reading followed Pater in its celebration of the solipsistic experience of art, then Orage, with his view of literature as an instrument by which the experience of 'truth' could be made common, was firmly Arnoldian in his allegiances.

In spite of these differences, the common theme linking the work of all three critics is their elevation of judgement over knowledge, with the capacity to judge (in an echo of Arnold's formulation of the critic's task as 'simply to know the best that is known and thought in the world'[12]) securing the critic's authority. This emphasis on judgement means that the criticism they produced was, for the most part, resolutely unacademic, calling on values that could not be synthesised with the developing norms of professionalisation and specialisation and using a range of rhetorical techniques to draw attention to their own critical status. While both Murry and Orage attempted to identify certain objective principles by which criticism could be seen to operate, neither succeeded in doing this in a manner that would enable the act of criticism to be taught or examined.

Virginia Woolf: Criticism as private experience

It is difficult to approach Virginia Woolf without being conscious not only of her Modernism, but also of her relationship to the concept of a feminine sensibility. Because many of Woolf's subjects are women, and because the method of reading she advocates is linked closely to her attempts to explore the 'unknown and uncircumscribed spirit'[13] of woman, it is easy to see how her criticism has been read as wholly feminist in direction, devoted to a concern for women writers and women's experiences. Such a view – whether it focuses on her opposition to the male-dominated world of the universities, her recovery of the 'lives of the obscure' or the importance she places on the role of subjectivity in creating a feminised method of reading – is emphasised by her critics and biographers, and casts an uneasy shadow over any attempt to see Woolf in a different light. Rachel Bowlby has summarised the ways in which differing interpretations of Woolf have been made to serve a feminist agenda:

> She is celebrated as a modernist breaking with formal literary conventions, and thereby also with the normative structures of patriarchal- or phallocentric-language; she is also celebrated as a realist, by appeal to her authentic description of women's lives and experiences, and her commitment to the end of patriarchal society [...] There is also the question of biography [...] in the very extremity of its outlines, the tale can become either a demonstration of common female oppression – the norm revealed at its outer edges – or proof of her exceptional status.[14]

Such interpretations extend to Woolf's criticism and to the methods it employs. Hermione Lee, for example, sees Woolf's critical writing in terms of its opposition to the '(male) cultural coteries' of 'professors, editors [and] literary hacks'; an opposition in which Woolf asserts the importance of 'a kind of reading as a woman which is different from "the man's way"', metaphorised in feminine terms as 'slipping, skipping, loitering'.[15] Maria DiBattista's reading of Woolf is less explicitly gendered, yet still draws attention to the 'otherness' of Woolf's criticism in describing the 'necromantic powers' that allow her to revive the lives of forgotten authors.[16]

It is important to emphasise that I do not seek to negate the importance of gender as a dominant force in Woolf's literary criticism. Indeed, there are certain, and crucial, points when gender and critical method are inextricable, most obviously in *A Room of One's Own*, where the narrator's exclusion from the male-dominated world of the university and the fact that she has consequently 'been drawing a picture where I should, like my neighbour, have been writing a conclusion'[17] act as an appropriate symbol of Woolf's decision to approach her subjects through image and metaphor rather than conventional academic prose. Where my interpretation differs is in attempting to interpret Woolf's literary writings in the context of the changing nature of criticism as a whole, rather than in terms of a simple gendered opposition. DiBattista's claim that Woolf was 'somewhat dazed, as both novelist and reviewer-critic, by the break up of the reading public into a "bewildering variety" of audiences', and that she reacted to this by demonstrating 'the special authority and unique advantage of those stationed on the periphery of officialdom', attests to the ways in which she was influenced by the decline of the certainties of the Victorian men of letters, and the increasing importance of academic literary criticism – a form of 'officialdom' to which Woolf was clearly opposed.[18] However, while this 'officialdom' may have been predominantly masculine, Woolf's opposition cannot just be seen in terms of gender: it has much in common, for instance, with the early work of John Middleton Murry and with a tradition of aesthetic criticism that stretches back to Pater in its resistance of academic norms. Seen in this light, Woolf's criticism appears less of an isolated phenomenon than many readings of her work might suggest.

Two recent studies of Woolf's writing have offered different approaches to the feminist interpretations outlined above, setting Woolf's non-fiction in its cultural and generic contexts with regard to conventions of both journalism and essay-writing. Elena Gualtieri's *Virginia Woolf's Essays: Sketching the Past* (2000) focuses initially on Woolf's anxiety about whether she was able to convey the 'true reality' of life or whether she was simply writing about herself.[19] Gualtieri uses these doubts to place Woolf within a Continental tradition of thought that emphasises the nature of the essay as 'pure discourse', a form that calls attention to its own status as art as well as to its content. Drawing on the words of Georg Lukács, Gualtieri describes the essay as a kind of writing that 'asks the fundamental ontological questions, "what is life, what is man, what is destiny?", but provides them not with "the answers of science or, at purer heights, those of philosophy" but with a form, a "symbol" '.[20] Gualtieri's work also draws on Graham Good's *The Observing Self* (1988) in describing the essay's mimicking of 'a scattered and only loosely connected self' as making it 'the most suitable form with which to combat both the homogenisation of individual consciousness by mass culture and the systematic reduction of that consciousness to an abstract entity in the theories of the human sciences'.[21] Gualtieri's analysis therefore places Woolf's essays at 'the intersection between a feminist critique of patriarchal power structures and a Marxist analysis of the ideological formations of capitalism',[22] seeing them as an anti-authoritarian form of writing that foregrounds conversational and personal modes of thought and address.

A more documentary approach is taken by Leila Brosnan, whose *Reading Virginia Woolf's Essays and Journalism* (1997) highlights Woolf's ambivalent relationship to the world of journalism. Brosnan points out that while Woolf's letters and diaries indicate that she was acutely conscious of her dependence on editors and publishers, her fame as a journalist also brought her considerable pleasure.[23] Woolf's diary of 1918 records her feelings of being 'pressed & important & even excited a little' on being asked to write reviews, and in her more optimistic moments she saw such work as 'a great stand by – this power to make large sums by formulating views on Stendhal & Swift'.[24] Brosnan also argues that while it is easy to see the male-dominated world of literary journalism as a restrictive force, contemporary editorial practices led Woolf to develop an allusive, metaphorical style that would allow her to express a range of potential meanings, forming 'a suggestive subtext that undercuts [her essays'] surface conformity to editorial expectations'.[25] For Brosnan, the 'inventive rewriting'[26] that Woolf carried out in her reviews was a liberating force, unleashing a subjective voice that was able to claim a particular kind of writerly authority for itself.

Brosnan's work is important in that it represents a revisionist attempt to see Woolf's literary journalism as benefiting from, rather than being stifled by, the circumstances in which it was written. It also uses substantial historical evidence to break down simplistic views of a gender-based opposition between Woolf and her editors, arguing that the world of the Edwardian literary periodicals was shaped by class and family allegiance rather than gender.[27] As a result, it offers a way of reading Woolf's work against a background of conventions and expectations that I shall return to later. Nevertheless, both Brosnan and Gualtieri stop short of carrying out a detailed examination of Woolf's relationship with academia. While Gualtieri's highly theoretical approach does encompass Woolf's engagement with the practices of contemporary journalism, it does not deal in detail with Woolf's equally complex relationship with the normative structures of the new academic disciplines. Brosnan, meanwhile, does refer briefly to the emergence of English studies, claiming (in a discussion of the generic conventions of the essay) that the rise of English 'saw the rebirth of the essay as an instrument of [. . .] literary criticism'.[28] She also draws attention to George ('Dadie') Rylands's feeling of being 'unsettled' by Woolf's essay 'On Not Knowing Greek', seeing his comment that Woolf 'read[s] Greek differently' and his querying of her omission of Pindar as representing a clash of expectations between Rylands's scholarship and Woolf's emphasis on subjectivity.[29] Nevertheless, this latter incident is treated rather as a collision between two opposing views of the essay – a *generic* opposition – rather than as an *institutional* clash between the values of amateur and professional. While the two are easy to conflate, I want to argue that separating them allows Woolf's critical strategy to be seen less as the product of individual choice than as part of an ongoing struggle between two differing views of critical authority, one of which includes Woolf but is by no means restricted to her. Placing Woolf in this institutional context may deny her the pioneering role that many feminist interpretations have sought to bestow on her, but it also restores a sense of her historicity – and raises the largely ignored question of how her criticism was shaped by her awareness of the practices that were developing in the universities.

Woolf's sense of her distance from the status and privilege represented by the universities is easy to document. One of the most famous images in her writing is of the narrator of *A Room of One's Own*, forced to remain outside the libraries of Oxbridge: conversely, her letters and diaries are full of examples of the scorn Woolf felt for professional scholars and the institutions to which they belonged. On the one hand, Woolf protested that 'I do not believe that gifts, whether of mind or character, can be weighed like sugar and butter, not even at Cambridge, where they are so adept at putting people into classes and fixing caps on their heads and letters after their names.'[30] She also boasted that she had persuaded T. S. Eliot 'to go some way with me in denouncing Oxford & Cambridge', and noted with pleasure that they had 'agreed about the infamy of teaching English; the idiocy of lectures; the whole hierarchy of professor, system & so on'.[31] This 'infamy' was something on which Woolf was prepared to elaborate at length. In a letter to her nephew Julian Bell about Dadie Rylands's election to a lectureship in English at Cambridge, she commented that 'all one can do is to herd books into groups, and then these submissive young, who are far too frightened and callow to have a bone in their backs, swallow it down; and tie it up; and thus we get English literature into ABC; one, two, three; and lose all sense of what its about'.[32] She also knew, however, that this world was one in which she could not participate and that this exclusion placed certain limits on the critical methodologies available to her. The student at the British Museum, criticised in *A Room of One's Own* for 'wear[ing] a ready-made tie' and breathing noisily, nevertheless possessed 'some method of shepherding his question past all distractions as a sheep runs into its pen', while for the untrained researcher 'the question far from being shepherded into its pen flies like a frightened flock hither and thither, helter-skelter, pursued by a whole pack of hounds'.[33] Similarly, for all Eliot's sympathy with her views, Woolf had to concede that 'I daresay though he will become Prof of Poetry at Oxford one of these days'[34] – a recognition that Eliot was able to move in circles from which Woolf herself was excluded.

Nevertheless, the techniques adopted by Woolf suggest that she was able to use this sense of exclusion as a means of creating a different kind of literary criticism. It is significant, for example, that Woolf's critical personae are often leisured, free of the pressures of time and procedure to which journalists and academics were subjected. Many of her essays mention acts such as looking up from a book, gazing out of the window and listening to the sounds of the world outside, with their casual, almost careless nature standing in marked contrast to the developing norms of academic study. In 'How Should One Read a Book?' Woolf's images are drawn from the leisured and relaxed rhythms of her everyday life, placing reading within a domestic and unstructured sphere in a passage that begins with a very Paterian formulation:

> We must pass judgment upon these multitudinous impressions; we must make of these fleeting shapes one that is hard and lasting. But not directly. Wait for the dust of reasoning to settle; for the conflict and questioning to die down; walk, talk, pull the dead petals from a rose, or fall asleep. Then suddenly without our willing it, for it is thus that Nature undertakes these transitions, the book will return, but differently. It will float to the top of the mind as a whole. And the book as a whole is different from the book received currently in separate phrases. Details now fit themselves into their places. We see the shape from start to finish; it is a barn, a pig-sty, or a cathedral. Now then we can compare book with book as we compare building with building.[35]

That this persona is also gendered must not be forgotten: this essay was first delivered as a lecture at a private girls' school at Hayes Court in Kent in January 1926, and this context suggests an advocacy of a kind of reading that is implicitly more suited to the lives and minds of women. Yet it is clear that alongside this gendering is an awareness of the reader's amateur status, reflecting Woolf's validation of ways of reading that are distanced from the professional processes of the university. Much of her critical work, as Brosnan indicates, takes the form of an imaginative engagement with the text that enables the reader to apprehend the 'essence' of an author, and thereby to enter into the relationship with the past that Woolf placed at the centre of her artistic philosophy. A common Woolfian strategy is to create an impressionistic vision of an author's life as a means of illustrating their preoccupations and the influence of the age in which they lived. In her essays, authors are given a new sense of being through narratives that recreate an impression of their inner lives. Of Jane Austen, she writes that one of those fairies who perch upon cradles must have taken her a flight through the world directly she was born. When she was laid in the cradle again she knew not only what the world looked like, but had already chosen her kingdom. She had agreed that if she might rule over that territory, she would covet no other. Thus at fifteen she had few illusions about other people and none about herself [...] Her gaze passes straight to the mark, and we know precisely where, on the map of human nature, that mark is. We know because Jane Austen kept to her compact; she never trespassed beyond her boundaries. Never, even at the emotional age of fifteen, did she round upon herself in shame, obliterate a sarcasm in a spasm of compassion, or blur an outline in a mist of rhapsody. Spasms and rhapsodies, she seems to have said [...] end *there*; and the boundary line is perfectly distinct. But she does not deny that moons and mountains and castles exist – on the other side.[36]

Because of its focus on women's experience, it is easy to see this technique as evidence of the gendered nature of Woolf's criticism. However, it may also owe something to Woolf's reading of Pater, and in particular to her interest in his depiction of the luminary qualities of the artist in 'Notes on Leonardo da Vinci', which she saw as being more important than empirical 'fact': 'it is not knowledge of Leonardo that remains with us, but a vision'.[37] This quotation could easily stand as a manifesto for Woolf's own criticism, a vindication of the impressionistic style that she herself chose to adopt. Even so, it is important to recognise that Woolf's comment is based, to some extent, on a misreading of Pater, as the kind of 'vision' he communicated in *The Renaissance* was inevitably grounded in knowledge, and in a concept of the 'scholar writing for the scholarly'.[38] It is also clear that Woolf's reading of Pater is a feminised one. Pater's ideal of scholarship was essentially masculine, as he makes clear in 'Style':

The literary artist is of necessity a scholar, and in what he proposes to do will have in mind, first of all, the scholar and the scholarly conscience – the male conscience in this matter, as we must think it, under a system of education which still to so large an extent limits real scholarship to men.[39]

In contrast, Woolf privileges a more instinctive form of sympathy that is emphatically non-scholarly, existing beyond the reach of any system of education. However, the Paterian elements of Woolf's thought are important, as they link her to the aesthetic theory of the late nineteenth century and to the early attempts to separate the private sphere of aesthetic experience from the more public concerns of academia. This private sphere is often foregrounded through Woolf's emphasis of the sensual pleasure associated with the act of reading, with the use of plural pronouns drawing the reader into the narrator's own reactions to the text. When reading George Eliot's early novels, for example,

> we feel the delicious warmth and release of spirit which the great creative writers alone procure for us. As one comes back to the books after years of absence they pour out, even against our expectation, the same store of energy and heat, so that we want more than anything to idle in the warmth as in the sun beating down from the red orchard wall.[40]

In Woolf's work, the effect of such a technique is to present the reader with what could be described as the 'emotional truth' of a particular experience of reading, as opposed to the objective 'truth' represented by a form of academic enquiry that privileged empirical research, verifiable evidence and the accumulation of facts. The centrality of this 'emotional truth' stems from Woolf's concern with the 'moments of being' that she famously saw as a truer record of an individual's essence than the dry facts of 'clock-time'; an attempt to bring to life the 'luminous halo' of individual existence.[41] Using a distinction drawn from Gertrude Stein's 'What is English Literature?', DiBattista has described this critical method as Woolf's attempt to present literature as 'a history of you', not 'a history of it': an unmistakable return to the primacy of the individual and to a form of authority that was opposed to that which was represented by the structures and methods of academia.[42] As well as validating a concern for the 'inner lives' of her subjects, Woolf was also attempting to validate an approach to literature that lay outside the bounds of academic inquiry.

In doing this, Woolf's criticism builds, whether consciously or not, on Pater's engagement with changing forms of intellectual authority. Pater's definition of the aesthetic experience as lying within the act of perception rather than in the art-object itself has been described by Ian Small as being central to his 'attempt to relocate the authority for the assessment and appreciation of a work of art within the individual',[43] a vital part of Pater's challenge to the development of disciplinary structures. Faced with the decline in eminence of the mid-Victorian man of letters, and the absence – as yet – of an adequate academic alternative, Pater, in the 1870s, was evolving a form of writing that sought to eschew the scholarly devices of the newly professionalised discipline of history, such as the use of externally verifiable sources and reliable methods of citation and annotation. Small interprets this as an unwillingness 'to seek in or grant to that academic community a final intellectual authority';[44] and such a reading of Pater may help to explain Woolf's desire to locate the significance of an author in the relationship between text and reader, which emphasises the value of individual acts of reading. Woolf's own hostility towards the academic world, and her use of domestic images and metaphors of leisure and idleness, can therefore be seen as a revisiting of Pater's methods and concerns.

The common reader: Leisure and idealism

Woolf's attempt to validate a non-academic approach to literature is best exemplified by her championing of Samuel Johnson's figure of the 'Common Reader'. For Woolf, this figure 'dignifies [the] aims' of the 'private people' who read in rooms 'too humble to be called libraries', the mass of ordinary, non-academic readers.[45] The common reader differs from 'the critic and the scholar' in that he is

> worse educated, and nature has not gifted him so generously. He reads for his own pleasure rather than to impart knowledge or correct the opinions of others [...] Hasty, inaccurate, and superficial, snatching now this poem, now that scrap of old furniture, without caring where he finds it or of what nature it may be so long as it serves his purpose and rounds his structure, his deficiencies as a critic are too obvious to be pointed out; but if he has, as Dr. Johnson maintained, some say in the final distribution of poetical honours, then, perhaps, it may be worth while to write down a few of the ideas and opinions which, insignificant in themselves, yet contribute to so mighty a result.[46]

The common reader is distinguished by qualities that set him in direct opposition to the professional literary critic: the new importance of attention to detail is countered by his inaccuracy, and academic specialisation by his haphazard pursuit of his own tastes. Indeed, this last point allows Woolf to mount a further challenge to the values of disciplinary English, as she opposes the official hierarchy of the canon with a defence of the delight of 'rubbish-reading' – the letters, memoirs and biographies of uncanonised authors, a common literary history that was able to accommodate all that had been left out of the new English Literature degrees.[47] This sense of the value of an unstructured programme of reading is apparent in Woolf's impressionistic technique (a very nineteenth-century habit), and in the emphasis that this technique places on the authorial persona, meaning that many of Woolf's reviews actually say very little about the work she is ostensibly reviewing (a further reflection of nineteenth-century practice). A review of Ellis H. Chadwick's biography *Mrs. Gaskell*, to take one example, says a lot about Woolf's opinion of Gaskell, but nothing about Chadwick's book.[48] The effect of this is to recreate a sense of the personal authority of the man of letters Woolf wished to emulate, an authority that was sustained by a sense of the mystique of the critic rather than the critic's possession of a certain body of knowledge. If Woolf portrays herself as having a privileged access to the 'truth' of a particular author, or a superior right to pass judgement on a text, then this is entirely the product of her own rhetoric: in aligning herself with the amateur, she consciously lays aside the sources of authority to which academics could lay claim.

Yet the concept of the 'common reader' is a complex one, relating to a figure that is often confused with the notion of the mass of readers, and – particularly in Woolf's case – with a certain condescension for the ordinary person. Both of these interpretations are problematic. Hermione Lee argues that far from having the elitist overtones that some readers have detected, the adjective 'common' refers to how Woolf saw herself as a reader: 'non-specialist, adventurous, and open'.[49] In addition, Woolf was careful to distinguish between her ideal 'common reader' and the public at large, reflecting Q. D. Leavis's sense that 'the general public – Dr. Johnson's common reader' had been seduced by the mass market and the availability of publications that appealed to more immediate tastes.[50] The 'rubbish-reading' advocated by Woolf was very different from the newspapers, magazines and bestsellers made available for these readers by the advent of cheaper methods of publishing and distribution: Woolf also stated that the common reader had read more than 'could be expected of a working man, or any but a very exceptional bank clerk'.[51] Moreover, the common reader is also identified with a different kind of reading. Woolf's descriptions in both series of *The Common Reader* of idling in the warmth of the sun and waiting for the 'dust of reasoning' to settle represent a different kind of leisure to that which the 'masses' were popularly believed to enjoy, characterised by superficial distractions and mindless entertainment. Q. D. Leavis's analysis of the pastimes of working people made the point that modern methods of production had changed the working day from 'a sequence of interests to a repetition of mechanical movements of both body and mind': while such work did leave time for leisure, the working day was so exhausting that leisure time was spent in recovery, rather in any meaningful pursuit.[52] As a result, the new mass market publications had to be 'designed to be read in the face of lassitude and nervous fatigue',[53] read – in the words of one critic – 'not with any artistic, spiritual, moral, or informative purpose, but simply in order to pass time'.[54] Woolf's 'common reader' may have been 'hasty, inaccurate, and superficial', but he was nevertheless 'guided by an impulse to create [...] some kind of whole', an aim that distinguished his reading from the mere pastime of the masses.[55]

It is difficult, then, to align Woolf's 'common reader' with the mass of readers, as the kind of reading with which the common reader is identified – despite Woolf's references to 'hastiness' – is one that is based on having the time to engage with and think about texts, drawing from them a sense of the 'wholes' that Woolf saw as so important. Yet Woolf is often surprisingly reticent on the subject of the mass market, reserving her scorn for the class of readers she described as 'middlebrow'. Indeed, in a letter written (but not sent) to the editor of the *New Statesman*, and later published as 'Middlebrow' in *The Death of the Moth*, she describes 'lowbrows' and 'highbrows' as sharing similar qualities: the former's 'thoroughbred vitality' and the latter's 'thoroughbred intelligence'; the fact that the highbrow 'rides his mind at a gallop across country in pursuit of an idea' while the lowbrow 'rides his body in pursuit of a living at a gallop across life'.[56] This similarity brings Woolf to a definition of the two groups' mutual dependence:

> Lowbrows need highbrows and honour them just as much as high-brows need lowbrows and honour them. This too is not a matter that requires much demonstration. You only have to stroll along the Strand on a wet winter's night and watch the crowds lining up to get into the movies. These lowbrows are waiting, after the day's work, in the rain, sometimes for hours, to get into the cheap seats and sit in hot theatres in order to see that their lives look like. Since they are lowbrows, engaged magnificently and adventurously in riding full tilt from one end of life to the other in pursuit of a living, they cannot see themselves doing it. Yet nothing interests them more. Nothing matters to them more. It is one of the prime necessities of life to them – to be shown what life looks like. And the highbrows, of course, are the only people who can show them. Since they are the only people who do not do things, they are the only people who can see things being done.[57]

Neither are the two groups defined along the lines of social class: Woolf claims to have known 'duchesses who were highbrows, also charwomen', the two linked by 'that vigour of language which so often unites the aristocracy with the working classes'.[58] Yet both are insistent in their distaste for the middlebrow, defined by Woolf as

> the man, or woman, of middle-bred intelligence who ambles and saunters now on this side of the hedge, now on that, in pursuit of no single object, neither art itself nor life itself, but both mixed indistinguishably, and rather nastily, with money, fame, power, or prestige.[59]

And while Woolf identifies the highbrows with both taste and leisure, stating rather archly that as she writes she is 'breakfasting, as usual, in bed', the middlebrows are associated with 'sham antiques', 'first editions of dead writers – always the worst' and a lack of leisure: 'poor middlebrow [. . .] has to keep at it scribbling away, year in, year out, while we highbrows ring each other up, and are off for a day's jaunt into the country'.[60]

The middlebrows so despised by Woolf bear certain similarities to Arnold's 'philistines', a group almost coterminous with the middle classes.[61] Their class also links them to the late nineteenth-century expansion of higher education, and to a group of people who Woolf viewed as possessing the outward appearance of culture with none of its spirit. The 'middlebrows' were associated with an attempt to be cultured that is also latent in Woolf's description of the ready-made tie worn by the 'ungentlemanly' scholar at the British Museum:[62] they are the owners of 'Queen Anne furniture (faked, but nonetheless expensive)' and 'bound volumes of the classics behind plate glass'.[63] Nevertheless, for Woolf, their lack of genuine taste and leisure time meant that they could never be identified with the common reader, an idealised figure who, like Arnold's 'alien', was neither a scholar nor part of the 'masses'. For the common reader, the acquisition of culture was a random and haphazard project, made possible by the availability of a certain amount of leisure: the middlebrow, like the scholar, simply had to work too hard.

Woolf and Murry: Impressionism and authority

Woolf's opposition to scholarship and the canon, and her upholding of a method of reading that was emphatically non-institutional, make her search for an authorial persona and an appropriate critical methodology seem less the product of gender alone than the result of a complex set of intellectual and institutional factors, in which gender nevertheless played an important part. It is certainly significant that there are parallels between Woolf's criticism and that of John Middleton Murry, who was also faced with the 'bewildering variety' of audiences that resulted from the break-up of the reading public, and who experienced his own sense of exclusion from many of these audiences. The diversity of Murry's career reflects the multiplicity of critical forms that existed in the early twentieth century, and hints that the easy division between 'man of letters' and academic is difficult to sustain. He edited the Modernist periodical *Rhythm* from 1911 to 1913 and the *Athenaeum* from 1919 to 1921; he founded the *Adelphi*, and published a vast number of essays in journals that included the *Times Literary Supplement* and the *Nation*. He also wrote monographs such as *Fyodor Dostoevsky* (1916) and *Keats and Shakespeare* (1925), and was invited to deliver a series of lectures to undergraduates in the School of English at Oxford in the summer of 1921, which were later published as *The Problem of Style* (1922).

This multiplication of roles can be linked to the search for an audience that has been identified by Josephine M. Guy and Ian Small as the central problem facing the 'amateur' (or non-academic) critic in the early twentieth century.[64] The general public could no longer be seen as the natural audience for literary criticism, and the withdrawal of intellectual debate into the academic community meant that the amateur critic was becoming increasingly marginalised. Murry's journalism and editorial work coincided with a time when the circulation figures for literary periodicals were in decline: the *Adelphi* struggled financially under his editorship, and the *Athenaeum*'s circulation fell significantly. He also felt, for most of his life, that his background and ideals made him an 'outsider'. He was not part of the 'intellectual aristocracy' to which Woolf belonged, but neither was he willing to embrace the opportunities offered by the expanding market for 'lowbrow' journalism, as indicated by his rejection of the 'bitter world of the cash-nexus' and lament for the loss of the 'precise and exacting standards of honour and integrity'[65] that he saw as an essential element of journalistic dignity. Yet Murry was also sceptical about many of the practices and values of academic literary criticism, especially its attempt to lay claim to the objectivity possessed by other disciplines. In *The Problem of Style*, he rejected 'the fantastic dream that [criticism] might be reduced to the firm precision of a science', and drew attention to the fascination of a form of criticism whose terms were 'fluid and uncertain', defined not by academic convention but by the 'invention' of the individual critic.[66] Elsewhere, in an essay entitled 'The Courage of Criticism', he argued that criticism should be open to all, rather than 'a highly specialised profession like medicine or the law': 'Every reader is a potential critic, and in so far as he reads well an actual one.'[67]

Murry's assertion that every reader had the potential to be a critic was shaped by the particular intellectual circumstances in which he was working. Guy and Small state that 'the obvious response to [the processes of professionalisation and specialisation] was to redefine the nature of literary value so that it drew upon "common" (that is, non-specialized) knowledge and experience';[68] and it is significant that much of Murry's work, like Woolf's, draws attention to a kind of reading that takes place in a quotidian setting and is underpinned by values that are personal rather than institutional. The essays collected in *Pencillings* (1923), which Murry originally published in *The Times*, the *Nation* and the *Athenaeum*, are written in a gossipy, confidential tone that recalls Woolf's emphasis of the personal, domestic nature of reading, foregrounding the persona of the author as he overhears conversations in the street, ponders the connection between Dr Johnson and a flight of swallows, and turns to popular fiction after suffering from 'a surfeit of literature'. In these essays, Murry depicts reading as a pleasurable, humanising force that operates through a close relationship between the text and a reader who, like Woolf's 'common reader', possesses a certain amount of leisure. When writing on Dickens, for example, Murry grounds his appreciation in emotion, rather than in an intellectual reaction:

> Jonas Chuzzlewit makes our nights miserable, and Mrs. Gamp our days a delight [...] we simply know that we enter an amazing and extraordinary world, and that once we have abandoned ourselves to it the only wonder is that we could ever have been such fools as to remain outside, even for a single year.[69]

If the tone of such statements recalls that of the old men of letters, then this may not be accidental. The subtitle of this volume, 'Little Essays on Literature', makes it sound like the reminiscences of a much older man, even though Murry would only have been in his early thirties when the essays it contains were written. While he notes that the title was not his own choice, it certainly suggests a conscious re-creation of the values of a previous age.

The importance of difficulty

On one level, it is easy to see both Murry's humanism and Woolf's visions as a means of self-promotion, resting as they do on a personal engagement with the text rather than the detached, analytical methods of the newly professionalised humanities. This, of course, leaves both Woolf and Murry open to many of the charges levelled at literary criticism when its entry into university syllabuses was first mooted: that it was gossipy, subjective and required no intellectual skills other than those gained in the nursery. Certainly, Woolf herself was aware that her methods were haphazard, her only 'training' the sheer amount of reading in which she engaged. In her diary, commenting on her writing of *The Common Reader*, she asks herself 'Shall I plunge into early Elizabethans, of whom I am appallingly ignorant? What happened between Chaucer & Shakespeare?'.[70] An earlier entry records her enjoyment of 'the exercise of my wits upon literature – reading it as literature. And I think I can do this the better for having read through such a lot of lives, criticism, every sort of thing.'[71]

However, while Woolf's approach may make it all too easy to see 'amateur' criticism as unintellectual, both Woolf and Murry defined criticism as involving a particular kind of difficulty. For Murry, this was a difficulty that stemmed from his desire to draw on common experiences and concerns: the Arnoldian problem of negotiating a role for literature at a time of immense social and political change. For Woolf, the difficulty of criticism took the more Paterian form of the rigour of reading properly. Both authors were able to use these definitions of criticism to create an alternative form of critical authority for themselves: one that rested not on the structures and processes of academia, but on a different conception of the value of literary knowledge.

An important dimension of this redefinition of critical authority is how it emphasises the intellectual demand of reading and how it draws on certain elements of Pater's aesthetic philosophy in order to do this. In the late nineteenth century, the growing gap between professional academic practice and the artistic appreciation of the aesthete was exploited (as Ian Small has shown) by satirists such as George du Maurier, who depicted the aesthete as effete and solipsistic, judging art by entirely personal criteria.[72] One way in which aesthetic critics responded to this was by defining artistic perception in a way that emphasised its difficulty, insisting that it was not simply a process that could be undertaken by anyone, but that it required a certain kind of temperament and a certain set of skills. We have already seen how Pater emphasised the need for the critic to be alert to the 'challenge for minute consideration' posed by the author, and his definition of the function of the aesthetic critic in *The Renaissance* involves a careful anatomising of the elements and feelings bound up in the act of criticism. Rather than being passive, Pater's critic is an active participant who is required to discriminate carefully between different sets of impressions:

> to distinguish, to analyse, and separate from its adjuncts, the virtue by which a picture, a landscape, a fair personality in life or in a book, produces this special impression of beauty or pleasure, to indicate what the source of that impression is, and under what conditions it is experienced.[73]

Ironically, Pater borrows the language of scholarship in order to assert this claim: the vocabulary used (here, 'impression', and elsewhere, 'sensation') is imported from the new discipline of psychology, lending a scientific tone to Pater's description of perception which in turn gives it further validity.[74]

For Woolf, the demands of reading were slightly different, but no less stringent. 'How Should One Read a Book?' emphasises the need for the reader to play an active role in the creation of 'meaning', becoming the author's 'fellow-worker and accomplice'.[75] Reading was not simply an act of decoding, but 'a difficult and complex art': 'You must be capable not only of great fineness of perception, but of great boldness of imagination if you are going to make use of all that the novelist – the great artist – gives you.'[76] Such statements are undoubtedly fuelled by Woolf's sense of herself as an author, by her desire to be understood and her hatred of unsympathetic or dismissive readings, the 'crimes of criticism' of which she was often all too aware. For Woolf, this need for understanding was also rooted in her awareness of herself as belonging to a particular – and very narrow – social group. She was conscious of the hostility towards 'Bloomsbury' and the public's image of a self-serving, self-obsessed coterie, producing difficult books and difficult art for a small and equally self-absorbed audience. Yet as we saw earlier, Woolf also sought to distance her reading and writing from the activities of the 'middlebrows'.[77] Significantly, this class included literary scholars, whose profession – 'teaching and [. . .] writing books about Shakespeare'[78] – is seen purely as a means of subsistence, in stark contrast to the leisured reading enjoyed by Woolf herself.

Woolf's depiction of reading as an act that was implicitly 'amateur' must also be balanced against her claim that a true engagement with the text was a rigorous process, requiring time and attention if it was to be accomplished properly. Even though reading was not necessarily 'work' (for this would associate it with the financial motives of both professional academia and mass market publishing) it was a pursuit that involved a definite and advanced set of skills. These skills set it apart from the reading of the masses, to whom reading was a mere pastime, a temporary diversion from the exhaustion of working life. The spread of literacy hastened the need for reading to be defined in terms of a particular set of qualities. If reading was reduced to a simple matter of decoding words, then potentially anyone could do it, with mass education and its vision of universal literacy bringing this form of leisure within everyone's grasp. Conversely, if a distinction was made between different levels of reading, then the claims to superiority of a cultural elite could be justified.

Woolf's criticism, then, can be characterised by a number of tensions and contradictions. First, it is built in opposition to a world that Woolf both scorned and felt excluded from. In addition to this, it defines reading as a leisured activity, yet also as an act that involves a certain amount of difficulty. Woolf's identification with the 'common reader' is therefore ambiguous: this figure may have been untutored and undirected, but it was also difficult to reconcile with the actual 'common readers' who made up the mass reading public of the early twentieth century. In addition, while Woolf sought to define her criticism using Paterian terms, her sense of the difficulty of reading seems to be located in the act of engagement – the 'fineness of perception' and 'boldness of imagination' advocated in 'How Should One Read a Book?' – rather than in the rigorous and scholarly self-awareness that Pater recommends. It is clear that this act of engagement brought its own kind of insight and authority – an authority that enabled Woolf to speak confidently as a critic outside the world of the universities.

Murry and Orage: Editors and sages

If Woolf's criticism was Paterian in its vision of the relationship between reader and text, then that of Murry, and his fellow editor A. R. Orage, was firmly Arnoldian. Both saw literature as essential to the upholding of a certain set of values, generally characterised in terms of an appeal to 'truths' that could rescue the age from the social and spiritual problems it faced. Indeed, Orage chose an explicitly Arnoldian formulation in describing culture as 'the disinterested pursuit of human perfection', with literature – a 'valuable instrument of truth' – being uniquely able to make this 'truth' part of humanity's common experience.[79] For Murry, literature could fulfil spiritual and emotional needs that were no longer assuaged by 'social or religious security': in *The Problem of Style*, he described a respect for Thomas Hardy as evidence of 'a hunger, if not for religion, for the peace of an attitude of mind which might with some truth be called religious'.[80]

This Arnoldian vision of the redemptive power of criticism had obvious consequences for the critic's role. While Murry believed that every reader had the potential to be a critic, he also insisted that the critic possessed a set of skills that elevated him above the ordinary reader. On one level, these skills consisted of the capacity to act as a mediator in performing an explication of the text, helping the reader to understand 'the unique and essential quality of his author' by removing 'some of the obstacles that stand in the way of an immediate contact between this quality and the reader's mind' and offering a privileged insight into the 'truth' contained within the text.[81] In addition, the critic also acted as an evaluator. The lectures that make up *The Problem of Style* are peppered with terms that attest to this role: authors are seen in terms of their 'vitality', 'perfection' or 'triviality'; novels are divided simply into 'good' and 'bad'; a passage of Arnold Bennett displays 'downright wickedness'.[82] In a similar way, Orage saw 'truth' as linked inextricably to the concept of 'common sense', being something that 'everybody knows but needs to be reminded that he knows'.[83] These 'reminders' needed to be issued by critics able to recognise and communicate this truth, people who were both part of the common domain of humanity yet also set apart from it by their possession of a superior kind of knowledge. In turn, this knowledge had to be communicated in a manner that was 'capable of being understood by the jury of mankind': the images of judge and jury that pervade his critical writing reflect the seriousness with which he saw literary criticism, a process vital to the health of society.[84]

Both Murry and Orage, then, elevated the critic above Woolf's 'common reader' and gave him the role of sage, a figure endowed not just with knowledge, but also with wisdom. Significantly, this was a role they also claimed for themselves. They did this partly through their criticism, but also – perhaps more crucially – through their work as editors, a task which gave their critical work a more specific context and direction.

It is important to note that the journals Murry and Orage edited were not exclusively literary, but contained articles on a range of topics felt to be relevant to the issue of culture and society. Orage, whose weekly magazine *The New Age* has been described by Wallace Martin as 'an unparalleled arena of cultural and political debate',[85] was vehemently anti-specialist, criticising both the narrow-mindedness of 'aesthetic fastidiousness' and the 'dull' outlook that resulted from an overemphasis of 'history, foreign affairs, [and] economics'.[86] During his editorship of

The New Age, which lasted from 1907 to 1922, Orage aimed to bring together politics, literature and the arts in an attempt to address the social, cultural and economic problems of the time through a coherent philosophy of life rather than in empirical terms. In doing this, he also hoped to counter the fragmentation that had been brought about by the specialisation of academic disciplines and the diversification of the arts. Consequently, *The New Age* was intended to appeal to a broad social spectrum: both the new thinkers and readers created by the growth of secondary and higher education, and the old audiences of the Victorian periodicals, dissatisfied by the way that these journals had modified their content to keep up with the demands of the mass market.[87] This non-specialist aim was shared by Murry in his editorship of the *Adelphi*, a journal that consciously played on its audience's sense of urgency at the supposed breakdown of an educated reading public and the displacement of criticism into academic analysis. Even when Murry resigned as editor, it is significant that his successors, Max Plowman and Richard Rees, were keen to advertise their desire to carry on his work rather than creating a break with his aims, presenting the *Adelphi* as part of a humanist attempt to seek 'a sense of values commensurate with the glory of life and the majesty of death' in a battle against 'cynical indifference, superficial wit, [and] otiose amiability'.[88]

Such sentiments are clearly part of what Stefan Collini has described as an early twentieth-century nostalgia for the ideal of the coherent Victorian reading public, an important strand of which was an insistence on the 'debased' nature of the contemporary media and the lack of seriousness engendered by the popular press and its focus on leisure and amusement.[89] It is therefore all the more significant that Murry's criticism and presence continued to dominate the *Adelphi* even after his editorship ceased. In the year after Murry's resignation, the *Adelphi* contained essays by Murry on the influence of Lord Northcliffe and on modern religion, as well as a series of reminiscences of D. H. Lawrence; he was to contribute more articles and reviews in the future. In addition, Plowman and Rees did their best to consolidate Murry in the role of sage. Their first editorial described his resignation as a release from 'humbler duties', allowing him to devote his time to the more important tasks of literary and cultural criticism.[90] In a review of Murry's *Discoveries* and *Studies in Keats*, Plowman described him in terms that foreground his humane qualities rather than any academic achievements, seeing his 'simple sincerity', 'reverence for common things' and 'quiet depth of feeling' as revealing a truth whose value was, implicitly, much more substantial.[91] According to Plowman, *Discoveries* contained the sober evaluations of a widely informed, even learned mind. It is beautifully written, in that it is 'the complete and coherent utterance of a man who feels and sees and thinks clearly and is convinced that his feeling and vision and thought is worth utterance'. Each essay fulfils the author's intent in being 'the adventures of a man's soul among books', and surpasses that intention by adventuring deeply into the souls of those who wrote the books. The discoveries are not the usual discoveries of the modern essayist – of mare's nests facetiously disguised – but are genuine and personal discoveries, of purpose, felicity and meaning, which reveal different aspects of truth as it appears in great work.[92]

In *Studies in Keats*, meanwhile, Keats was 'not disintegrated by analysis, nor intellectualised into a poetic cypher, but better known both in his likeness and in his unlikeness to ourselves'.[93] Such statements posit an opposition between academic analysis and the more spiritual (and, implicitly, more far-reaching) criticism of those who were prepared to meet literature on its own terms, making themselves humble before the 'greatness' of the text. In contrast to the analytical techniques associated with academic criticism, Murry's work was 'an adventure of the soul, a delivery of himself up to the test all great literature makes of those capable of its appreciation'.[94]

It is clear from such statements that the authority Plowman claimed for Murry was grounded in non-specialist skills and values. Murry himself saw the source of critical authority as an important topic and was frequently scathing about the value of scholarship, emphasising instead a form of knowledge that could not be generated by academic analysis. In a review of *The Wheel of Fire*, Murry criticised the Shakespeare scholar G. Wilson Knight for wanting 'to prove too much, to delve too deep', and commented that 'he does not deepen, but does violence to our immediate impression of Shakespeare's plays'. Furthermore, he claimed that Shakespeare 'is to Mr. Wilson Knight different from what he is to me. I can scarcely recognise some of the plays after they have passed through the process of "interpretation" to which he submits them.'[95] What Murry considered important was not the professional validity of Wilson Knight's work, but the protection of Shakespeare's integrity: the critic must be careful to restrict his or her work to an investigation of the humane elements of literature, balancing the desire for knowledge against the need to produce interpretations that will sustain and give hope.

Orage was also keen to reject the notion that literary analysis had to be scholarly. In an article in the *New English Weekly* in 1932, he dismissed an argument put forward by Sir Josiah Stamp (then Governor of the Bank of England) that called for the revival of a form of intelligence defined by 'the application of scientific methods to a continually widening area of human experience', stating that scientific reason was only one form of reason.[96] This drew on his earlier desire to use *The New Age* to advance the idea that reason itself was only one faculty among many, none of which should be ignored. In 1917, he had urged readers of *The New Age* to 'suspend final judgment until complete harmony has been established, until, in short, the brain and the heart are of one mind'.[97] In emphasising the role of the heart as well as that of the brain, Orage was able to ground criticism in qualities that were easily rendered mysterious, stating that the 'message' of the greatest books could only be grasped intuitively. In an editorial written in 1919, he claimed that 'the "subconscious" of every great book [...] is vastly greater than its conscious element [...] We may be unable indeed to put into words any of the ideas we have gathered.'[98] If one consequence of academic professionalisation was to make disciplines more conscious of the methods and procedures they adopted, then Orage was taking criticism in quite the opposite direction: his insistence that it rested on processes that could not be articulated meant that it was not available for further analysis, placing it beyond the scope of academic enquiry.

The mysteriousness with which Orage surrounded the act of criticism can be interpreted as a response to a dilemma that Guy and Small have detected in the work of both Orage and Murry, namely that while both critics attempt to authorise their judgements through an appeal to common values and experience, they also had to claim for themselves the privileged insight that would justify and protect their role.[99] Both Orage and Murry stated that everyone had the potential to be a critic, with the 'common sense' upon which criticism rested being latent in the minds of everyone. In 1918, Orage wrote that right judgement was never purely personal: 'Its essential character [...] is simply that it is right; right however arrived at, and right whoever arrives at it.'[100] But if everyone could act as their own critic, then the status of the sage would be undermined. As we have seen, one potential solution was to invest this role with a set of skills that would separate it from the lesser capacities of the leisured reader. However, attempts to carry this out often led to further contradictions. While Orage, for instance, claimed that 'the best judgements commend themselves to the common sense of even the average jury', that 'any average body of readers could be brought to appreciate the justness of every sound literary judgment', he also dismissed the idea that 'Tom,

Dick and Harry' should be invited to 'offer their opinions as of equal value with the opinions of the cultivated'.[101] There is a certain slippage between these two positions: the former elevates the 'mass' of ordinary readers, while the latter (influenced perhaps by Orage's distaste for the very real phenomenon of the mass market) dismisses the ordinary reader's capacity to make critical judgements.[102] The situation that results from this is highly problematic: while the average reader is unable to produce the kind of judgements made by the cultivated critic, these judgements needed to be secured by the assent of the average reader in order to have any kind of validity.

This dilemma over the status of the critic often leads to a particular self-consciousness about language and method. In Murry's *The Problem of Style*, this self-consciousness takes the form of an attempt to find a precise language in which to define the critic's role. Murry's initial statements about criticism appear as a celebration of its vagueness, which is presented as a positive alternative to the 'ideal of definition' by which the critic is often preoccupied:

> The critic becomes dissatisfied with the vagueness of his activity, or his art; and he will indulge the fantastic dream that it might be reduced to the firm precision of a science. He may even, during this period of dissatisfaction, forget that half the fascination of his task lies in the fact that the terms he uses are fluid and uncertain, and that his success depends upon the compulsive vigour with which he impresses upon them a meaning which shall be exactly fitted to his own invention and unmistakable by his audience.[103]

On one level, this definition of criticism acts as a justification of Murry's right to define 'style' on his own terms: as a non-academic critic speaking in an academic setting, he speaks out on behalf of the authority of the individual. This can, in turn, be read as a vindication of Murry's right to be taken seriously. If critical authority rests on individual skill rather than the fact of institutional employment, then the amateur critic still has a role to play. Yet elsewhere in these lectures, Murry's celebration of the 'fluidity and uncertainty' of critical expression is replaced by an attempt to isolate a more precise kind of language in which critical judgements can be uttered. The need for this precision is hinted at early on, in Murry's definition of the critic's task as 'to recreate in his reader the peculiar emotion aroused in him by a work of literature'[104] – to convey, as precisely as possible, the effect of reading a particular text. And as Murry goes on, his search for this method of 'precise communication' involves the use of algebraic formulae, as he strives to articulate the difficulty of achieving such a form:

> To [communicate an emotion], I have to find some symbol which will evoke in [the reader] an emotional reaction as nearly as possible identical with the emotion I am feeling. Do not mistake me when I say symbol; I use the word because I cannot think of a better at the moment; I mean to include in it any device of expression which is not merely descriptive [...] But on both sides there is unfortunately an unknown quantity: my temperament is an x, my reader's is a y. The product that results from the combination of those given circumstances with x may be, probably will be, very different from their combination with y.[105]

Murry's initial rejection of 'the firm precision of a science' is therefore replaced by a sense that the conventional vocabulary of literary criticism lacks the precision that is required for such complex definitions: the essential problem facing Murry is the problem of style itself. In turn, it seems that Murry's attempt to explain this problem becomes a further way of securing his authority. In working at this metacritical level, Murry suggests that he has a wider grasp of what the critic's role involves that allows him to move from the particular to the general, making oracular statements about the task of both the critic and the creative artist. And in addition, the task of criticism is given a status that takes it beyond mere impressionism: when we analyse style, 'we are making not so much a literary as a scientific or even an ethical judgement'.[106] Murry's rhetoric therefore helps to consolidate his authority by drawing attention to his own perception of the task in which he is engaged: his audience is kept constantly aware of both the importance of this task and the difficulty of performing it correctly.

In spite of the diversity of their practices and beliefs, what links the criticism of Woolf, Murry and Orage is a shared emphasis on knowledge and processes that remained intangible. Woolf's impressionism and the focus on judgement shared by Orage and Murry both located the importance of the text in its effect on a particular kind of reader, positioned between the scholars and the masses: either as part of a pleasurable yet rigorous experience or within a project of cultural renewal. Their own critical pronouncements rested, moreover, on forms of authority that were personal rather than professional, underpinned by rhetoric and by an appeal to a kind of knowledge that was shrouded in mystique.

As a result, none of these writers produced a model of literary criticism that was teachable. Instead, they occupied a varied range of positions in which literary criticism was neither an academic discipline nor a form of leisure: it was too important to leave either to the whims of the masses or to the misdirected pedantry of scholarship.

5
Methods and Institutions: Eliot, Richards and Leavis

My discussion of the work of Woolf, Murry and Orage in the previous chapter indicates that the personal authority of the Victorian men of letters continued to be used well into the twentieth century, to underwrite judgements about literature that were set in opposition to the values of scholarship. All three of these critics drew on a rhetoric that helped to surround their status with a certain mystique, allowing little room for dissent. In doing this, they asserted the validity of a form of criticism that could not be made to cohere with developing frameworks of disciplinary practice. Their preferred model of criticism rested on qualities that were somehow indefinable, and as a result, they did little to make criticism teachable: while they helped to sustain a sense of the importance of literary criticism in the face of challenges from the mass market, they did little to support its emergence as an academic discipline.

In contrast, the work of T. S. Eliot, I. A. Richards and F. R. Leavis is widely seen as having had a lasting impact on both the subject of English and the broader concept of literary criticism. Chris Baldick, for instance, groups Eliot, Richards and the Leavises along with Arnold as 'the acknowledged leaders of English critical thought'. For Terry Eagleton, Richards and Leavis were both 'architects of the new subject at Cambridge' and a vital force in shaping the manner in which English would be taught in other institutions.[1] Such is the enormity of these claims that it is easy to see why Eliot, Richards and Leavis have come to dominate studies of literary criticism in the twentieth century, appearing as a commanding triumvirate who it is impossible to omit. Nevertheless, it is significant that many studies of their work have focused not on their contribution to the academic discipline of English, but on what Baldick has termed the 'social mission' that their writings address. Pamela McCallum's *Literature and Method: Towards a Critique of I. A. Richards, T. S. Eliot and*

F. R. Leavis (1983) concentrates on the attempts of all three critics to tackle a central paradox in Arnoldian thought: namely, that culture had become progressively isolated from the society whose problems it was meant to resolve, and was therefore left with the problem of how to reinsert itself into society in order to carry out Arnold's regenerative vision.[2] Baldick's own treatment of their work, in *The Social Mission of English Criticism*, is driven by his desire to draw attention to 'the views taken by the founders of modern English Studies and literary criticism regarding the wider social effects and aims of this activity', focusing on Eliot's concept of order, the Leavises' critique of popular culture and Richards's belief in the importance of literary study as 'an indispensable agent of social cohesion'.[3] And Francis Mulhern, in *The Moment of 'Scrutiny'* (1979), offers an analysis of Leavis's journal as an example of cultural and political discourse, focusing on the journal's broader concerns and philosophies rather than seeking to place it within a specifically academic framework.[4] In all three studies, the notion of discipline-formation is present, but not central: where the university does figure, it is as a place where attempts to resolve McCallum's 'Arnoldian paradox' might be fostered, not as the location of specialist scholarship and research.

Such studies, of course, reflect an important element of the thought of all three critics. Their desire to resolve the Arnoldian paradox is present in the sense of urgency with which they articulate their belief in the value of criticism: in Eliot's reference to Charles Eliot Norton's sense of the impending destruction of the institutions in which civilisation was embodied; in Richards's desire for *Principles of Literary Criticism* to guide readers through the difficult choices occasioned by recent social, political and technological changes; and in Leavis's view of English as offering 'a real and potent force in our time'.[5] Yet such statements have often been interpreted in a manner that conflates a belief in the power of criticism with support for the existence of a specialist discipline of English. Consequently, Eliot, Richards and Leavis have suffered from the same analytical blurring as the discipline of English itself. In such interpretations, these three critics are seen as important figures in the history of academic English purely because of their belief in the social necessity of literary criticism. And as we have seen, many nineteenth-century commentators made out similar cases for the study of English and the practice of criticism, but these arguments alone were not strong enough to secure English its place on university syllabuses. In order for this to be achieved, the supporters of academic English needed to address questions of form and method, and of the nature and value of specialist research, as well as those of ideology.

My analysis of Eliot, Richards and Leavis in this chapter will therefore focus not on their politics (an issue that has already been well documented), but on the complex relationships between their proposals for literary criticism and the academic discipline of English. What I aim to demonstrate is that for all three critics, criticism was so important that it could not possibly be conceived of as a narrow academic specialism: its true purpose could only be fulfilled within the wider sphere of life. Education did form an important part of their attempts to resolve the Arnoldian problematic, but this was education at a broad and general level: questions of academic specialism were of secondary importance. As a result, what is significant about the work of Eliot, Richards and Leavis is that in spite of its perceived centrality to the history of academic literary study, it occupies an ambivalent position in relation to that study itself. Regardless of their politics, and leaving aside their belief in the importance of criticism *per se*, none of these critics made a convincing argument in favour of the specialist academic study of literature.

An important starting-point for my discussion of Eliot, Richards and Leavis is Louis Menand's claim that Eliot's criticism – which 'could be understood as presenting a highly disciplined theory of poetic and critical method' – was successful 'not simply [because of] what Eliot had to say, but [...because of] the institutional needs his writing was able to serve'.[6] The implication is that Eliot's criticism could be adapted, and used as a model, by departments of English seeking to give the study of literature intellectual rigour, a difficulty of a kind that had previously been supplied only by the adoption of alternative disciplinary paradigms. It might be expected that Richards and Leavis – critics who were influenced by various aspects of Eliot's philosophy, and who did much to promote his work throughout the 1920s and 1930s – were at the forefront of attempts to adapt Eliot's criticism to suit these 'institutional needs'. Both began their careers in Sir Arthur Quiller-Couch's Cambridge: Richards, whose degree was in Moral Sciences, was appointed to lecture on criticism and the modern novel in Quiller-Couch's English School in 1919, while Leavis took Part Two of the English Tripos (in 'English Literature, Modern and Medieval') in 1921.[7] Nevertheless, as Mulhern has pointed out, both also belonged to a new generation of Cambridge academics and to a very different social class from that represented by Quiller-Couch himself. Consequently, they might reasonably be seen as ideally placed to instigate a new, more systematic form of literary study, 'subverting the ideal of the scholar-gentleman' that had been promoted by Quiller-Couch and replacing it with a different set of methods and values.[8] Yet paradoxically, Richards and Leavis can also be seen (in a manner that is admittedly much more radical) as contributing little to the notion of English as a specialist academic pursuit, preferring instead to conceive of criticism as a much more generalised activity. Consequently, their relationship with the discipline of English emerges as much more problematic than many commentators have admitted.

Eliot and his influence

The relationships between the work of all three critics are complex. Only seven years separated them in age. Eliot and Richards were close friends whose correspondence spanned some forty years; Leavis was deeply influenced by both Eliot's poetry and his analysis of the development of the literary tradition; and Leavis and Richards were contemporaries at Cambridge, although relations between them were strained (Leavis felt that Richards should have given him more help in securing a permanent post in the Cambridge English Faculty, while Richards, who detested the academic politics of Cambridge, suspected that Leavis ridiculed him in lectures).[9] Yet while there are certain similarities between the work of all three, it is difficult to prove that Richards and Leavis adopted their ideas in a direct response to Eliot – that Eliot was the direct influence that Menand describes. It is, perhaps, more accurate to state that some of the concepts that are present in Eliot's work were developed, in differing ways, by both Richards and Leavis, although whether this was part of a conscious attempt to build on Eliot's philosophy is not always certain.

It is also important to recognise that Eliot's prose writings do not, in themselves, express a single, unified theory of criticism. These writings – spanning literature, religion and society, and made up of a vast number of articles, books and lectures written over a period of forty years – are notoriously difficult to summarise, and attempts to do so can seem highly reductive. Menand's description of Eliot's critical method as 'highly disciplined' is contradicted by his later statement that rather than possessing an 'interlocking and highly developed set of aesthetic criteria', Eliot's criticism was made up of a group of ideas that were under continual revision, making attempts to identify a consistent set of critical principles problematic.[10] Certainly, the circumstances in which Eliot worked – publishing in periodicals such as the *Adelphi*, the *Athenaeum* and the *Times Literary Supplement* as well as the *Criterion*, and writing to make a living rather than with a consistent philosophy in mind – highlight the need to avoid projecting a retrospective cohesion onto his critical canon. Graham Hough, sounding a cautionary note common to much writing on Eliot's prose, asserts that 'what has been received as a considered literary programme was in origin something far more fortuitous', written 'from necessity and under pressure' rather than with a consistent critical philosophy in mind.[11] As a result, any attempt to isolate Eliot's critical method needs to proceed with care.

One way of side-stepping this difficulty – and resolving the apparent contradiction in Menand's comments on Eliot's critical philosophy – is by focusing not so much on the internal consistency of Eliot's ideas, as on the specific areas of his thought and practice that could be adopted by academic departments of English. Consequently, my emphasis in the first part of this chapter will be on two separate elements of Eliot's criticism. The first consists of what might be interpreted (as in Menand's analysis) as those elements of Eliot's criticism that were most amenable to the 'institutional needs' of the universities: his doctrine of impersonality, his rejection of subjectivity and his analysis of form and language. The second, in contrast, involves a set of values that are much less 'academic', seeing Eliot adopting the kind of subjectivity that some of his early criticism, in particular, is keen to reject: a subjectivity that relies on an apparently innate sense of judgement, and therefore rests not on scholarship, but on a more personal form of authority.

Eliot and scholarship: Method and judgement

Eliot had his own doubts about the desirability of an academic form of literary criticism. His misgivings stemmed, in part, from his belief that the qualities needed to be a critic included a kind of taste that developed in a gradual, organic manner, rather than being a skill to be taught. In the Introduction to *The Use of Poetry and the Use of Criticism* (1933), Eliot stated that he was uncertain as to 'whether it is possible to explain to schoolchildren or even undergraduates the differences of degree among poets, and whether it is wise to try', doubting 'whether the attempt to teach students to *appreciate* literature can be made at all'. Such appreciation rested not on education but on the wider development of character, requiring a breadth of perspective and 'experience of life' rather than the 'sham acquisition' of taste.[12] Implicitly, the formal study of literature was only tangential to such a development: the capacity for the kind of objective judgement that Eliot required, a 'pure contemplation' in which personal emotion was set aside, arose 'only very slowly in the course of living' and could not be accelerated.[13]

These doubts about the nature of criticism can be linked to Eliot's conception of the purpose of criticism, and its relationship with creative artistic practice. In 'The Function of Criticism' (1923) Eliot established a vision of criticism and creation as interdependent processes, insisting that the 'frightful toil' of authorship is 'as much critical as creative', and attacking 'the thesis that the great artist is an unconscious artist, unconsciously inscribing on his banner the words Muddle Through'.[14] Indeed, Eliot admits that 'at one time I was inclined to take the extreme position that the *only* critics worth reading were the critics who practised, and practised well, the art of which they wrote', suggesting that an isolated form of critical practice would be limited in use.[15] In his 1942 lecture 'The Music of Poetry', Eliot used this notion of isolation to distinguish between the scholar's awareness of versification – seen in terms of a knowledge of 'the names of feet and metres, [and...] the accepted rules of scansion' – and his own, more instinctive assimilation of verse forms, suggesting that the rhythms of English poetry could be best preserved through 'a deeper imitation than is achieved by analysis of style'.[16]

However, Eliot was not prepared to state, unequivocally, that scholarship was futile. Earlier in the same lecture he had argued that 'the critic, certainly, should be something of a scholar, and the scholar something of a critic', describing W. P. Ker – to whom this lecture was dedicated – as showing an attention to 'problems of historical relationship' that was also interfused with 'the sense of value, the good taste, the understanding of critical canons and the ability to apply them, without which the scholar's contribution can be only indirect'.[17] In a lecture on Milton, delivered to the British Academy in 1947, Eliot described both scholar and practitioner as dedicated to the understanding of the literary tradition, albeit in different ways:

> The scholar is more concerned with the understanding of the masterpiece in the environment of its author: with the world in which that author lived, the temper of his age, his intellectual formation, the books which he had read, and the influences which had moulded him. The practitioner is concerned less with the author than with the poem; and with the poem in relation to his own age [...] The scholar can teach us where we should bestow our *admiration* and *respect*: the practitioner should be able, when he is the right poet talking about the right poet, to make an old masterpiece actual, give it contemporary importance, and persuade his audience that it is interesting, enjoyable, and *active*.[18]

Eliot's definition unites both scholar and practitioner in the important task of promoting the living tradition of art: while the practitioner concentrated on the contemporary application of the literary tradition, the scholar aimed to analyse this tradition in a way that was commensurate with the early Cambridge ideal of uniting 'literature, life and thought'. And importantly, the work of both was also infused with a sense of rigour, placing it beyond the realm of subjectivity.

This rigour meant that the relationship between criticism and creation required a certain balance. Eliot's analysis of a range of 'flawed' critical styles, in 'The Perfect Critic' and 'Imperfect Critics', includes a warning against the subordination of criticism to an impulse towards creativity, a failing he blames for the degeneracy of modern criticism. The critical work of the Decadent writer Arthur Symons is denounced as little more than 'the faithful record of the impressions [. . .] upon a mind more sensitive than our own', with these impressions reflecting the 'incomplete artist[ry]' of one who is neither purely analytical nor a true creator.[19] The 'tumultuous' and 'undisciplined' style of Algernon Charles Swinburne, meanwhile, is used as the basis of an exploration of an alternative kind of criticism that emphasises tradition and analysis over pure subjectivity. Swinburne, so Eliot tells us,

> might as a poet have concentrated his attention upon the technical problems solved or tackled by these men; he might have traced for us the development of blank verse from Sackville to the mature Shakespeare, and its degeneration from Shakespeare to Milton. Or he might have studied through the literature to the mind of that century; he might, by dissection and analysis, have helped us to some insight into the feeling and thought which we seem to have left so far away. In either case, you would have had at least the excitement of following the movements of an important mind groping towards important conclusions. As it is, there are to be no conclusions, except that Elizabethan literature is very great, and that you can have pleasure and even ecstasy from it, because a sensitive poetic talent has had the experience.[20]

The alternative proposed by Eliot involves a willingness to set aside the personal and subject oneself to the higher scale of values by which art should be judged, showing a belief in the authority and objectivity of classical order and a sense of the importance of the past to the present. For if 'the forces of the past' could not be brought to bear on 'the present problems of art', criticism was little more than a temporary diversion.[21] The undirected enthusiasm of Symons, Swinburne and their fellow 'imperfect critics' was only a starting-point in the development of a critical sensibility in which 'the original intensity of feeling' needed to be tempered by 'a more intellectual addition', allowing the critic 'to classify and compare his experiences, to see one in the light of others', and therefore 'to understand each more accurately'.[22]

This description of the process of classification and modification echoes Pater's belief in the importance of discrimination, of the need ' "to see the object as in itself it really is" [...] to know one's impression as it really is, to discriminate it, to realise it distinctly'.[23] Yet while Pater's emphasis was firmly on the relationship of art to the self – on the effect of the art object 'on me'[24] – Eliot's was on the place of both text and reader within a much more objective system, that of the critical tradition. In turn, Eliot's notion of this tradition – and of the ability to compare and reorder on which it relies – can be seen as underpinning what appears to be a particular model for the academic study of literature, resting on both a breadth of literary knowledge and the beginnings of a critical methodology. Such a model is hinted at in Eliot's review of A. H. Cruickshank's *Philip Massinger*, in which he praises Cruickshank's scholarship for bestowing on the reader 'a method, rather than a judgment' and describes his scholarship as being of a kind 'that professed critics ought more willingly to undertake'. Cruickshank's historical breadth receives a particular measure of approval: in Eliot's opinion, 'to understand Elizabethan drama it is necessary to study a dozen playwrights at once, to dissect with all care the complex growth, to ponder collaboration to the utmost line'.[25]

This emphasis on breadth is apparent in a number of Eliot's essays. In 'The Function of Criticism', it is seen as being crucial to an understanding of the 'organic wholes' within which 'individual works of literary art, and the work of individual artists, have their significance', while in 'The Perfect Critic' it underwrites Eliot's description of the mental processes involved in the ideal act of criticism:

> There is not merely an increase of understanding, leaving the original acute impression unchanged. The new impressions modify the impressions received from the subjects already known. An impression needs to be constantly refreshed by new impressions in order that it may persist at all; it needs to take its place in a system of impressions. And this system tends to become articulate in a generalized statement of literary beauty.[26]

Interestingly, Eliot believed that this broad sweep of knowledge was essential to the work of the practitioner, as well as that of the critic.

Indeed, Eliot's 'manifesto' for a poetic training, expressed in his 1947 British Academy lecture in the statement that 'a knowledge of the literature of their own language, with a knowledge of the literature and the grammatical construction of other languages, is a very valuable part of the poet's equipment', echoes the syllabus that was in place at Oxford in the early twentieth century, in which English was accompanied by the study of classical and modern languages.[27] If poetry was to fulfil the task Eliot set out for it in *The Use of Poetry and the Use of Criticism*, acting as a living force that was able to counter the potential barbarism of a society that 'ceases to care for its literary inheritance', then both poet and critic would need to base their work on a broad understanding of literature, rather than on the narrowness of personal opinion.[28]

Eliot's doctrine of impersonality and historical breadth can therefore be interpreted as giving literary criticism both a body of knowledge and a sense of rigour, emphasising the need for an awareness of the development of a literary tradition that was also simultaneous with the present, and for a critical method that allowed no space for the impressionism of misplaced creation. His emphasis on poetry and verse drama, and on the literature of the sixteenth and seventeenth centuries, gave his criticism an additional measure of difficulty. This can be linked to the early degree courses in English that were discussed in Chapter 2, which focused on poetry and drama – and avoided the literature of the more recent past – as a means of distancing themselves from the taint of 'home reading'. In Eliot's work, verse was also the subject of a close verbal and metrical analysis that foreshadowed later developments in formalist criticism, giving substance to Eliot's approval of the adoption of 'method, rather than [...] judgment' as a means of approaching the text. In the Preface to the 1928 edition of *The Sacred Wood*, Eliot justified such criticism by drawing attention to poetry's stylistic properties, defining poetry as 'excellent words in excellent arrangement and excellent metre', and rejecting Arnold's idealistic conception of poetry by stating that it was not 'the inculcation of morals, or the direction of politics; and no more is it religion or an equivalent of religion, except by some monstrous abuse of words'. He also went on to argue for the autonomy of poetry in claiming that it was 'something over and above, and something quite different from, a collection of psychological data about the minds of poets, or about the history of an epoch'.[29] This opened the way for a form of criticism based on close verbal analysis rather than historical or other extralinguistic studies, involving the rigorous examination of expression and versification.

This dimension of Eliot's criticism is perhaps most apparent in his essays on Renaissance dramatists and in his work on Donne and

Milton, where Eliot demonstrates a form of criticism in which judgements are based on a close analysis of imagery and versification. In 'Notes on the Blank Verse of Christopher Marlowe', Eliot uses a series of quotations to analyse Marlowe's conscious reworking of elements of Spenser's lyricism, using this analysis to demonstrate his sense of Marlowe's energy: 'Marlowe gets into blank verse the melody of Spenser, and he gets a new driving power by reinforcing the sentence period against the line period.'[30] A similar level of detail is present in the 1936 essay 'A Note on the Verse of Milton', a piece contributed to the English Association's *Essays and Studies*, in which Eliot's thesis that blank verse never recovered from the 'Chinese wall' of Milton rests on his observation that Milton's syntax emphasises 'musical significance [...] the auditory imagination, rather than [...] the attempt to follow actual speech or thought'. Milton's privileging of the auditory imagination is seen by Eliot as creating a separation between the surface of his verse and the 'inner meaning': while Eliot admits that he can 'enjoy the roll' of Milton's verse, he also feels that it is 'not serious poetry', leading nowhere 'outside of the mazes of sound'.[31] Eliot saw his close analysis of Milton's style as a crucial part of his reassessment of the poet's status: if his analysis was not to be seen as 'wanton iconoclasm', it would need to make its methods and assumptions absolutely clear.[32]

Personal authority and the retreat from scholarship

Such a focus on language gives many of Eliot's writings a characteristic structure that is at once an echo of Walter Bagehot's notion of the 'review-like essay',[33] and a potential blueprint for an academic essay that could demonstrate the capacity for judgement as well as knowledge that he praised in the work of W. P. Ker. Eliot's early periodical essays typically begin by quoting an accepted view of the writer in question, and then examine its validity through a close analysis of style and theme, a technique described by F. W. Bateson as embodying a scepticism whose 'continuous invitation [...] to dig below the verbal or conventional surface' gave Eliot's early work much of its rigour.[34] Yet this rigour is not consistent in its application. At many points in Eliot's work, quotations are used not as the starting-point for an analysis of language and form, but as a means of justifying evaluative comments that are presented as objective, all-encompassing truths. When comparing Massinger to Shakespeare, Eliot opines that 'while the lines of Massinger have their own beauty', they remain inferior:

'a "bright exhalation" appeals to the eye and makes us catch our breath in the evening; "meteor" is a dim simile; the word is worn'.[35] The normative use of plural pronouns gives Eliot's judgements an authoritative sweep that elevates them above the purely personal, echoing the rhetoric of the 'men of letters' in its attempt to create a sense of objectivity. Later in the same essay, Eliot's judgements become more expansive, encompassing not just stylistic technique but the whole of an author's vision:

> Marlowe's and Jonson's comedies were a view of life; they were, as great literature is, the transformation of a personality into a personal work of art, their lifetime's work, long or short. Massinger is not simply a smaller personality: his personality hardly exists. He did not, out of his own personality, build a work of art, as Shakespeare and Marlowe and Jonson built.[36]

Here, beliefs about the relationship of text and author, and about the relative success of the authors Eliot mentions, are asserted with the impersonality of fact. For J. Hillis Miller, such impersonality is purely illusory, a trick of rhetoric that substitutes the appearance of a universal mind for the private mind of Eliot himself: 'in neither case can there be an encounter with anything other than mental'.[37] Yet this impersonal rhetoric is an important factor in maintaining Eliot's critical authority. The broad historical range of his work, together with his presentation of tradition as an order and a system of which he had a complete understanding, gives his criticism a sense of objectivity that seems to expect no dissent. The importance Eliot placed on judgement – on 'the critic's ability to tell a good poem from a bad one' – adds to this air of confidence: while it is unspoken, Eliot's belief in his own ability to carry out this task is apparent throughout his work.[38]

This belief in the centrality of judgement often leads Eliot to adopt a critical position that seems entirely at odds with the authority of the academic. While many of his essays do draw attention to judgements that are rooted in factual knowledge, others seem to revel in exposing gaps in this knowledge, even flaunting them as evidence that the critic has a right to voice judgements even when they are unsupported. His discussion of versification in 'The Music of Poetry' is accompanied by the admission that 'I have never been able to retain the names of feet and metres, or to pay the proper respect to the accepted rules of scansion.'[39] In *The Use of Poetry and the Use of*

Criticism, Eliot's attitude towards Coleridge's theory of imagination seems decidedly casual:

> I have read some of Hegel and Fichte, as well as Hartley (who turns up at any moment with Coleridge), and forgotten it; of Schelling I am entirely ignorant at first hand, and he is one of those numerous authors whom, the longer you leave them unread, the less desire you have to read. Hence it may be that I wholly fail to appreciate this passage. My mind is too heavy and concrete for any flight of absolute reasoning. If, as I have already suggested, the difference between imagination and fancy amounts in practice to no more than the difference between good and bad poetry, have we done more than take a turn round Robin Hood's barn?[40]

Such claims may well have been disingenuous, an attempt to lessen the gap between Eliot and his audience rather than a genuine admission of ignorance. Yet it is important to note that Eliot's brusque rejection of Coleridge's philosophy (and the knowledge that supported it) places him firmly in the camp of the generalist: one who may be rescued by his own authority as a poet, but who nevertheless is emphatically not an academic specialist.[41] This personal stance is also apparent in Eliot's discussion of Shelley, in which he makes it perfectly plain that he is approaching Shelley as an interested amateur rather than a scholar: 'I find his ideas repellent [...] the man was humourless, pedantic, self-centred, and almost a blackguard.'[42]

Eliot's overt rejection of scholarly knowledge highlights his ambivalence about the value of a form of criticism that was dominated by the needs of specialisation. Chris Baldick points out that while the 'university English Studies movement' was able (as Louis Menand has claimed) to 'expand upon Eliot's early promise [by] appropriating his critical innovations [...] and using them for its own purposes', this process of appropriation was 'often against [Eliot's] will', taking criticism in a direction of which Eliot would not have approved.[43] One of the most pertinent examples of this is in the formalist analysis that E. M. W. Tillyard defined as a major influence on the work of I. A. Richards. For Tillyard, 'the change of taste typified and promoted by Eliot, the reaction from Romantic emotionalism to more cerebral types of poetry, fostered the urge towards practical criticism because it directed attention to a kind of literature for which minute exegesis was especially apt'.[44] Yet Eliot himself felt that such exegesis did not necessarily assist the ordinary reader, as it carried with it an assumption that poetry was invariably difficult – thus throwing the reader into 'a state of consternation very unfavourable to poetic receptivity'.[45] He also believed that the critic must bear in mind the relevance of the knowledge he or she sought to produce. In 'The Function of Criticism', he insists that while the critic's chief tools are comparison and analysis, 'it is obvious indeed that they *are* tools, to be handled with care, and not employed in an inquiry into the number of times giraffes are mentioned in the English novel'.[46] A similar view, albeit more soberly phrased, is expressed in 'The Perfect Critic', in which technical criticism is seen as 'limited' in its aims.[47] Meanwhile, in 'The Frontiers of Criticism' (1956), Eliot acknowledged that while 'most of the really interesting criticism to-day is the work of men of letters who have found their way into the universities, and of scholars whose critical activity has first been exercised in the classroom', the resulting level of specialisation threatened to deaden true critical insight, producing a kind of knowledge typified by the 'explanation by origins' of John Livingston Lowes's *The Road to Xanadu*, or by 'the lemon-squeezer school' of Practical Criticism. Neither approach would succeed in fostering a genuine understanding of literature. The former – like the 'bogus scholarship' of Eliot's own notes to *The Waste Land* – offered little more than a puzzle invented 'for the pleasure of discovering the solution', accumulating knowledge yet failing to use this for any real purpose.[48] The latter closed off the possibility of individual thought by claiming to offer a single, univocal interpretation of the text: 'There are many things, perhaps, to know about this poem, or that, many facts about which scholars can instruct me which will help me to avoid definite *mis*understanding; but a valid interpretation, I believe, must be at the same time an interpretation of my own feelings when I read it.'[49] Perhaps more important, however, was the sense that such approaches also pointed to a loss of critical direction. Recognising the changing nature of the 'serious' reading public, and the narrowing of the potential audience for criticism, Eliot wondered 'whether the weakness of modern criticism is not an uncertainty as to what criticism is for [. . .] what benefit it is to bring, and to whom'.[50] If criticism was to carry out its task of reasserting and reinterpreting the literary tradition to a world in crisis, it had to avoid both the subjectivity of aestheticism and a retreat into academic isolation.

Eliot's criticism therefore offered a number of methods and philosophies to academic departments of English. Its early insistence on rigour and impersonality, and on the importance of critical method, gave implicit support to the subject's claims to disciplinarity: to read Eliot's criticism is to be aware of an activity that was at once wide-ranging, difficult and important. Yet this importance brought responsibility, and this responsibility – to a society constantly depicted as in danger of losing its sense of its culture – could not be fulfilled if English was allowed to remain a purely specialist pursuit. For criticism to carry out its 'social mission', it would need to have a wider audience and a wider frame of reference.

I. A. Richards: Meaning and value

Eliot's rejection of the 'lemon-squeezer school of criticism' also adds an ironic twist to Tillyard's claim that Eliot was himself a central figure in the development of such a school, promoting critical rigour and the need for the 'minute exegesis' of difficult texts. By 1956, Eliot had become convinced that criticism should be directed towards enjoyment as well as understanding, and was afraid that analysis would put the ordinary reader's experience of the text in jeopardy, hinting at a level of difficulty that was not necessarily present. Yet this was also a view that Richards himself came to espouse. In a conversation in December 1968, Richards stated that 'making [English] into an academic subject has not increased the amount of enjoyment taken in the poems [...] I think we're burying the valuables under a whole load of derivatives'.[51] Eliot's reduction of practical criticism to mere 'lemon-squeezing' was also based on a misreading of Richards's aims. While Richards did indeed see a structured, analytical approach to literature as important to an understanding of the text, this was formulated not in specialised, academic terms, but as the only appropriate response to the crisis faced by literature in the modern world – a crisis that had also been perceived by Eliot himself.

The precise extent of Eliot and Richards's influence upon each other is difficult to isolate. John Paul Russo, Richards's biographer, suggests that their effect on each others' criticism and philosophy 'cannot be asserted with assurance', but nevertheless concedes that 'it cannot be said that they arrived at certain positions without studying each others' work'.[52] Even so, critics have differed in their evaluation of this study. While Tillyard saw Eliot's direction of attention to 'more cerebral types of poetry' as crucial to the emergence of practical criticism, John Constable has argued that Richards (unlike many of his Cambridge contemporaries) did not use *The Sacred Wood* as a 'primary text' in the development of his own critical method, with his textual annotations being 'short and dismissive'.[53] Eliot and Richards also disagreed on several points. In his Norton Lectures, Eliot was openly critical of Richards's recommendation of a set of 'spiritual exercises' designed to heighten the reader's response to poetry.[54] Earlier, in an article in *The*

Dial, he had heaped scorn on Richards's belief that poetry 'is capable of saving us': 'Poetry "is capable of saving us," he says; it is like saying that the wall-paper will save us when the walls have crumbled.'[55] Richards was more muted in his censure of Eliot's work, but still disagreed with aspects of his style and practice, commenting in a marginal annotation in his copy of Eliot's *Homage to John Dryden* (1924) that 'T. S. E. always writes as tho' he were God. Here the fact that HE is going to say something about Dryden is going to alter everything for ever.'[56] Yet importantly, both men saw criticism as a rigorous process that involved careful comparison and analysis, with Richards's formulation of criticism as 'the endeavour to discriminate between experiences and to evaluate them' both echoing Pater's emphasis on discrimination and foreshadowing Eliot's description of the classification and comparison of experiences in *The Use of Poetry and the Use of Criticism*.[57] In addition, both men also conceded that literary criticism had to involve a wider analysis of society and its values. While Eliot sought to protect poetry from the belief that it could be 'religion or an equivalent of religion', he later stated that 'it is impossible to fence off literary criticism from criticism on other grounds [...] moral, religious and social judgments cannot be wholly excluded'.[58] And while Richards's concept of 'pseudo-statements' led him to challenge the belief that poetry could offer the same kind of verifiable truths as science, he also emphasised that literature and morality were intimately related: 'The common avoidance of all discussion of the wider social and moral aspects of the arts by people of steady judgment and strong heads is a misfortune.'[59] Indeed, this philosophy of the arts came to underpin Richards's sense of the importance of interpretation: for Richards, the interpretative act was central to a complete grasp of the value of all art.

Nevertheless, Richards also shared with Eliot certain doubts about the value of academic literary study. He was convinced that interpretation should be the focus of academic attention, and was scathing about the cursory treatment it had previously been given, commenting in *Practical Criticism* that

> one would expect that our libraries would be full of works on the theory of interpretation, the diagnosis of linguistic situations, systematic ambiguity and the functions of complex symbols [...] Yet, in point of fact, there is no respectable treatise on the theory of linguistic interpretation in existence, and no person whose professional occupation it is to inquire into these questions and direct study into the matter.[60]

However, he also made it clear that such an inquiry should not be limited to the study of literature, pointing out that 'direct training in reading' would also be beneficial to 'such studies as economics, psychology, political theory, law or philosophy'.[61] In addition, the study of interpretation was not to be confined to academia, but extended to society at large through programmes of education at all levels. Indeed, Richards stated, at a meeting of graduate students at Harvard in 1969, that graduate programmes in English 'should be dropped altogether', as scholarship and criticism were a special calling that could only be enjoyed by a select few: global literacy and high-school teaching (of the kind promoted by Richards's work on 'Basic English') were far more important than the specialist pursuit of writing 'books-about-books-about-books and reviews of them'.[62]

The fact that the development of English as an academic discipline was not one of Richards's specific aims means that his relationship with the subject is problematic. His belief in the importance of interpretation, and his formulation of a methodology for the systematic investigation of meaning, may well have helped to give literary criticism a rigour that it did not otherwise possess, focusing on the text itself rather than the investigation of sources, analogues and bibliographical matters that was emphasised by academic textual study. Yet Richards's emphasis on interpretation was not strictly concerned with literature alone. Instead, it reached beyond literature into the wider sphere of experience, a sphere also stressed by the rhetoric of Hugh James Rose and John Churton Collins. Their desire to give criticism a wider role paradoxically hindered its achievement of the academic status that rested on its capacity for specialisation. In Richards's formulation, the need for criticism and interpretation to be of wider use creates a constant tension between specialism and utility – and in Richards's own career, the latter eventually won.

Richards's sense of the importance of interpretation, expressed in both *Principles of Literary Criticism* (1924) and *Practical Criticism* (1929), was driven by the need to define a set of standards by which the value of the arts could be expressed. In *Principles of Literary Criticism*, this value is seen as being threatened by two specific forces: the 'narrowing and restriction' to which art had been subjected by aesthetic philosophy, and the more general debasing and commercialisation of culture that was taking place within contemporary society, resulting in the decreasing merit of ' "best-sellers" [...] magazine verses, mantelpiece pottery, Academy pictures, Music Hall songs, County Council buildings, [and] War Memorials'.[63] These forces had brought about the urgent need for 'a general theory of value' that was able to account for 'the place and function of the arts in the whole system of values', defending the arts from the values of both capitalism and an empty aestheticism.[64] Richards's sense of the importance of such a project is apparent in the metaphors of attack and defence in the following passage:

> We need weapons with which to repel and over-throw misconcep-tions. With the increase of population the problem presented by the gulf between what is preferred by the majority and what is accepted as excellent by the most qualified opinion has become infinitely more serious and likely to become threatening in the near future. For many reasons standards are much more in need of defence than they used to be [...] To bridge the gulf, to bring the level of popular appre-ciation nearer to the consensus of best qualified opinion, and to defend this opinion against damaging attacks [...] a much clearer account than has yet been produced, of why this opinion is right, is essential. [...] The expert in matters of taste is in an awkward position when he differs from the majority. He is forced to say, in effect, 'I am better than you. My taste is more refined, my nature more cultured, you will do well to become more like me than you are'. It is not his fault that he has to be so arrogant. He may, and usually does, disguise the fact as far as possible, but his claim to be heard as an expert depends upon the truth of these assumptions. He ought then to be ready with reasons of a clear and convincing kind as to why his preferences are worth attention.[65]

Such language attests vividly to Richards's sense of threat, and also to a certain insecurity about the role of the 'expert in matters of taste', whose uneasiness is presented as ample justification for the theory of value Richards proposes. Significantly, while this 'expert' is not defined in academic terms, it is important to note that what Richards is calling for is a means of securing expert authority and defining it as concerned with something that is more objective than the simple assertion of personal taste. Richards was some way from formulating the detailed methods of analysis proposed in *Practical Criticism*, but he was, never-theless, carrying out what Francis Mulhern has described as a 'deliberate repudiation of the amateurism of belles lettres', emphasising the need to shift criticism onto more objective grounds.[66]

Richards's work on interpretation, seen by Ian MacKillop as providing 'new, basic concepts for criticism',[67] aimed to secure this objectivity by drawing on his belief that language could be analysed according to clear, scientific principles. Such a belief would help to locate judgement

(and therefore evaluation) in the process of analysis, a meticulous investigation of the text's formal properties and their shaping of meaning.
Richards's 1926 work *Science and Poetry* (later reissued as *Poetries and
Sciences*) argued for a dramatic change in the way in which the language
of poetry was discussed, complaining that 'we think and talk in terms
which merge and confound orders which must be distinguished'.[68] To
combat such confusion, Richards proposed a method of inquiry that
would unite psychology and literature in a task for which neither the
professional psychologist nor the man of letters had so far been
equipped: a systematic analysis of the experience of reading. Richards's
attempts to outline this process of inquiry show a clear desire to establish a set of scientific principles appropriate to the description of literary
meaning. His set of specialised quotation marks, developed in *How to
Read a Page* (1943) and included in his 1970 Commentary to *Poetries and
Sciences*, represents an attempt to distinguish between different types of
meaning, such as ambiguities, specialised meanings, and words requiring
particular attention.[69] In addition, his description of the reading process
demonstrates his desire to draw on the language and conceptual models
of psychology, with reading being defined in terms of a process of
'agitation' set up by 'the impression of the printed words on the retina',
and continuing with the separation of this 'agitation' into intellectual
and emotional streams. For the mind, 'a system of very delicately
poised balances', each experience requires a rearranging of thought and
emotion in order to achieve a state of harmony, with poetry being
regarded as particularly effective in creating a state of mental equilibrium.[70] The poet's capacity for ordering speech, and the reader's ability
to interpret this order, thus become central to Richards's concept of
poetic value: poetry is, in effect, representative of a wider capacity for
the ordering of experience that is essential to the attainment of mental
stability.

It is important to note here that Richards's theory of value differs
from a concept of value that is based on the morality inherent in the
literary text, of that kind envisioned in the Marxist model of English
studies as an aggressive means of promoting a certain kind of culture.
His description of critical method rarely turns to individual authors;
and indeed in *Practical Criticism* he shifts the focus of questions of value
from the text itself to the mind of the reader:

> Instead of an illusory problem about values supposed to inhere in
> poems [...] we have a real problem about the relative values of different
> states of mind, about varying forms, and degrees, of order in the

personality. [...] It is less important to like 'good' poetry and dislike 'bad,' than to be able to use them both as a means of ordering our minds.[71]

Crucially, it is this sense of order that is of lasting benefit to the reader, and which will be carried out into the world at large. In the closing pages of *Practical Criticism* Richards expresses this philosophy through a quotation from Matthew Arnold: a 'commerce with the ancients' appears to Arnold to produce, 'in those who constantly practise it, a steadying and composing effect upon their judgment, not of literary works only, but of men and events in general'.[72] Richards's emphasis on the ordering of experience also recalls Eliot's focus on the reordering of tradition, with both processes foregrounding the need for impersonality and discrimination. For both Eliot and Richards, the importance of poetry lay in its rigorous organisation of both language and experience, rather than in the crude communication of a definite set of morals and values.

Poetries and Sciences, then, represents Richards's attempt to formulate a model of reading that was based on scientific principles, drawing on his background in the moral sciences – a background that gave Richards a unique position within Cambridge's English Faculty – to 'evaluat[e] the precise activity of the human mind'.[73] However, in *Practical Criticism*, Richards acknowledged that communication and interpretation are not always precise, straightforward processes. His study of the 'protocols' produced by his audience uncovers and enumerates the different types of 'misreading' that occurred amongst his group of respondents, classifying these into such categories as 'stock responses', 'technical presuppositions', sentimentality and inhibition.[74] Yet while Richards was concerned with the number of misreadings that his respondents produced, he also believed that 'the deficiencies so noticeable in the protocol writers [...] are not native inalterable defects in the average human mind. They are due in a large degree to mistakes that can be avoided, and to bad training.'[75] To address this lack of analytical training, Richards proposed a model of reading that turned the study of texts into a question of exegesis, involving 'an intellectual analysis of the Total Meaning' into its contributory components of sense, feeling, tone, intention and form.[76]

This method of reading diverged radically from the Cambridge model of 'literature, life and thought', as it isolated the text from its historical and biographical contexts and placed the emphasis firmly on the reader's interpretative capacity. This anti-historicism was perhaps inevitable, given Richards's dislike of history as both an academic discipline and a way of understanding the world, and his mistrust of biographical approaches.[77] Even so, it did not prevent his critical method from being adapted by the new Cambridge English Faculty when it was founded in 1926. The revised English Tripos of that year gave a central place to practical criticism, in the form of a compulsory paper entitled 'Passages of English Prose and Verse for Critical Comment'.[78] This was to be the first stage in a process that would see practical criticism becoming a staple method in the teaching of English at both school and university level, offering self-contained exercises that emphasised rigour, difficulty and exactitude. Richards has subsequently come to be seen as a central figure in the development of English critical methodology, offering 'a precisely articulated theory of criticism, together with an analytical method for its classroom use'.[79] Indeed, in the words of Wallace Martin, Richards's conception of criticism is 'almost without precedent in the English-speaking world': innovative, far-reaching, and a crucial contribution to the disciplinary development of English.[80]

Such claims on behalf of Richards are common, and it is sometimes difficult to see him in any other light than as the founder of modern English studies, contributing a precise, scientific method to a subject that had still not found a unified academic identity. Nevertheless, it is important to recall Richards's own intentions in formulating practical criticism. He did not want his techniques to be applied in a programmatic manner, and felt that criticism required a 'subtle sense' of meaning and intention rather than the crude application of a fixed method.[81] He also expressed a profound mistrust of approaches that offered 'statistical inquiries into the "efficiency" of different forms of composition, into types of imagery, into the relative frequency of verbs and adjectives'.[82] His vision of interpretation was one that he wished to communicate to society at large, rather than restricting it to the narrow world of academia: it is important to note that it was a theory of interpretation *per se*, and not specifically one of literary interpretation. However radical it may have been, a critical method that had no influence outside the universities would have been a failure, judged by Richards's own criteria.

As a result, Richards's contribution to the academic study of English must be assessed with caution. Practical criticism was an important innovation in critical method, especially in a faculty that was increasingly concerned with the need to bring rigour and objectivity to English studies.[83] Yet Richards intended it to be a generalist technique rather than part of a specialist programme of study. The uncovering of meaning, through a meticulous process of interpretation, was essential to Richards's conceptions of value, experience and the mind, and was therefore central to his hopes for the regeneration of humanity: it could not be seen as a mere scholarly pursuit.

F. R. Leavis: The university and the sage

Richards's sense of the narrowness of literary scholarship is apparent in the direction taken by his career. After the publication of *Practical Criticism* in 1929, he spent relatively little time in Cambridge: in 1934, he was commissioned by the General Education Board in New York to recommend a set of improvements in the teaching of interpretation, and subsequently directed his energies towards the definition and teaching of 'Basic English'. In contrast, F. R. Leavis's career was much more firmly rooted in the routine of academic life: in teaching, lecturing, and holding the small-group tutorials for which he became well known.[84] Yet Leavis shared Richards's distaste for a form of literary criticism that was directed entirely towards the needs of academia, and felt that the 1926 reform of the English Tripos encouraged little more than a 'narrow academicism'.[85] Rather than forming the basis of a specialist discipline, criticism should offer itself as 'the best possible training for intelligence – for free, unspecialized, general intelligence, which there has never at any time been enough of, and which we are particularly in need of today'.[86] Leavis's conception of criticism consequently represented an attack on two fronts: not only against what Mulhern has described as 'the palsied cultural regime of post-war England',[87] but also against the formal, centralised structures that dominated the new Cambridge English Faculty.[88]

Such an attack drew its motivation from a particular image of Cambridge, and of the ideal university Leavis wished to promote. In his 1967 Clark Lectures, published in 1969 as *English Literature in Our Time and the University*, Leavis presented the earliest version of Cambridge's English Tripos in terms of a 'distinctive tradition' that had made 'the intelligent study of literature possible'.[89] This notion of 'intelligence' is set in stark contrast to the 'academic ethos' of Oxford, summed up by what Leavis described as 'compulsory Anglo-Saxon and the naïve associated notions of "language" and "discipline"'.[90] While Oxford's English School was dominated by a nineteenth-century belief in the importance of philology, Cambridge's early English Tripos was modern, 'distinctly literary' and humane.[91]

Nevertheless, this ideal had been undermined by what Leavis perceived as a certain kind of institutional interference from the Cambridge English Faculty, and by changing conceptions of higher education and its purpose. The increasing specialisation of academic life meant that Cambridge's English Faculty had become populated by '"brilliant" charlatans' and 'dull mediocrities': the university was 'no longer a centre of life and hope', but was threatened by a 'vacuity' that was identified both with the influence of America and with Leavis's fear of the 'technologico-Benthamite' forces with which society was threatened.[92] *English Literature in Our Time and the University* is, in essence, a plea for the 'real' university to avoid the utilitarianism of mechanistic learning and research, and to become instead a 'centre of consciousness and human responsibility for the civilized world [...] a creative centre of civilization'.[93] Thus envisioned, the university would become the embodiment of Arnold's critical spirit, a place where the play of the mind could be brought to bear on the problems of modernity.

Leavis's sense of the crisis facing the universities, made urgent by the beginnings of student unrest and by the 'blankness [...] that characterizes our civilization', is apparent in his belief in the importance of the present as a point where culture is crystallised.[94] In *English Literature in Our Time and the University*, this belief is used to articulate a sense of the importance of English, which 'has its reality and life (if at all) only in the present'.[95] In a formulation that recalls Richards's description of disturbance and equilibrium, Leavis states that this reality changes 'as the inner sense of stress, tension and human need changes', meaning that each age needs to discover the 'significant relatedness' of literature in 'an organic whole, the centre of significance being (inevitably) the present'.[96] Consequently, the task of the undergraduate was not to master a particular body of knowledge, but to form a sense of this whole, and therefore to become part of a wider realisation of literature's potential:

> At any point in his student career his 'English Literature' will be patchy and partial, but, properly guided, he will in acquiring his knowledge of his selected areas and themes be forming a sense of the whole to which they belong and which they implicitly postulate. [...] He will at the same time be developing a strong sense of himself 'belonging' as he reads and thinks and works at organizing his knowledge and thought; and this sense – one of belonging to a collaborative community, the essential nucleus of which is the permanent English School – will play a very important part in the force and effectiveness with which he realizes the fact, and the nature of the existence, of 'English Literature'.[97]

'English' under such a description becomes detached from its institutional existence and becomes, instead, a mode of life and thought, a way of helping the student to make sense of and contribute to the present. If McCallum's 'Arnoldian paradox' (that of how to reintroduce an increasingly isolated culture into society at large) was to be resolved, then Leavis's university – with the English school at its centre – was presented as the site of this resolution.

Leavis's reference to the idea of an 'organic whole' inevitably recalls Eliot's concept of the reordering of experience, and of the need for criticism to be a constant process of reinterpretation. Indeed, Eliot is a frequent presence in Leavis's work. In *The Common Pursuit* (1952), whose title was taken from Eliot's definition of criticism as 'the common pursuit of true judgment',[98] Leavis's concept of the interaction between literature and society – one in which artists exist as part of a tradition they can modify and challenge, but not escape – has clear parallels with Eliot's own philosophy of tradition. Leavis's desire to assess the contribution of various texts to the literary tradition, represented by *New Bearings in English Poetry* (1932), *Revaluation* (1936) and *The Great Tradition* (1948), is a profoundly Eliotian task, influenced by Eliot's sense of criticism as 'a process of readjustment between poetry and the world in and for which it is produced'.[99] And, in *Education and the University: A Sketch for an 'English School'* (1943), Eliot lies behind Leavis's attempt to address the problem of methodology that dominates the 'Arnoldian paradox', shaping the 'sketch for an English school' that Leavis offers therein. Leavis's ideal course, which was also influenced by the work of the American educationalist Alexander Meiklejohn, would lead to examinations in practical criticism, Dante, French literature, the seventeenth century in England, and the transition from the seventeenth century to the modern period, echoing both Eliot's sense of the centrality of seventeenth-century literature and Meiklejohn's conviction of the need to study a culture in relation to its formation. Students would have to sit an oral examination and write reviews of a number of books, an activity that seems to have been motivated by Leavis's opinion that commercial reviewing was a 'literary racket' that lacked honesty and intelligence.[100] They were also required to take part in discussions and seminars, reflecting Leavis's conviction that examinations merely tested 'examinability'.[101] Leavis recognised that the process of discussion was always, invariably, both tentative and incomplete, and acknowledged that such a course would not offer security, resting on a mode of thought that involved questions and challenges rather than the mechanical acquisition of knowledge. However, he also believed that this incompleteness was superior to the 'spirit of strict scholarship', a spirit that could be 'vicious, a mere obstructiveness, a deadness, and an excuse for pusillanimity'. Instead, Leavis's scheme would foster 'a scrupulously sensitive yet enterprising use of intelligence', offering a liberal ideal that aimed to promote the values of a humane culture.[102]

In some respects, Leavis's ideal English school did offer to unite scholarship with a more personal form of criticism. Its emphasis on discussion would help to foster individual judgement in the manner Quiller-Couch had intended at the time of the English Tripos's inauguration, and drew on Leavis's own encouragement of critical debate (a process that also fostered the student's sense of belonging to a community of thinkers). Its historical breadth, its inclusion of Dante and French literature, and its use of practical criticism offered both a sense of rigour and the familiar 'borrowing' of other disciplines. Moreover, it was 'specialist' in its view of the university as a centre for intellectual debate. Yet this was where its specialism ended, as Leavis did not intend to train a school of academics. Instead, as with Richards's promotion of interpretation as the key to an appreciation of value, Leavis's school of criticism was ultimately generalist in aim. His course was intended to offer an advanced programme that students would follow after studying a different discipline (MacKillop compares it to Part Two of the Cambridge Tripos, taken in the final year of a degree course after two years of preliminary study) and as a result he treated English as 'a crossroads subject, signing to routes out and on from itself', rather than as an independent discipline.[103] Yet while *English Literature in Our Time and the University* spoke of the need to make English 'a real and potent force in our time',[104] Leavis's earlier work on education insisted that English should not be seen as anything more than an example of the kind of thought the university should encourage: 'to say that the literary-critical part of the scheme is the crown of the whole, and that the training and testing of judgment on pieces of literature is the ultimate end in view, would be to misrepresent my intention'.[105] Leavis's sketch of an English school was less a plan for 'a discipline of scholarly industry and academic method' than a process of training a mode of thought, providing 'a discipline of intelligence and sensibility' that would act as a 'focus of the finer life of cultural tradition'.[106]

This generalist emphasis means that Leavis's English school shares more with Richards's practical criticism than Leavis himself would probably have acknowledged, given the strength of his objection to the 'Neo-Benthamism' of Richards's critical method.[107] Yet Leavis's concept of the process of criticism was articulated in terms that were much less precise than Richards's. His emphasis on the importance of interpretation, present in his borrowing of Eliot's image of the 'organic whole' and the need to reinterpret literature for the current age, casts the critic in the role not of the academic expert but of the sage, endowed with the wisdom that is needed to detect the needs of the present and reshape the literary tradition accordingly. Yet the exact nature of the qualities needed by such a critic is left indistinct. English, being 'at the other extreme from mathematics', is based – so Leavis argues – on 'kinds of judgment of quality and value that don't admit of demonstrative enforcement', and is therefore surrounded in a vagueness and a mystique that recall those created by Orage and Murry.[108] This vagueness continues in Leavis's subsequent descriptions, which define the skills acquired by students in resolutely circuitous terms. According to Leavis, students of English are essentially learning 'what reading is and what thinking is [...] By "reading" and "thinking" I mean the kinds characterizing the discipline of intelligence that belongs to the field of literary criticism.' The student's initiation into 'reading' and 'thinking' will come about 'by the time he has come to intelligent critical terms with, and made himself, with personal conviction, intelligently articulate about, two or three of the great Shakespeare plays, two or three major novels, and some poems of diverse kind by great poets'. Such a programme would form the first stage in 'a development of powers and interests and understanding that *is* education as "university" promises it', continuing the liberal ideal established in *Education and the University*.[109] Yet in Leavis's work, terms such as 'intelligence' and 'conviction' – while conveying a moral seriousness that befitted the important role criticism could play in modern society – are allowed to pass undefined, acting as general terms whose meaning, so Leavis implies, should be obvious to those who possess a true understanding of them. Consequently, they represent a critical tradition that stands in opposition to the scholarship of Oxford, with its much more mechanistic motion of disciplinarity.

The distinction Leavis makes between Cambridge and Oxford echoes the opposition drawn by Wallace Martin between 'criticism' and 'scholarship', and their corresponding concepts of knowledge as underpinned by either scientific or personal 'canons of truth'. Leavis's elevation of the latter is clear throughout *English Literature in Our Time and the University*: he deplores 'the thought-frustrating spell of "Form", "pure sound value", prosody and the other time-honoured quasi-critical futilities' (an analysis of which had helped English to secure its disciplinary status), and describes *Scrutiny* as representing a kind of skill that was 'not regarded by the actual profession as professional. [...] The professional spokesmen, the institutional powers and authorities, the rising young men and the recruits for co-option regarded such skill as offensively *un*professional'.[110] This defence of *Scrutiny*'s anti-academic nature was also apparent in the journal itself, as Leavis sought to dissociate *Scrutiny* from 'the view that criticism can be a science': indeed, Leavis wanted to make it clear that the journal had never 'done anything but discountenance the ambition to make it one or to win credence for the pretence that something of the nature of laboratory method can have a place in it'.[111]

Leavis's feeling of being regarded by the profession as 'unprofessional' is difficult to separate from his sense of injustice at the problems he experienced in securing a permanent post in Cambridge's English Faculty.[112] Yet it is also true that much of Leavis's criticism appears 'unprofessional' in tone and technique, drawing on the rhetoric of personal authority as a means of securing its judgements. R. P. Bilan has singled out Leavis's 'failure at times to state *any* reasons for his judgment and, allied to this, his tendency to offer rhetoric in place of reason' as important weaknesses in *The Great Tradition;*[113] Ian MacKillop argues that *Revaluation* is dominated not by an actual theory of evaluation but by Leavis's desire to be received by readers who would recognise what he was looking for without needing explicit guidance.[114] Indeed, it is fair to say that Leavis's critical rhetoric often recalls that of critics who appealed to personal forms of authority. Often, he relies on the Woolfian technique of offering an imaginative reconstruction of the minds of his chosen authors. Of a short passage from 'The Fall of Hyperion', Leavis states that 'the facts, the objects of contemplation, absorb the poet's attention completely. [...] His response, his attitude, seems to us to inhere in the facts, and to have itself the authenticity of facts.'[115] The tone of *The Mill on the Floss*, meanwhile, 'strikes us as an emotional tone. We feel an urgency, a resonance, a personal vibration, adverting us of the poignantly immediate presence of the author. [...] The emotional quality represents something, a need or hunger in George Eliot, that shows itself to be insidious company for her intelligence – apt to supplant it and take command'.[116] What is on display is not knowledge, but sensibility, of a kind that is remarkably 'generalist' in tone.

For Pamela McCallum, Leavis's emphasis on this sensibility – and on the individual reader – weakens his capacity to address the Arnoldian problematic, creating a paradigm in which isolated individuals are able to respond to culture through their possession of a particularly receptive consciousness, but which offers no methodology for the reintroduction of culture to a wider society, beyond the sharing of ideas and ideals that was fostered by the kind of intellectual community represented by *Scrutiny*. According to McCallum's criteria, Leavis's work was therefore less successful than Richards's; for Richards was at least able to devise a methodology that conceptualised 'meaning' in a more objective manner, and could therefore be taught to others in a more systematic way. For Leavis, 'meaning' appeared through the lived experience of the text, rather than through any kind of analytical process. McCallum sees such an experience as lacking the distance necessary for a balanced process of judgement or analysis, reflecting 'not so much the intransigence of genuine critical thinking as a kind of blind vitalist intuitionism without theoretical understanding'.[117]

Crucially for my analysis, this means that while Leavis's criticism offers both a concept of literary value and a broad justification for literary study, it does not formulate this study in terms that are congruent with the needs of a specialist academic discipline. Neither does it exemplify the practices that such a discipline might involve. Leavis saw the university as a place where discrimination and judgement could be fostered, and where the processes of discussion, reading and thinking could contribute to the formation of responsive minds. However, his ideal university was a liberal community of thinkers rather than a centre for scholarship and research. In emphasising the need for the former, Leavis dismisses – with varying degrees of explicitness – the need for the latter.

At the beginning of this chapter, I signalled my intention to focus on a different set of questions about Eliot, Richards and Leavis, concentrating not on the politics of their literary criticism but on its relationship to academic literary study. While their criticism faces the 'Arnoldian problematic' of reintroducing an alienated culture into society, it also embodies another, much less widely recognised paradox: that in making criticism both socially and politically engaged, it also denies its status as a specialist academic discipline. Inherent in the work of all three critics – in Eliot's comments on the limitations of technical criticism;[118] in Richards's sense of the futility of 'books-about-books-about-books';[119] and in Leavis's critique of the 'academic ethos' of Oxford[120] – is a sense that the specialist nature of academic literary criticism undermined its capacity to be useful. What is significant is that for all three critics, it was social utility – rather than academic specialism – that won. All three continued to draw on nine-teenth-century arguments about the importance of judgement, the inculcation of morality and the relationship between criticism and 'right thinking'[121] as a means of promoting criticism. Yet they were also united in their opposition to a form of criticism that remained within the university, serving only the needs of an academic community. Chris Baldick's statement that 'the innovations of Eliot and Richards enabled what had been suspected of being a soft option, a frivolous subject, to adopt that appearance of strenuousness and difficulty proper to a serious branch of study'[122] therefore misses the point. Eliot and Richards may well have contributed to the development of critical rigour, but the consolidation of English as a specialist academic discipline was never their main intention. Instead, it was criticism's wider social role that was felt to be more important.

Part III

Current Debates

6
Revising English: Theory and Practice

The difficulty of resolving the 'Arnoldian paradox' – of closing the gap between culture and society so that the former could be brought to bear on the problems of the latter – remained an important theme in the literary criticism of the 1960s and 1970s. During these decades, the need for a stable, humane culture was given a new sense of urgency. For some, this stemmed from the threat of the Cold War: the critic C. L. Mowat claimed that a renewed sense of a common culture was potentially 'our last, best hope on earth'.[1] For others, this urgency was prompted by the debasing of popular culture, and the consequent need for critics who could keep alive what Lionel Trilling referred to as 'the cultural mode of thought'.[2] The critic, charged with the task of interrogating modern culture and finding ways in which literature could continue to be made meaningful, was invested with a level of responsibility that far exceeded that of the scholar. And while the critic may indeed be an academic specialist, the task he or she faced was of a scale that rendered questions of disciplinarity irrelevant: 'We are all specialists now: and what we need is to rediscover what is common between us.'[3]

This book has focused, up to this point, on the disparities between the academic study of English literature and the ways in which literary criticism was theorised and practised by a number of influential critics in the late nineteenth and early twentieth centuries. It would now seem logical to turn my attention to the developments that took place in criticism and scholarship between the 1950s and the 1980s, developments which have arguably done more than any other to exacerbate the gap between the lay reader and the professional scholar. A detailed study of this period – from, say, the end of *Scrutiny* in 1953 to the publication of Terry Eagleton's *Literary Theory: An Introduction* 30 years later – might take a number of courses. It might look at the work of the journal *Critical*

Quarterly, which was founded in 1959 and aimed to address 'the great central values and insights of our culture and of our common humanity alike', reinterpreting the literary tradition for an audience that encompassed 'everyone whose I.Q. is good and whose education, in whatever discipline or specialism, has been worthy of the name'.[4] It might address the impact on English of the rise of cultural studies and the work of Raymond Williams and Richard Hoggart. It would certainly take in the work of Terry Eagleton, Terence Hawkes and Catherine Belsey in popularising – and making available for student consumption – the developments made in European and North American literary theory, through texts such as *Structuralism and Semiotics* (1977), *Critical Practice* (1980) and *Literary Theory: An Introduction* (1983), and through Hawkes's work as editor of the 'New Accents' series. Such work offered its own ways of modifying and reinterpreting the literary tradition, 'question[ing] those arrangements of foregrounding and backgrounding, of stressing and repressing, of placing at the centre and restricting to the periphery, that give our own way of life its distinctive character'.[5] Indeed, for Terence Hawkes, the arrival of structuralism marked the potential democratisation of critical activity, resting as it did on principles that could be 'systematically set out, taught, and learned' rather than on what appeared to be 'qualities you had to be born with'.[6] However, the consequences of literary theory for the academic discipline of English – consequences that included the overturning of former certainties about the primacy of the canon and the stability of meaning – were not universally welcomed. Hayden White, writing in 1977, highlighted the loss of cohesion and lack of shared purpose that many saw as a threat to the subject's disciplinary identity: 'Modern literary critics recognize no disciplinary barriers, either as to subject matter or to methods [...] This science of rules has no rules. It cannot even be said that it has a preferred object of study.'[7] And while this erosion of boundaries could be experienced as liberating, the complexity of much literary theory – the abstruseness of its discourse, its removal from common experiences of reading and its reliance on philosophy – meant that it could easily become divorced from any concept of utility. Academic literary criticism had arrived at a level of specialisation that could only be comprehended by a small circle of readers: the Arnoldian concept of the critic as mediating between the text and the educated general public had been left far behind.[8]

In this final chapter, however, I intend to explore another field in which the tension between scholarship and criticism has been particularly apparent, namely that of secondary education, and more specifically, of A-level English Literature. This course is, effectively, the first 'point of entry' to the discipline for the literary critics of the future, being a prerequisite for the majority of degree courses in English at British universities. Yet the versions of literary study embodied by A-level syllabuses – the models of criticism that they establish and validate – have, until recently, received relatively little attention from the subject community as a whole. Nevertheless, A-level English Literature has become a particularly rich forum for debates about the nature and purpose of literary study; and it is for this reason that it provides a fitting subject for the closing chapter of a book on the ways in which literary criticism has been defined, discussed and contested, especially in the context of education.

Many of the debates about A-level have focused on the same opposition between personal and professional knowledge that I have traced in the development of English at university level. These debates were highlighted by the reform of A-level English Literature that took place in 2000, as part of the wider restructuring of post-16 education throughout England and Wales. The new specifications in English Literature that were introduced in September 2000 promised, initially, to bring A-level English into line with the practices and philosophies that shape English in higher education (in particular, the challenges posed by literary theory and its questioning of the status of the text and the nature of interpretation). These changes raised a number of arguments that hinted at a continuing anxiety about literary criticism and the nature of literary knowledge, leading ultimately to the question of what it is that A-level English Literature should be aiming to do.

The problematic nature of the relationship between school and university English stems largely from increasing governmental intervention in the shape of the school curriculum. Since the introduction of the National Curriculum in 1989, English teachers in maintained schools throughout England and Wales have had to follow a prescribed framework and draw on a fixed canon of texts: all secondary school pupils in England, for example, must study two plays by Shakespeare; the work of two major novelists and four major poets published before 1914; and poetry, fiction and drama by at least seven major writers published after 1914.[9] The public examination system has also been brought under greater governmental control. For much of the twentieth century, this system was the responsibility of the universities, through the work of organisations such as the University of Cambridge Local Examinations Syndicate, the University of London Examinations and Assessment Council and the Joint Matriculation Board, run by the universities of Birmingham, Leeds, Liverpool, Manchester and Sheffield. These organisations drew up syllabuses, appointed examiners and regulated assessment, and were therefore able to control the transition from A-level to higher education by specifying the depth and content of A-level courses. In 1988, however, qualifications became subject to the regulations of the Schools Examinations and Assessment Council, which was merged with the National Curriculum Council in 1993 to become the Schools Curriculum and Assessment Authority. In 1997, this body was amalgamated with the National Council for Vocational Qualifications to create the Qualifications and Curriculum Authority (QCA), charged with the accreditation of all academic and vocational qualifications in England and Wales. QCA provides exam boards with the outline for every qualification in every subject, and monitors their work to ensure that these are implemented correctly: these outlines are also subject to the approval of the Secretary of State for Education. This increasing centralisation is also reflected in the fact that there are now only four main A-level examining bodies in England and Wales: the Assessment and Qualifications Alliance (AQA), Oxford, Cambridge and RSA Examinations (OCR), the Welsh Joint Educational Committee (WJEC) and the former London board, now called Edexcel.

Much attention has been drawn to the effects of this political intervention. In *Cox on the Battle for the English Curriculum* (1995), Brian Cox, chair of the first National Curriculum Working Group for English, documents the attempts made by successive Conservative governments to prescribe certain approaches to the teaching of language and literature, creating a 'Revised English for Little England' that privileged Standard English, rote learning and a traditional canon of texts.[10] Deborah Cameron has drawn attention to the way in which debates about the teaching of language have been dominated by misconceptions about the nature of grammar, which has been made to act as a metaphor for morality, discipline and social control.[11] And Peter Hollindale, former senior lecturer in English and Education at the University of York, has stated that 'no other subject has attracted such a battery of amateur political interference, or been subjected to such quango-led manipulations, or excited such displays of ignorance and prejudice'.[12] Yet such interference has not, for the most part, been extended to the universities. While governments have attempted to impose increasing uniformity on universities in the form of standardised subject benchmarks and the documentation of aims and objectives, university syllabuses are not subjected to the same kind of centralisation as the school curriculum: individual departments are still free to set and examine their own courses, along lines that reflect both the specialisms and the philosophies of their staff and the needs of their students. As a result, a gap has opened up between the heritage-dominated National Curriculum that operates in schools and the multiplicity of forms that the subject takes in higher education. A-level – the bridge between the two – therefore offers itself as a particularly contentious site for debates about the nature of literary study.

A-level reform: A brief introduction

The introduction of Curriculum 2000 was the result of a long period of debate about post-compulsory education in England and Wales. The changes it implemented were intended to broaden the post-16 curriculum and increase the number of students choosing to stay on after GCSE. The main focus of its attention was the A-level, a qualification introduced in the 1950s and aimed then at the small proportion of students who intended to go on to university. The expansion in degree level provision (and the intention of the Labour Prime Minister, Tony Blair, to bring about a further increase in the number of 18 30 year olds in higher education) meant that an exam originally aimed at 10 per cent of the school leaving population was no longer appropriate for the majority of post-16 students: the traditional three-subject A-level model was also felt to be too narrow and specialised. Curriculum 2000 would replace this three-subject model with a four- or five-subject structure that would allow students to maintain greater breadth.[13] Each subject would be divided into six units, and three of these units would be examined at the end of the Lower Sixth, giving the student a qualification at Advanced Subsidiary (AS) level. In the following year, students would be allowed to specialise, pursuing three of their original subjects and sitting exams in the remaining three units at a level known as A2. Marks for both AS and A2 would be aggregated to make up the student's final A-level grade. Terminology would also change: A-levels would now be called 'Advanced GCEs' and syllabuses would be referred to as 'specifications', although in practice, only the latter would be adopted with any consistency.

The introduction of these changes was to prove problematic. Workloads for both students and teachers would increase dramatically; the organisation of an additional set of public examinations created difficulties for schools and awarding bodies; and many people complained that post-16 education had been reduced to a matter of examinations and league tables, leaving little time for genuine intellectual exploration. However, in English Literature, such concerns were accompanied by an additional set of uncertainties that related to the nature of the academic discipline that the new specifications enshrined. When the new A-level courses were made public, they appeared to represent not just the structural changes that applied to every subject, but also a set of philosophical changes as to what was to be considered valid and appropriate academic knowledge. What appeared to be taking place was a revision of the activity of literary criticism. It was this revision that led Peter Buckroyd, of the Northern Examinations and Assessment Board, to warn teachers that their best candidates would fail if schools continued to teach English in 'conventional' ways: it seemed that the 'new' English was to be nothing short of revolutionary.[14]

At first glance, the new specifications seemed to be based on a relatively conservative canon. At AS level, students would cover a minimum of four texts, including a play by Shakespeare and at least one other text published before 1900. These would be supplemented at A2 by at least four further texts, including one published before 1770 and one before 1900. All texts should have been originally written in English, and all 'should be of sufficient substance and quality to merit serious consideration'.[15] The difference that Buckroyd alluded to – a difference that would lead students to fail if they were taught in 'conventional' ways – lay instead in the way in which these texts were to be approached. The new specifications were to be underpinned by five Assessment Objectives (AOs): these objectives would be applied (with varying levels of emphasis) to the assessment of all six units, and would therefore dictate the manner in which individual set texts would need to be taught and studied. The first three AOs were relatively uncontentious, relating to the student's capacity to structure written arguments, respond to texts of different types and periods, and analyse the ways in which meanings are shaped by language, form and structure. AOs 4 and 5, however, were to prove more controversial. These specified that students should be able to analyse the contexts in which texts were written and interpreted, making judgements that were 'informed by different interpretations of literary texts by other readers' and evaluating 'the significance of cultural, historical and other contextual influences on literary texts and study'.[16] In this new version of the subject, students would have to learn about 'the importance of cultural and historical influences on texts and the relevance of the author's life and his/her other works'; 'the significance of literary traditions, periods and movements in relation to texts studied'; and 'the ways in which texts have been interpreted and valued by different readers at different times, acknowledging that the interpretation of literary texts can depend on a reader's assumptions and stance'.[17]

Some of the principles that underpinned the new specifications had actually been present in A-level syllabuses for some years. Even before Curriculum 2000, candidates had been expected to show 'knowledge of the contexts in which literary works are written and understood' and 'an ability to discuss their own and other readers' interpretations of texts'.[18] Indeed, Jenny Stevens, a teacher of English at Godolphin and Latymer School in London, pointed out that 'nothing in the pre-2000 syllabuses [...] prevented us from trying out the textual approaches needed to fulfil the now famous AO4 and AO5':[19] a common point made at support meetings for the new specifications was that it is difficult to teach texts at A-level without setting them in context, whatever the focus of assessment might be. Yet the new subject criteria for English also reflected a belief that the theorisation of the A-level syllabus – in a manner that was much more rigorous and insistent than what had gone before – was essential if students were to make a smooth transition to the study of English at degree level. Robert Eaglestone, a key voice in the attempt to increase awareness of literary theory in schools, stated that ' "theoretical" ideas and questions now generally taken for granted in HE have been very slow to influence A-level [...] A-level is very far from matching – in an appropriate way – the shape of the discipline in HE [...] However the new [specifications] do seem to have been designed to begin to bridge this gap.'[20]

This attempt to rewrite what it meant to study English Literature at A-level offers obvious parallels with my study of the process of discipline-formation in the late nineteenth and early twentieth centuries, when the shape of academic English was being disputed and defined. In stating that students would need to show an awareness of different interpretations of texts by other readers, and of cultural, historical and other contextual influences, QCA appeared to be calling for an increased level of specialisation, giving the study of English a body of knowledge that drew on other disciplines (specifically, history) for its authority, and could be examined in objective terms. The objections to this call – from teachers who believed that an increased need for specialist knowledge would detract from the student's personal communion with the text – reflected earlier attempts, by critics such as Pater, Bradley and Woolf, to reclaim criticism as a more personal activity that was beyond the reach of institutional methods and values. My study of these earlier processes and arguments therefore provides a context within which the reform of A-level English Literature can be interpreted. Consequently, the arguments raised by these reforms can be seen in terms of a much older set of debates about what the study of literature should involve.

The reform of A-level English also has a more recent set of contexts, relating to the place of English in schools and the political and educational factors that have influenced its current forms. I have already mentioned the reactions of Brian Cox, Deborah Cameron and Peter Hollindale to the Conservative government's interventions in the English curriculum in the late 1980s and early 1990s, and its demand for traditional texts and prescriptive grammar. Yet it would be misguided to assume that what the Government prescribes is uniformly and unquestioningly taught. For many years, debates about the teaching of English have pointed to the existence of a plurality of philosophical and pedagogical approaches rather than a single, dominant model. This reflects the multiplicity of roles English is expected to play. The Bullock Report (*A Language for Life: Report of the Committee of Inquiry*) of 1975 identified three major functions of English: it fostered personal growth, provided children with skills of literacy and oracy and acted as an instrument of social change.[21] In 1989, the Cox Report (*English for Ages 5–16*) distinguished between five possible models of the subject, which focus respectively on personal growth, cross-curricular needs, adult needs, cultural heritage and cultural analysis.[22] More recently, Bethan Marshall has identified five broad categories of English teacher, to whom she has given the titles 'Old Grammarians', 'Liberals', 'Technicians', 'Critical Dissenters' and 'Pragmatists'.[23]

It is worth looking at these different subject models and philosophies in more detail, since the conflict between them is at the root of many of the recent disagreements about the reform of A-level. The 'conventional' approach identified by Peter Buckroyd can, for example, be identified with Cox's 'cultural heritage' model of English, a tradition that reaches back to Leavis, Arnold and the Newbolt Report of 1921 in its valorising of the civilising power of literature. Such an approach also overlaps with a philosophy of personal growth, involving methods of analysis and judgement which – in their emphasis on objectivity and disinterestedness – were intended to foster a certain attitude of mind. Yet such growth is clearly determined by a particular set of values, often articulated through the kind of rhetoric that was used to promote the subject's original liberal aims. The Newbolt Report, for example, recommended that the national language and literature should be used to encourage a sense of national pride, seeing the rise of organised labour movements and the resistance of literary culture as pointing to a 'morbid condition of the body politic which if not taken in hand may be followed by lamentable consequences'.[24] Meanwhile, in the current National Curriculum for English, personal growth is determined by a view of what it means to be an active citizen: one who can reflect on questions of right and wrong, work collaboratively and 'participate fully in the wider world beyond school, in public life, and in decision making'.[25] Personal growth is thus defined by a particular set of social objectives, with the English curriculum – and, specifically, the literary canon – being used as a means of inducting the individual into a certain kind of culture.

Over the last few decades, this 'cultural heritage' model of English has been challenged by two distinct movements that have aimed to foster personal growth through a deconstruction of the traditional canon. The first is a liberalism often identified with the 1960s and 1970s, founded on personal freedom and an authentication of pupils' own experiences. Bethan Marshall sees this liberalism as having its roots in the philosophy of Edmond Holmes and John Dewey, and defines its central method as the use of English as a means of 'exploring thoughts and emotions [... and] promoting empathy, understanding and tolerance', using 'the literature of social realism' to explore issues close to students' own concerns, and therefore prioritising content and 'message' over style and form.[26] Such a curriculum might include the study of texts such as Barry Hines's *A Kestrel for a Knave*, John Steinbeck's *Of Mice and Men* and William Golding's *Lord of the Flies*, taught for their perceived relevance to pupils' own lives and concerns and their insights into the nature of humanity and society.[27] This liberal approach has often been felt to be particularly suitable for less academic pupils, allowing for an exploration of thought and feeling through texts that are used in appropriate, accessible ways. The progressivist work of David Holbrook, for example, used Shakespeare to provide a literary experience that would enable the child to discover his or her 'authentic self', concentrating on the pupil's own experience of the text rather than any analytical process imposed by the teacher, the curriculum or any notion of 'literary criticism'.[28]

The second challenge to 'cultural heritage' is a version of English that has been influenced by elements of critical theory, developing a view of English as an instrument of challenge and empowerment, and identifiable with both the Cox Report's category of 'cultural analysis' and Marshall's group of 'critical dissenters'. This model of the subject is aligned with the political Left, especially in its opposition to the National Curriculum's increasing emphasis of the English literary heritage, and has been given concrete form through the work of organisations such as the National Association for the Teaching of English. Paradoxically, this version of English offers to deconstruct the very discipline on which it is based. Nick Peim, one of the dissenting model's supporters, states that 'the identity of English has been and is founded on premises that are no longer viable', with the National Curriculum in English 'proposing quite specific values and beliefs [...which] tend in general to devalue, or at least to exclude, the cultural experiences of most of its subjects'.[29] As a result, such a view places great emphasis on what is often referred to as 'critical literacy', legitimising students' own knowledge and experiences and encouraging methods of reading 'against the grain'. Its exponents have sought, in particular, to present literary criticism as a means of rejecting works as well as accepting them, allowing students 'to deconstruct texts, knowingly to debunk the canon and find alternative texts that had been omitted'.[30]

The dissenting model's emphasis of the student's own experience is founded on a much more oppositional stance than that which underpins more liberal philosophies of personal growth. Bethan Marshall sees this model's central feature as its awareness of 'the political context and connotations' of literature, an awareness that sets it apart from the liberal emphasis on the 'personal level' of the issues literature raises.[31] To illustrate this, Marshall cites the work of Peter Griffiths, whose *English at the Core: Dialogue and Power in English Teaching* (1992) argues that personal growth 'has frequently (though not invariably) tended to be construed as individual in an atomistic sense [...] What English teachers might profitably attempt to do is to work with a much more dialogic and social model of [...] personal growth [...] one which fully recognises the constraints of the institutional nexus of the school, the curriculum, and the State.'[32] This radical approach is clearly motivated by a sense of unease about the values that traditional humanism (and its more aggressive political and institutional embodiment in the National Curriculum) have sought to advance. Nevertheless, Jay Snow – himself a supporter of the radical model – has drawn attention to the fact that its goal of social transformation is itself informed by a very specific set of values that are by no means universal: 'If the project of Arnold and Newbolt was to create a particular kind of society through the educational production of individuals as subjects, it is possible that critical literacy might involve a similar subjugation to "the overall goals of national reconstruction".'[33]

In spite of these differences, what unites both the liberal and the radical models of English is their common opposition to the institutional and political authority invested in canonical texts, syllabuses and examinations, and the narratives that are used to justify their status. This opposition has drawn much criticism. The right-wing British journalist Melanie Phillips has denounced both models for their refusal to uphold established norms and values, citing such strategies as part of a relativist erosion of educational standards. Referring to a month-long seminar for

English teachers held at Dartmouth College in America in 1966, Phillips states that

> not only did this meeting equate responses to literature with reaction to films, TV plays and the students' own personal writings or spoken narratives, it also invited the reader to redefine the value of a text in the light of his or her own experience. The process was seen as an explicit means of challenging the forces of 'powerful institutional centres'. Relative values were turning into a political weapon.[34]

For Phillips, the source of such atrocity was to be found in critical and cultural theory, which 'provided the opportunity for cultural revolutionaries to claim that great literature was a means of political domination':

> Under the impact of a relentless cultural relativism, in which no absolute values could any longer be asserted, the whole aesthetic culture started to disintegrate. It wasn't just the validity of language or teaching that came under fatal attack but the validity of the texts themselves. Intellectuals were no longer content to draw from classic texts the lessons of antiquity. In the modern spirit of individualistic hubris, they believed they could improve on them. So the literary canon was recreated, in accordance with the doctrine that creativity was the highest form of human activity, and to promote the ideologies of gender, race and class.[35]

Similar attacks also came from politicians and from those invested (despite their lack of specialist knowledge) with the responsibility for overseeing curricular development.[36] Brian Cox's account of the revisions of the National Curriculum that took place under the Conservative government of the late 1980s and early 1990s tells of how the National Curriculum Council's view of literature was informed by a belief in the centrality of the canon and the danger of approaches that involved popular culture and a plurality of interpretations. John Marks, one of the Committee's sub-chairs and actually responsible for Mathematics, went so far as to claim that teachers of English were intent on rejecting Shakespeare and the classics, thus denying children 'access to the riches of English literature and our cultural heritage'.[37] Such beliefs, while based on exaggeration and prejudice, nevertheless exerted a powerful influence on educational policy, leading to the publication in 1993 of a revised version of the National Curriculum that sought to impose a narrow canon of prescribed reading and a belief that 'there are fixed responses [to literary texts], which are either right or wrong'.[38] For Cox, this represented an extremist response to the relativism of literary theory, and threatened to undermine the teaching of literature by imposing canonical texts on students at an age that was far too early. Cox himself upheld the opposing view that teachers should not 'succumb to bardolatry' when teaching Shakespeare: '"Cultural analysis" of the values implied in his plays is an essential part of good English teaching.'[39]

The debates that Cox refers to focus on the curriculum followed by pupils from the age of five to sixteen, and make no reference to the teaching of English at A-level. Nevertheless, arguments about the post-16 reforms have drawn on an equally diverse range of beliefs about the place of English in contemporary education, and the values it is felt to encode. The need to maintain the 'gold standard' of A-level has been challenged, for example, by the increasing importance of accessibility, especially in view of Curriculum 2000's aim to increase the numbers of students staying on at school after GCSE: while this latter is not a subject-specific argument, it has been made more pointed in English by the anti-elitism of Marshall's 'critical dissenters'. In addition, the heritage-based approach of the National Curriculum has been balanced against a desire to bring A-level English closer to the developments in literary theory that have shaped the subject in higher education. The new specifications – based on a core laid down by the Qualifications and Curriculum Authority, and interpreted in differing ways by the various examining bodies – were therefore shaped by a range of different philosophies, with their content and methods of assessment bearing the traces of both political conservatism and a number of rather more radical elements.

The new A-level: The treatment of contexts

Reactions to the revised specifications were mixed. One English teacher, Pamela Bickley, described QCA's new version of English Literature as 'positively encouraging'. Its emphasis on contextuality made it a welcome alternative to 'the A-Level tendency to study a work of literature as a discrete entity that springs to life fully formed' and offered 'far less possibility for indulging in the "This poem makes me feel sad" school of literary criticism'.[40] However, many were more cautious. Some teachers objected to the stipulation that all students should study four pre-twentieth-century texts: such requirements were felt to alienate less able students and contradict the inclusive spirit of Curriculum 2000. Others were concerned about the prescriptive nature of the Assessment

Objectives, and whether they would lead to a programmatic 'A-level by numbers'. And teachers also worried about the amount of time they would need to devote to re-reading (and perhaps reinterpreting) set texts, feeling that their existing subject knowledge had been rendered obsolete. In addition to these fears, there have been a number of objections to the critical principles that the new specifications embody. One of these objections concerns the handling of literary contexts, and challenges the new A-level's claim to radicality by questioning the rigour of its theoretical basis.

As stated earlier in this chapter, an understanding of the contexts of production and reception was present in A-level syllabuses before the introduction of Curriculum 2000. The mark scheme for the Oxford, Cambridge and RSA Board's 'legacy syllabus' in English Literature of June 2001, the final sitting of the 'old' A-level, stated that a knowledge of 'social and political norms and mores, religious beliefs, customs and all aspects of cultural background' would naturally underpin the study of particular texts: 'Questions which involve character and relationships, social and financial hierarchies, marriage and the position of women, kingship and political manoeuvring, education and so on, are obviously dependent upon such knowledge.'[41] What was intended to make the new specifications different was that rather than treating these contexts as a general prerequisite of literary study, they would emphasise specific types of contextual knowledge in certain questions on certain texts. At AS level, for instance, students following AQA Specification A would not need to show any contextual knowledge at all in their responses on the modern novel (Unit 1) or Shakespeare (Unit 2): such knowledge would only be required in Unit 3, which would involve the study of one pre-twentieth-century text and one text written after 1900. At A2, pre-1770 drama would be assessed in its critical context, while Romantic poetry would be studied in the light of its historical, social and cultural contexts.[42] It is not surprising that George Keith, co-writer of AQA's Specification B and one of its chief examiners, commented that 'The plain fact is that you cannot even pass an A-level examination on just being a good reader': success would now depend not just on the quality of a student's response, but on a constant juggling of assessment objectives on the part of both teachers and their classes.[43] Many English teachers worried about the precise extent of the contextual knowledge students would require: whether they would need to quote specific critics, or learn set pieces of information. Such concerns were heightened, rather than allayed, by the appearance of a rash of new publications aimed at helping students and teachers to cope with the demands of these objectives. The 'Cambridge Contexts in Literature' series, endorsed by OCR and edited by Adrian Barlow, its Chief Examiner in English Literature, was presented as having been 'carefully planned to help students evaluate the influence of literary, cultural and historical contexts on both writers and readers'.[44] Frank Myszor and Jackie Baker, authors of *Living Literature: Exploring Advanced Level English Literature*, stated that their book was 'closely linked to the Assessment Objectives [...] The most important word here is *context* because it crops up explicitly or implicitly in most of the objectives. It is this word that has strongly influenced the organisation of this book.'[45]

This new method of dealing with contextual knowledge involves a selectiveness that undermines the new specifications' claim to theoretical rigour. QCA's decision to restrict the assessment of contextual knowledge to certain papers implies that such knowledge can sometimes be dispensed with: that texts can be understood without any reference to the circumstances in which they are written and read. This interpretation of 'contexts' is markedly different from that provided by Rob Pope, who argues in *The English Studies Book* (a popular undergraduate introduction to critical theory) that contexts constitute both the text and the reader's understanding of it. Modern literary theory, states Pope, rejects the idea that contexts can ever be dismissed or ignored: that 'literature is somehow distinct or detachable from the social and historical conditions in which it is produced and received', and that 'the primary object of study is "the text in itself", with the context (including intertextual relations) being treated as merely secondary or even optional'.[46] Pope goes on to say that for contemporary literary historians, the text is less 'the expression of some uniquely individual genius' than 'an expression of the interplay of contextual conditions and social-historical forces': it cannot be detached from the circumstances of production and interpretation.[47] However, such a detachment is precisely what some of the new specifications have sought to achieve, restricting students to certain kinds of response in a manner that has no apparent literary rationale. AQA Specification A, one of the most popular specifications, discourages students from exploring cultural and historical contexts in its A2 unit on 'Literary Connections', even though many of the specified areas of study – which in 2002 included 'History in Literature', 'A Woman's Struggle' and 'Experiences of India' – seem to demand such an investigation. The study of Shakespeare at AS level shows particular inconsistencies, as a knowledge of contexts is prohibited by some boards yet actively rewarded by others. Edexcel, for instance, sets AO5 ('show understanding of the contexts in which literary texts are written and understood') as a dominant objective, saying that students must comment on how their chosen play 'was affected by the social or theatrical conditions of the time'.[48] Yet AQA Specification A states that tasks on Shakespeare should not 'encourage critical reading and background reading': instead, the focus should be on the play itself. AQA does provide a pedagogical rationale for this decision, stating that students cannot necessarily cope with the intellectual demands of contextual study at this stage in the course,[49] but this belief is clearly not shared by other boards, who see their students as fully capable of rising to this challenge. (Incidentally, even at GCSE, students are asked to 'relate texts to their social, cultural and historical contexts and literary traditions'.)[50] This confusing situation is rendered even more bizarre by the fact that many teachers will nevertheless want to introduce elements of contextual knowledge in order to develop students' understanding of the text, reasoning that it is difficult to teach (for example) *The Merchant of Venice* without referring to the play's stage history and critical legacy, even though such topics may not be explicitly required for the final examination. As a result, students are then involved in a strange form of 'doublethink', in which the knowledge they acquire in class has to be hidden in the exam – lest it should prevent them from fulfilling the assessment objectives on which they will eventually be tested.

It is worth looking at AQA Specification A in more detail, since this specification's treatment of contextual knowledge has been particularly ambivalent. The way in which Specification A has implemented AOs 4 and 5 represents not so much an embracing of such knowledge, as a retreat from it: consequently, this retreat can be seen as embodying both a fear of academic literary knowledge and a desire to reinstate in the A-level curriculum a more 'amateur' set of values. This emphasis on the heuristic function of literature results, effectively, in a crude reduction of scholarship to a kind of Gradgrindian fact-grubbing. The implication is that to focus on knowledge is to close down the imaginative possibilities of the text – and thereby any opportunity for personal growth.

The hesitant approach of AQA to AOs 4 and 5 is perhaps most apparent in Specification A's treatment of Romantic poetry and pre-1770 drama, both of which are examined through an A2 unit called 'Texts in Time'. The board's Specimen Papers for this unit, released to give teachers an impression of what the new system would involve, seemed to ground this paper in a definite body of scholarship. A sample question on *Othello*, in the 'Texts in Time' paper, asked: 'In the opinion of F. R. Leavis, "Iago's power is that he represents something that is in Othello." To W. H. Auden, however, Iago was "a portrait of a practical joker of an appalling kind." Discuss these and other ways of regarding Iago's role in the play.' The marking grid for this question stated that students would need to show 'a reasonable understanding of the views of Leavis and Auden about Othello' to achieve as little as seven marks out of a possible twenty, the equivalent of a bare pass: to achieve an A, students would need to show a 'grasp of the significance of the issues raised by Leavis, Auden and other readers'. Meanwhile, students writing on Wordsworth were invited to consider the extent to which the poetic philosophy expressed in the Preface to *Lyrical Ballads* was put into practice in Book II of *The Prelude*. To achieve a pass, it seemed that students would need a substantial knowledge of relevant criticism and the historical, cultural and social backgrounds of their set authors: to reach the highest grades, judgements would need to be underpinned by a kind of knowledge that was 'specific, detailed' and 'mature, sophisticated, confident, even scholarly'.[51]

This emphasis on the understanding of contexts – rather than on the individual reader's relationship with the text – can be interpreted in a number of conflicting ways. On one level, it can be viewed as part of the attempt to lessen the gap between A-level and degree level study by drawing on aspects of post-structuralist theory, encouraging students to see texts as generated by specific historical, social and cultural formations rather than as the discrete and de-historicised products of 'genius', and to examine their own interpretive stances and assumptions. Conversely, it is also possible to see it as part of a bureaucratic movement that emphasises the use of precise learning objectives as a means of regulating the 'quality' of educational provision. Simon Dentith has described this movement in terms of an 'audit culture' that is radically opposed to the existence of an 'autonomous unregulated "professional" sphere', evidence of a profound mistrust of the notion of academic freedom.[52] And Dentith's argument hints at a further conservatism that lies beneath the new assessment objectives, which can be seen as part of a backlash against the perceived undermining of scholarship represented by the liberal and radical Englishes of the last two or three decades. This backlash can, in turn, be linked to a more abstract kind of anxiety about the value attributed to English in contemporary education. In Curriculum 2000, as in the late nineteenth century, the knowledge represented by the contexts of literature seemed to offer an attempt to address the problem of defining what 'doing English' – a notoriously diffuse practice – was to involve.

Nevertheless, the reality of AQA Specification A turned out to be rather different from the version of English encoded in the new subject criteria. The early sittings of the exam were marked by an extremely cautious approach to AOs 4 and 5. To some extent, this caution was motivated by an understandable desire to discourage the simple regurgitation of unassimilated secondary material. In 2001, after the June sitting of the first AS level exams, AQA reminded schools that 'it should not be forgotten that the text remains the primary focus of every answer; knowledge of context is addressed *via* knowledge of the text itself'.[53] Successful candidates, therefore, 'kept the text at the forefront of their answer and integrated contextual information when it was appropriate': less successful answers consisted of 'biographical accounts which paid minimal attention to the [text] itself'.[54] However, AQA's approach also betrayed an ambivalence about the value of contextual knowledge, suggesting that such knowledge could be considered superfluous to the 'sound knowledge and understanding' required to reach the highest grades.[55] While the 'Texts in Time' specimen paper had demanded a detailed knowledge of the work of named critics, the papers that were eventually set involved a much more subjective approach that actually required very little discussion of critical sources. Questions typically invited students to consider two opposing quotations and then articulate a personal viewpoint: 'One critic describes Portia as "a great lady who brings to the play a dignity, an authority and good breeding." Another sees her as "insensitive and cruel in both word and deed." What evidence is there in the play for both of these views? What kind of character do *you* think Shakespeare created in Portia?'.[56] None of these critical views were dated or attributed, and students were therefore not invited to discuss what kind of contexts might have shaped other critics' interpretations, or indeed their own – thus meaning that a significant aspect of the philosophy behind A2, the requirement that candidates should evaluate the significance of contextual influences on a text's reception over time, was not actually subject to any kind of formal examination.[57] In fact, in March 2002, AQA's Principal Examiner for the 'Texts in Time' paper informed schools that students would not need to read works of criticism in order to approach this paper:

> Good candidates who are not put off by the learned language used by some of the critics may well benefit by reading critical opinion, even critical theory. Most candidates, however, are better served by lively discussions in the classroom where different ways of looking at a play are encouraged. No critics are now named in the questions, and every attempt is made to ensure that their opinions are expressed in language which A level students really ought to understand.[58]

Subsequent pronouncements stated that the 'different interpretations' mentioned in the wording of AO4 could, in fact, be those voiced by other students in the candidate's own class – meaning that it would be entirely possible for a student to achieve Grade A at A-level without having read any literary criticism at all.

The resistance to knowledge

The reluctance of AQA Specification A to embrace the critical and theoretical possibilities of the new subject criteria came as no real surprise. Since the new specifications were launched, there have been a number of objections to the critical principles they represent: to the idea that the study of literature should involve anything other than a personal encounter with the text. This strand of complaint bears a number of similarities to the resistance to academic literary study mounted in the late nineteenth and early twentieth centuries; and as such, it is worth exploring in detail. What is perhaps most noteworthy is the way in which this resistance relies on an extremely reductive view of the knowledge associated with scholarship, and on a naïve elevation of the 'personal canons of truth' identified with criticism. The impossibility, for the resistance movement, of resolving the opposition between these kinds of knowledge serves ultimately to isolate A-level English Literature from other A-level subjects. It seems that as far as this movement is concerned, English Literature should be able to justify itself solely on heuristic grounds, without needing the same epistemological basis as other disciplines.

Much of the hostility towards the new specifications has focused on AOs 4 and 5, and their emphasis on the contexts of reading and writing. For some, these objectives marked a very clear desire to encourage a view of literature that was informed by a sense of historicity and plurality: the Oxford, Cambridge and RSA board (OCR) stated that teachers 'must be aware of the developing scope of literary studies, and the new emphases that have resulted'.[59] Yet this view of literary study was not universally welcomed. Mike Craddock, in an article in *The Use of English*, argued that the post-structuralist view of the text as a product of its contexts threatened the special status of literature as a 'transcendent object of value'.[60] The reading of literary criticism also came under attack. For Richard Hoyes, writing in the *Times Educational Supplement*, it encouraged a misplaced focus on secondary sources: students would spend so much time reading 'books about books' that they would forget about the books themselves.[61] Mike Craddock, meanwhile, saw it not as part of a legitimate study of alternative interpretations, but as a way of depriving students of their own voices, providing 'ready-made answers' that would 'pop up in essays' as 'mangled critical truisms'.[62] To encourage such reading was, effectively, to acquiesce in a form of spoon-feeding to which Craddock was passionately opposed: if students were to be engaged in 'the search for something more than a materialist world and consumerist age offers them', then they should be 'involved in that search so that they can find their own meanings and identities, not just [told] what to think'.[63]

Such views often display a problematic lack of awareness of their own ideological foundations. When Craddock urges the downgrading of contextual knowledge in favour of an understanding of the 'meanings, dreams, identities, realities, truths of one sort or another that *we* care about and need', he seems unaware of the totalising effect of his use of the plural pronoun: the fact that 'we' might not care about and need the same meanings, dreams and realities does not enter into his discussion.[64] Similarly, Craddock's belief that literature should be presented as something that students 'can own and make their own in a personal and creative engagement'[65] is not accompanied by any sense of the contexts by which these readings themselves are shaped, not the least of which is the institutional context represented by both individual schools and the wider educational system: it is difficult to imagine any reading produced in this context that is genuinely the student's 'own'. In addition, both Craddock and Hoyes offer a drastically simplistic view of the knowledge represented by the study of historical and critical contexts, suggesting as they do that such knowledge cannot possibly be utilised in any meaningful way. It is true that the reading of secondary sources presents teachers and students with a number of problems, and that students need to be introduced to ways of handling these sources that will not prevent them from articulating their own interpretations and drawing their own conclusions. But in this respect English Literature is no different from a wide range of other subjects – subjects which, significantly, locate themselves very clearly within a body of academic knowledge. The AQA specification for A-level History endeavours to enable candidates to 'understand the nature of historical evidence and the methods used by historians in analysis and evaluation'. It expects that students will develop the ability to read secondary sources – including academic monographs – in a 'discriminating and evaluative manner'.[66] The same board's A-level in Religious Studies aims to 'treat the subject as an academic discipline by developing knowledge and understanding appropriate to a specialist study of religion'. This knowledge includes an awareness of 'the contribution of modern scholarship', and an understanding of how different critical approaches can be applied to Biblical sources.[67]

It appears, then, that the concept of specialist knowledge occupies a much more vexed position in A-level English Literature than it does in other disciplines. Indeed, the distinction between academic specialisation and student-centred subjectivity seems so great that the possibility of a form of study that is alert to the student's own emotional life (and to what Derek Attridge has described as the 'singularity' of literature[68]) yet grounded in clear disciplinary thinking often appears to be very distant. Yet here again, there is a contrast between English Literature and other disciplines. The AQA specification for A-level Religious Studies states openly that the subject provides opportunities to 'address human experiences of transcendence, awe, wonder and mystery', and to 'explore their own beliefs, creative abilities, insights, self-identity, and self-worth'. Importantly, it sees no contradiction between such aims and the desire for students to take part in a 'rigorous study of religion'.[69] Meanwhile, anecdotal evidence suggests that many students of A-level English Language gain a strong sense of personal empowerment through the academic study of linguistic variation, which enables them to examine the place of language in their own relationships and communities, and to question the stereotypes imposed by prescriptive notions of 'correctness' (a process that seems all the more empowering from being rooted in academic evidence and debate, rather than simply the opinions of the layperson). However, in debates about A-level English Literature, the personal and the academic seem perpetually set at odds, as though there can be no possibility of a growth that occurs because of specialist knowledge, rather than being hindered by it.

Fortunately, such growth is made possible, every day, in the way in which the subject is 'actualised' in individual classrooms by individual teachers; and it seems that this 'actualisation' – a term that encompasses the pedagogical, intellectual and social choices that are made in bringing an academic discipline to life – would benefit from further consideration, in order to encourage a discussion of the processes by which the notoriously elusive practice of criticism is translated into particular readings of particular texts. Elaine Showalter's *Teaching Literature* (2003) calls for attention to 'the day-to-day life of the literature classroom' – and the pedagogical processes that underpin this life – as part of an exploration of how we teach students to 'think in the discipline': how we initiate them into the processes of reading, interpreting, questioning, dissenting and synthesising that make up the act of criticism, and how we find a place within these activities for our students' imaginative and emotional lives.[70] Philip Smallwood, meanwhile, has argued for the need to see the student critic as part of an extended community of critics in both the past and the present, and to draw on the support that this 'wider culture of criticism' can offer in enabling students to find their own critical voices and perspectives.[71] Such perspectives offer scope for a discussion of pedagogical processes (at both secondary and degree level) that engages with both the needs of students and the demands of academic specialisation, avoiding the two extremes (of bureaucratic performance descriptors on the one hand, and liberal subjectivity on the other) that have dominated many recent debates about English Literature at A-level. In short, what they address is how students can be given 'epistemological access'[72] to the discipline of English – a process that is clearly in need of attention.

The place of criticism: A wider view

What has emerged from this discussion of the reform of English Literature at A-level is that the tension between the specialist discipline of English and the private act of reading is still ongoing. In the late nineteenth and early twentieth centuries, this tension took two easily distinguishable forms: the intellectual authority that was used to underwrite the new literary scholarship was resisted by critics both inside and outside the universities, while the rhetoric that was used to sustain the importance of more 'personal' forms of criticism clashed with the emerging norms of academic practice. As discussed in Chapter 1, the paradigm of academic professionalisation sketched by T. W. Heyck suggests that at some point, this tension would be reconciled: that the philosophies and techniques of the amateur would eventually be superseded by the institutional authority of the professional. Yet contemporary debates about the nature and value of literary criticism suggest that specialist knowledge about literature is still the subject of suspicion. What such debates often involve is a resistance to the knowledge of the 'expert', and an assertion of the value of 'amateur' experiences of reading, which are seen as more authentic and direct. They are also fuelled by a belief in the importance of social utility and personal affect, arguing that in becoming more specialised, literary study loses its capacity to be relevant, meaningful and influential. The non-specialist reader is seen as engaging with the text in a manner that is not hindered or distorted by any extraneous detail: the academic, on the other hand, 'murders to dissect'.

This dismissal of specialist knowledge can be seen as part of a more widespread erosion of academic authority, or as evidence of a pervasive anti-intellectualism. Yet such claims need to be balanced against the fact that other disciplines have not suffered from the same kind of mistrust. History and the sciences have recently undergone a huge popularisation at the hands of writers such as Simon Schama, Anthony Beevor, Stephen Jay Gould and Richard Dawkins: Alain de Botton is starting to provide the same service for philosophy, and David Crystal, Bill Bryson and Simon Winchester have published highly accessible works on the English language, all aimed at the general reader. While not all of these writers are professional academics, what their works share is a focus on a body of knowledge that is beyond common experience, and which needs to be acquired before any further exploration of the subject can take place. The function of these authors is to provide their readers with such a body of knowledge, which is then used to elucidate ideas that are seen as valuable and worthwhile: the building of nations; genetics and evolution; human communication; and the 'meaning of life'. Moreover, for many readers, such texts will provide their only encounter with the academic field in question: they will not have the opportunity to explore historical documents or carry out laboratory based research. In contrast, literary texts can be read and understood without any apparent necessity for the secondary material of criticism and scholarship. While literature can, of course, be mediated to its audience in the same way as history and science, the need for this to take place is much less obvious. Martin Amis sees this process in terms of literature's greater accessibility, as 'words (unlike palettes and pianos) lead a double life: we all have a competence'.[73] And the relationship between the reader and the book is popularly seen as much more personal than encounters with other areas of knowledge, having a validity that exists independently of any kind of academic debate. As a result, the work of the literary scholar seems much less relevant to the public at large.

This mistrust of scholarship has become a common theme in popular discussions of literary criticism, which frequently depict university departments of English as engaged in an activity that is out of touch with the ways in which books are read – and enjoyed – by the population at large. In a review of Martin Amis's collection *The War against Cliché*, the journalist Natasha Walter claimed that academic literary criticism is dead, for the simple reason that 'outside the academic world, no one is interested'. For Walter, criticism in the universities has been reduced to mere 'intellectual buffoonery', characterised by 'a febrile kind of fascination' with deconstruction, feminism and other branches of literary theory. Such fields of knowledge, so Walter argues, are futile, as literary criticism is nothing more than a matter of personal opinion, a kind of 'shadow boxing' whose subjectivity means that it has no real target: in the end, 'there just isn't any final way to say a book is good except to point to it and to say, read it'.[74]

Walter's thesis is, of course, highly reductive, defining criticism as a simple process of evaluation and presenting a very narrow view of the kind of critical and scholarly activity that takes place in universities. It is also flawed in its treatment of Amis's argument, which offers a markedly different reason for the death of academic criticism. For Walter, such criticism is irrelevant because of its narrow institutional basis: it renders the discussion of literature deliberately theoretical, anti-humanist and obfuscatory. In contrast, Amis blames the decline of criticism on a pervasive democratisation of society that militates against the exaltation of literature through criticism and the canon, seeing as negative the same free play of personal opinion that Walter embraces. In the universities, Amis claims, this democratisation has led to a proliferation of critical approaches and the undermining of the traditional canon, bringing about a situation in which academic advancement 'will not come from a respectful study of Wordsworth's poetics; it will come from a challenging study of his politics – his attitude to the poor, say, or his unconscious "valorization" of Napoleon; and it will come still faster if you ignore Wordsworth and elevate some (justly) neglected contemporary, by which process the canon may be quietly and steadily sapped'. In a wider sense, it is epitomised by Amis's paraphrase of Gore Vidal's belief that 'nobody's feelings are more authentic, and thus more important, than anybody else's'. In other words, everyone has the capacity to be a literary critic – especially if criticism is, as in Walter's argument, little more than a matter of opinion, an individual encounter with the text that Amis sees as taking place 'without any reference to the thing behind [. . .] talent, and the canon, and the body of knowledge we call literature'.[75]

In another review of Amis's book, Lawrence Rainey has taken the author to task for his 'recycling [of] anti-intellectual clichés about academic critics'.[76] Such a charge could, of course, be brought against Walter as well; and there is certainly a hint of *reductio ad absurdum* about Walter's listing of representative critical topics and Amis's comments about academic preferment. Nevertheless, both Amis and Walter are writing as journalists, outside the boundaries of academic practice and with varying degrees of opposition to it. Perhaps more significantly, such sentiments are also a common feature of Harold Bloom's *How to Read and Why* and John Carey's *Pure Pleasure*, both written by professors of English (at New York and Oxford, respectively: Bloom is also Professor of Humanities at Princeton) and both aiming to act as a guide to literature for non-specialist readers. It is certainly important that Bloom's first instruction to his readers, Samuel Johnson's 'Clear your mind of cant', is given an explicitly anti-academic spin: 'Your dictionary will tell you that *cant* in this sense is speech overflowing with pious platitudes, the peculiar vocabulary of a sect or coven. Since the universities have empowered such covens as "gender and sexuality" and "multiculturalism," Johnson's admonition thus becomes "Clear your mind of academic cant." '[77] Particular scorn is directed at a university culture 'where the appreciation of Victorian women's underwear replaces the appreciation of Charles Dickens and Robert Browning',[78] and at the critical phantoms that Bloom sees as needing to be exorcised: 'One such phantom is the Death of the Author; another is the assertion that the self is a fiction; yet another is the opinion that literary and dramatic characters are so many marks upon a page.'[79] It is clear that for Bloom, such 'phantoms' represent a corruption of literature's primary humanist purpose, a sustaining and consolatory process that 'retains considerable continuity with the past, however [reading] is performed in the academies'.[80] Similarly, Carey states his aim as being the cultivation of 'pure reading-pleasure', a criterion ignored by 'the lists of "great books" concocted by panels of experts and published from time to time in the literary press'.[81] Carey is less vehement than Bloom in his opposition of academic practices, but the suspicion with which he treats the concept of 'great books' and his disparagement of the views of 'experts', make his intention to champion his own version of the 'common reader' quite plain.

Both Bloom and Carey espouse a view of reading that is essentially humanist, based on what Bloom describes as a 'solitary praxis' that is markedly different to the kinds of reading which takes place in institutional contexts.[82] Bloom's vision of reading is of a force that can 'strengthen the self, and [help us] to learn its authentic interests', making it 'the most healing of pleasures'.[83] For Carey, reading is valuable because it 'admits you to an inner space which, though virtually boundless, is inaccessible to the multitudes milling around'. In addition, it draws on an imaginative power that is intrinsically linked to 'the ability to empathize with other people'.[84] It is not surprising, therefore, that both authors draw attention to what they see as the timelessness of their chosen texts, drawing on a normalising use of pronouns to suggest a common, univocal response that transcends individual and cultural differences. Thus Bloom tells his readers, magisterially, that 'there are parts of yourself you will not know fully until you know, as well as you can, Don Quixote and Sancho Panza'.[85] While the Sherlock Holmes stories appear to us 'under the guise of science and reason', their actual appeal, says Carey, is to 'our appetite for wonder'. Chesterton's *The Man Who Was Thursday*, meanwhile, leads its readers 'back to a time when innocence, intelligence and hope went together'.[86] And we read Tennyson's 'Ulysses', ultimately, 'to find ourselves, more fully and more strange than otherwise we could hope to find'.[87]

The work of Carey and Bloom can be linked to the 'home-reading' that was often cited in the late nineteenth century as obviating the need for an institutional form of literary study, and which led to the publication of a large number of similar handbooks, guiding autodidactic readers through the literary canon and away from the cheap popular fiction that was leading to an increasing fragmentation of the reading public. It also promotes a vision of such reading as being not only more pleasurable but also more authentic than its academic counterparts, as indicated by Bloom's comment that 'those who read Austen "politically" are not reading her at all'.[88] As a result, it can also be placed within a tradition of dissent that stretches back through Woolf and Murry to critics such as Ker and Bradley. This tradition is characterised by two features: its mistrust of academic practices, and its conviction that reading outside these practices produces more valuable kinds of knowledge than those recognised within academic frameworks. In contrast, the knowledge associated with academia is seen as distracting, trivial or even pernicious.

There is a certain irony in the fact that Carey, as Merton Professor of English at Oxford, is explicitly recommending a philosophy of reading that was used to undermine English Literature's claim to disciplinary status at the time of the Merton Professorship's inception. While it is tempting to see *Pure Pleasure* and *How to Read and Why* as literary criticism's equivalent of popular science and history, their anti-institutionalism makes such an equation problematic. It is hardly surprising that Anthony Kearney has described Carey and Bloom as 'bit[ing] the hand that feeds them'.[89] Yet it also seems important to ask why such equivalents do not exist: why literary criticism lacks its Simon Schamas and Stephen Jay Goulds, popularisers who promote an interest in their subject that nevertheless does not involve a rejection of academic knowledge and beliefs. Clearly, the lack of such equivalents is not due to a lack of interest. The rising popularity of television adaptations of nineteenth-century novels, reading groups and forums for literary discussion on the Internet indicates that many people strive to gain the knowledge that is associated with literature. Nevertheless, this is not the same kind of knowledge as that which is generated by academic analysis. The apparent irrelevance of academic literary study to the reading public is highlighted by John Sutherland's observation that while an academic monograph on Dickens may sell as few as four hundred copies, Dickens's novels enjoy annual sales of over two million copies.[90] Sutherland, who was Professor of English Literature at University College London until 2004, has himself capitalised on the renewed public interest in 'classic' texts through his investigations of literary mysteries, collected under such titles as *Is Heathcliff a Murderer?* and *Will Jane Eyre Be Happy?* Such texts share Carey and Bloom's unacademic stance and aim to appeal to the 'ordinary' readers of the 'classics' who are the contemporary equivalent of Woolf's 'common reader':

> Such readers do not, I suspect, much worry about Deconstruction, New Historicism, or the distinction between extradiegesis and intradiegesis. But they do wonder, in their close-reading way, whether Becky killed Jos, exactly what nationality Melmotte is, what the 'missile' is that Arabella Donn pitches at Jude Fawley's head, what Heathcliff does in the three years which see him leave Wuthering Heights a stable-boy and return a gentleman, and what Paul Emanuel does in *his* three years' sojourn in Guadaloupe.[91]

The publishing company Penguin, meanwhile, has responded to this public interest in the nineteenth-century novel by re-marketing certain texts in its 'Penguin Classics' series, issuing them without scholarly apparatus and with redesigned covers in an attempt to appeal to readers who might find the notes and introductions of the standard editions off-putting. The 'blurbs' of these new issues are designed to highlight plot, character and drama, and carry recommendations by contemporary actors, writers and journalists: Beryl Bainbridge's comment on *Jane Eyre*, for instance, is 'They don't write them like this any more'.[92]

In pointing to the difference between the concerns of the academic and those of the 'ordinary' reader, Sutherland also highlights the particularly contested nature of the term 'literary criticism'. Within universities, literary criticism and literary scholarship take a number of different forms and philosophies, sometimes contradictory and often conflicting. Nevertheless, Sutherland's mystery-solving and Carey and Bloom's humanist explorations of reading would not – by their authors' own admission – be considered 'academic' ways of looking at literature. Even so, the fact that literary texts continue to be read and discussed outside academic departments of English means that the term 'literary criticism' also encompasses, in a wider sense, the activities and methods of inquiry promoted by Sutherland, Carey and Bloom, and by the more straight-forward expression of personal taste and engagement hinted at by Natasha Walter, and facilitated through reading groups, websites and other forums for discussion. The spectrum of activities covered by this more generalist definition of 'literary criticism' is therefore much broader – and requires much less specialist knowledge – than the activities encompassed by other academic disciplines.

Martin Amis's comment that where words are concerned, 'we all have a competence' therefore echoes the statement of Professor Mayo of Cambridge that the study of literature required little skill beyond the basic literacy that was learned in the nursery. Just over a century ago, the belief that literary criticism did not rest on any kind of specialist knowledge was used to argue against its institutionalisation in the universities. Today, it lies behind the designation of professional critics and scholars as 'book snobs', 'intellectual buffoons' and purveyors of 'academic cant' who seek only to deny 'common readers' a right to their opinion and enjoyment.[93] The recent reform of A level English literature has shown that the status of English within education is still dominated by the same arguments that circulated at the time of its entry into the universities: on the one hand, a desire to give English disciplinary status by grounding it in a recognisable body of scholarship; and on the other, a denial that English needs such a grounding, claiming that all it requires is a text and a sensitive reader. Literary study continues to find itself pulled between different conceptions of intellectual authority: the knowledge it produces and the purpose it is meant to serve are still the subject of debate.

Conclusion

The disciplinary history of English has often been dominated by one kind of story, a story that casts literary study in the role of villain. In this story, English is little more than an attempt to inculcate in its students a particular set of morals and values, promoting a spirit of nationalism and neutralising possible sources of resistance within the increasingly divided society of nineteenth-century Britain. This process of indoctrination is one in which institutions at all levels have been seen as complicit, creating a seamless continuum that links schools, universities and the adult education movement. In such a story, there is, implicitly, little to separate Matthew Arnold's call for 'the best which has been thought and said',[1] or John Churton Collins's emphasis on 'right feeling and right thinking',[2] from the most recent version of the National Curriculum. English may be an academic discipline, but its more important role in this story is as an agent of morality, spiritual growth and patriotic propaganda.

Yet there are other ways of telling the story of English that uncover different aspects of the subject's history: its problematic rise to disciplinary status, its institutional forms, and the debates and tensions that have surrounded its existence. While it would be naïve to deny that the study of English Literature has a political dimension, it is equally naïve to allow questions of politics to overshadow issues that are just as complex, and that are, indeed, inextricable from the ideologies located in nineteenth-century rhetoric about the teaching of English. For if English was intended to justify its existence by taking up a central role in a broad social project, it could not be a specialist academic discipline. In turn, if literary interpretation was made increasingly specialised, then this would lead to a devaluing of other forms of literary knowledge, dependent not on scholarship but on a more personal, intuitive engagement with

the text. While Heyck's paradigm suggests that other disciplines nego-
tiated the transition from amateur to professional, from generalist to
specialist, with relative ease, this was not the case with literary criticism.

In this book, my aim has been to explore a range of attempts to
define what it is that constitutes the discipline of literary criticism, and
some of the reactions that these attempts have provoked. What I have
found is that the years between John Churton Collins's campaign at
Oxford and F. R. Leavis's quest to redefine the ideal 'English School'
at Cambridge are marked by a constant circulation of the same debates:
about what kind of knowledge literary criticism involves, how specialised
this knowledge needs to be and whether this knowledge is actually
'useful'. My study of two aspects of contemporary literary criticism – the
rejection of specialism inherent in recent works by Harold Bloom and
John Carey, and the uneasy relationship between academic knowledge
and the reform of English Literature at A-level – indicates that these are
still contentious issues. For Stefan Collini, many of the controversies that
have faced literary studies can be understood in terms of 'the unresolved,
and perhaps unresolvable, tension between, on the one hand, being
simply one specialized activity alongside other specialisms [. . .] and, on
the other hand, still carrying the burden of being a kind of residual
cultural space within which general existential and ethical questions
can be addressed'.[3] The simplistic designation of English as an instrument
of ideological control often threatens to obscure this tension: the
subject's acquisition of disciplinary status did not solve these problems
of identity and purpose, but rather heightened them.

The chronological gap between Chapters 5 and 6 – between Leavis's
discussion of the role of English in the universities, and the introduction
of Curriculum 2000 – may make my final chapter seem something of
a coda, linked only tenuously to my main line of argument. However,
the recurring presence of the kinds of issues I have identified means
that my final chapter is less an afterthought than the entire *point* of this
book: that teachers and students of English Literature are still working
within a climate where the nature of specialist literary knowledge is
both questioned and doubted. The continuity that can be located
within English is therefore not so much a continuity of ideology as
a continuity of confusion. The story of English Literature's origins
as a discipline in the universities, and of the relationship of literary
criticism to this process, is therefore one of a struggle to define and
claim ownership of the knowledge that English represents: a knowledge
whose nature is still contested, and still indistinct.

Notes

Introduction

1. Quoted in James Morrison and Andrew Johnson, 'Inside Prince Charles' literary think camp', *Independent on Sunday* (6 October 2002), p. 5.
2. Deborah Cameron, *Verbal Hygiene* (London: Routledge, 1995), p. 94.
3. Charles, Prince of Wales, Annual Shakespeare Birthday Lecture, 22 April 1991, accessed online at http://193.36.68.132/speeches/education_22041991.html.
4. These reforms are discussed in detail in Chapter 6.
5. Remark made at the English Association Spring Conference for Teachers, St Catherine's College, Oxford, March 1999.
6. GCE Advanced Subsidiary and Advanced Level Specifications: Subject Criteria for English Literature (Department for Education and Employment/Qualifications and Curriculum Authority, QCA 991680144, 1999).
7. See, for example, the arguments put forward by Elaine Treharne in 'Balancing the English Degree Programme', *English Association Newsletter*, 166 (2001), p. 3; and by Patrick Parrinder in 'A View from the Bench', *English Association Newsletter*, 165 (2000), p. 2.
8. Martin Amis, *The War against Cliché: Essays and Reviews 1971–2000* (London: Jonathan Cape, 2001), pp. xiii–xiv.
9. I have confined my study to English universities because of the different intellectual traditions that prevailed elsewhere in the English-speaking world. In Scotland, the study of literature and rhetoric in the dissenting academies meant that English had a very different foundation. See, for example, Stephen Potter's *The Muse in Chains: A Study in Education* (London: Jonathan Cape, 1937); D. J. Palmer's *The Rise of English Studies* (Oxford: Oxford University Press, 1965); John Guillory's *Cultural Capital: The Problems of Literary Canon Formation* (Chicago and London: University of Chicago Press, 1993); and Robert Crawford's *Devolving English Literature* (Oxford: Clarendon Press, 1992) and *The Scottish Invention of English Literature* (Cambridge: Cambridge University Press, 1998). For accounts of the history of English studies in the United States of America, and of issues related to the teaching of English, see William E. Cain, *The Crisis in Criticism: Theory, Literature and Reform in English Studies* (Baltimore: Johns Hopkins University Press, 1984) and *Reconceptualizing American Literary/Cultural Studies: Rhetoric, History, and Politics in the Humanities* (New York: Garland, 1996); Gerald Graff and Michael Warner (eds), *The Origins of Literary Studies in America: A Documentary Anthology* (London: Routledge, 1988); Gerald Graff, *Professing Literature* (Chicago: University of Chicago Press, 1987); and Robert Scholes, *The Rise and Fall of English: Reconstructing English as a Discipline* (New Haven: Yale University Press, 1999).
10. Henry Butcher, Presidential Address to the British Academy, delivered 27 October 1909, *Proceedings of the British Academy* (1909–10), p. 23.

11. For an account of the rise of this mass market, see Richard D. Altick, *The English Common Reader: A Social History of the Mass Reading Public 1800–1900* (Chicago: University of Chicago Press, 1957).
12. Dr Mayo, speaking at a meeting on 8 December 1910. Quoted in *Cambridge University Reporter* (13 December 1910), p. 406.
13. Marjorie Garber, *Academic Instincts* (Princeton: Princeton University Press, 1999), p. ix.
14. F. R. Leavis, *English Literature in Our Time and the University* (Cambridge: Cambridge University Press, 1969), p. 2.
15. Harold Bloom, *How to Read and Why* (London: Fourth Estate, 2000); John Carey, *Pure Pleasure: A Guide to the Twentieth Century's Most Enjoyable Books* (London: Faber & Faber, 2000).

1   Histories of English: The critical background

1. Chris Baldick, *The Social Mission of English Criticism 1848–1932* (Oxford: Clarendon Press, 1983), p. 2.
2. The belief that the adult education movement sought to neutralise working-class activism is discussed in Jonathan Rose, *The Intellectual Life of the British Working Classes* (New Haven and London: Yale University Press, 2001), pp. 256–97.
3. Raymond Williams, *Culture and Society 1780–1950* (London: Hogarth Press, 1958).
4. See, for example, Brian Doyle, *English and Englishness* (London: Routledge, 1989); Terry Eagleton, *Literary Theory: An Introduction* (Oxford: Blackwell, 1983); Peter Widdowson, *Literature* (London: Routledge, 1999).
5. Eagleton, *Literary Theory*, pp. 25–6.
6. Widdowson, *Literature*, pp. 36, 42.
7. Doyle, *English and Englishness*, p. 12.
8. Ibid., pp. 17–18.
9. Eagleton, *Literary Theory*, pp. 23–4.
10. Matthew Arnold, *Culture and Anarchy* (London, 1869: Cambridge University Press, 1932), p. 6.
11. Widdowson, *Literature*, pp. 4–15.
12. Franklin Court, *Institutionalizing English Literature: The Culture and Politics of Literary Study* (Stanford: Stanford University Press, 1992), p. 6.
13. Matthew Arnold, quoted in Court, *Institutionalizing English Literature*, p. 8.
14. Court, *Institutionalizing English Literature*, p. 7.
15. By this time the new universities and university colleges included King's and University Colleges in London, and the civic colleges of Manchester, Birmingham, Leeds, Sheffield, Nottingham and Liverpool.
16. Widdowson, *Literature*, p. 59.
17. Doyle, *English and Englishness*, p. 3.
18. Josephine M. Guy and Ian Small, *Politics and Value in English Studies: A Discipline in Crisis?* (Cambridge: Cambridge University Press, 1993), pp. 161–4.
19. George Gordon, *The Discipline of Letters* (Oxford: Clarendon Press, 1946), p. 10. Quoted in Eagleton, *Literary Theory*, p. 23.
20. Eagleton, *Literary Theory*, p. 23.
21. Gordon, *Discipline of Letters*, p. 10.

22. Baldick, *Social Mission*, p. 105.
23. Bill Ashcroft, Gareth Griffiths and Helen Tiffin, *The Empire Writes Back: Theory and Practice in Post-Colonial Literatures* (London: Routledge, 1989), pp. 2–3.
24. Baldick, *Social Mission*, p. 61.
25. J. W. Hales, 'The Teaching of English', in *Essays on a Liberal Education*, ed. F. W. Farrar (London: Macmillan, 1867), p. 310. Quoted in Baldick, *Social Mission*, p. 62.
26. Baldick, *Social Mission*, pp. 63–4.
27. *Oxford Magazine*, 4 May 1887. Quoted in Baldick, *Social Mission*, p. 61.
28. Doyle, *English and Englishness*, p. 12.
29. T. W. Heyck, *The Transformation of Intellectual Life in Victorian England* (London: Croom Helm, 1982).
30. Quoted in Guy and Small, *Politics and Value in English Studies*, p. 52.
31. See the Epilogue to Sheldon Rothblatt, *The Revolution of the Dons: Cambridge and Society in Victorian England* (London: Faber & Faber, 1968).
32. Heyck, *Transformation of Intellectual Life*, p. 21.
33. Ibid., p. 82.
34. This process is dealt with in detail in Philippa Levine, *The Amateur and the Professional: Antiquarians, Historians and Archaeologists in Victorian England, 1838–1886* (Cambridge: Cambridge University Press, 1986).
35. T. B. Macaulay, *Critical and Historical Essays* (London: [n.p.], 1883), p. 51. Quoted in Heyck, *Transformation of Intellectual Life*, p. 122.
36. *Selected Essays of J. B. Bury*, ed. Harold Temperley (Cambridge: [n.p.], 1930), p. 22. Quoted in Heyck, *Transformation of Intellectual Life*, p. 122.
37. Stefan Collini, *English Pasts: Essays in History and Culture* (Oxford: Oxford University Press, 1999), p. 308.
38. Ibid.

2 English in the universities

1. Potter, *Muse in Chains*, p. 37.
2. Jo McMurtry, *English Language, English Literature: The Creation of an Academic Discipline* (London: Mansell, 1985), pp. 2, 5.
3. Baldick, *Social Mission*, pp. 60–2.
4. Alan Bacon, 'English Literature Becomes a University Subject: King's College, London, as Pioneer', *Victorian Studies*, 29 (1986), pp. 591–612.
5. Hugh James Rose, *The Tendency of Prevalent Opinions about Knowledge Considered* (Cambridge: Deighton; London: Rivington, 1826), p. 11. Quoted in Bacon, 'English Literature', p. 594.
6. See F. J. Hearnshaw, *The Centenary History of King's College, London* (London: Harrap, 1929), p. 124. Cited in Bacon, 'English Literature', p. 597.
7. Edward Copleston, review of *Letter to Mr Brougham on the Subject of a London University*, by Thomas Campbell, *Quarterly Review*, 33 (1825), p. 269. Quoted in Bacon, 'English Literature', p. 597.
8. Bacon, 'English Literature', p. 597.
9. Ibid., p. 605.
10. F. D. Maurice, 'Introductory Lecture by the Professor of English Literature and Modern History at King's College, London, delivered Tuesday, October 13',

Educational Magazine, n.s. 2 (1840), p. 276. Quoted in Bacon, 'English Literature', p. 607.

11. *Calendar of King's College, London* (hereafter *KCC*) (1903–4), pp. 84–5.
12. *Owens College Calendar* (hereafter *OCC*) (1881–2), pp. 30–1.
13. At King's, set authors between 1880 and 1900 included Langland, Chaucer, Shakespeare, Spenser, Milton, Bacon, Hobbes, Harrington, Locke, Defoe, Newton, Hume, Hartley, Gibbon, Addison, Swift, Johnson, Wordsworth, Coleridge, Byron, De Quincey, Carlyle and Ruskin. The only novelists listed were all from the eighteenth century: Richardson, Fielding, Smollett, Sterne and Goldsmith. At Manchester, set authors between these dates included Chaucer, Shakespeare, Spenser, Milton, More, Clarendon, Burnet, Pope, Addison, Goldsmith, Smollett, Johnson, Gibbon, Burke and Richardson. It is significant that both lists include philosophers and historians, figures who would today be seen as peripheral to a more 'literary' notion of the canon.
14. This course could be seen as evidence that attention was being paid to literary criticism as a distinct activity, with the theorisation of this activity being a topic of concern. However, the knowledge that students were expected to display – as indicated by questions asking them to identify which critical doctrines were associated with a number of writers, and to summarise the views of Aristotle, Horace and Longinus – does not appear to have included any kind of capacity to reflect on the nature of criticism, being instead a test of memory and factual knowledge. Significantly, the question attracting most marks (and which students seeking a First were strongly advised to attempt) involved the straightforward translation into English of a number of passages from the works of various French and German critics. *Victoria University of Manchester Calendar* (hereafter *VUC*), 1910–11, pp. lxiv–xv.
15. *KCC* (1892–3), pp. 116–17.
16. *VUC* (1910–11), pp. liii–lxviii.
17. Ibid., p. liii.
18. *VUC* (1882–3), p. cxxiv; *KCC* (1882–3), p. 636.
19. *KCC* (1882–3), p. 636; (1888–9), pp. 732–3.
20. *KCC* (1883–4), pp. 630–1; (1885–6), pp. 677–8.
21. Manchester's 1882 examination on 'The History of English Literature from Chaucer to Spenser' asked candidates to comment on the influence of Petrarch on the English sonnet-writers of the sixteenth century, and the influence of the Renaissance on any pre-Elizabethan poet. *OCC* (1882–3), pp. cxxxiv–cxxxv.
22. *VUC* (1910–11), p. liii.
23. *VUC* (1882–3), p. cxxiv; *KCC* (1881–2), p. 644.
24. *VUC* (1910–11), p. 188.
25. Such texts included Henry Morley's *A First Sketch of English Literature* (London: Cassell, Petter & Galpin, 1873); A. W. Ward's *A History of English Dramatic Literature* (London: Macmillan, 1875) and Leslie Stephen's *English Literature and Society in the Eighteenth Century* (London: Duckworth, 1903). Morley was Professor of English Literature at University College, London; Ward was Professor of English Literature and History at Owens College in Manchester. See *KCC* (1880–1), p. 325; (1882–3), p. 344.
26. *KCC* (1882–3), p. 636; (1900–1), p. lxxvi; *VUC* (1910–11), p. lxi.

27. E. A. Freeman, 'Literature and Language', *Contemporary Review*, 52 (1887), p. 562. Quoted in Baldick, *Social Mission*, p. 73.
28. Eagleton, *Literary Theory*, p. 27.
29. Guillory, *Cultural Capital*, p. 87.
30. Ibid., p. 168.
31. In 1882, students at Manchester were asked to comment on the characteristics of Spenser's style; in 1884, they were invited to comment on the metre of a range of quotations. *OCC* (1882–3), p. cxxxiv; (1884–5), pp. cxlvii–cxlviii. At King's, the 1884 exam contained questions on Langland's metre; a similar question was set in 1903 on Spenser. *KCC* (1885–6), p. 678; (1903–4), pp. cxx–cxxi.
32. *KCC* (1900–1901), p. cxxii; *VUC* (1910–11), p. liii.
33. Heyck, *Transformation of Intellectual Life*, pp. 72–3.
34. Alfred Barry, 'The Good and Evil of Examination', *Nineteenth Century*, 3 (1878), pp. 656 8.
35. For a detailed exploration of the reforms at Cambridge, see Rothblatt, *Revolution of the Dons*.
36. *KCC* (1880–1), p. 109.
37. *OCC* (1880–1), p. 38; significantly, the Science course was perceived as more specialised, preparing its students for 'pursuits and professions strictly scientific'.
38. *University College, Nottingham, Calendar for the Second Session* (1882–3), p. 14.
39. Terry Eagleton, *The Function of Criticism* (London: Verso, [1984] 1996), p. 76.
40. John Churton Collins, 'Can English Literature be Taught?', *Nineteenth Century*, 22 (1887), pp. 644–5.
41. Ibid., p. 651.
42. Ibid., p. 657.
43. John Churton Collins, 'The Universities in Contact with the People', *Nineteenth Century*, 26 (1889), p. 583.
44. A. C. Bradley, *Oxford Lectures on Poetry* (London: Macmillan, 1941), pp. 4–5.
45. Quoted in Palmer, *Rise*, p. 79.
46. Christopher Kent, 'The *Academy*', in *British Literary Magazines: The Victorian and Edwardian Age, 1837–1913*, ed. Alvin Sullivan (Westport, Connecticut: Greenwood, 1984), p. 3.
47. Henry Sweet, *Academy*, 27 (9 May 1885), p. 331.
48. Andrew Lang, *Academy*, 27 (20 June 1885), p. 439.
49. Henry Sweet, *Academy*, 27 (13 June 1885), p. 422.
50. See, for example, my analysis of the work of A. C. Bradley in Chapter 3.
51. See Palmer, *Rise*, p. 94.
52. Ibid., pp. 95–6.
53. Ibid., pp. 107–8.
54. Bodleian Library, Firth, b.36, quoted in Palmer, *Rise*, pp. 107–8.
55. Amendments dated 15 May 1894, one stating that students should show a 'competent knowledge of history' to support their study of literature, and the other demanding that there should be 'at least an elementary knowledge of Greek and Latin literature and languages in the new School'. Palmer, *Rise*, pp. 111–12.
56. This dependence on other subjects is reflected in the fact that it was not until 1926 that Oxford gained a separate English Faculty: the Final Honour

School of English Language and Literature was supervised by the Faculty of Literae Humaniores from its inception in 1894 to 1913, and then by the Faculty of Medieval and Modern Languages and Literature.

57. 'Guard Book' relating to the establishment of the King Edward VII Professorship of English Literature (Cambridge University Archives: CUR 39.46), p. 1.
58. Ibid., p. 2.
59. Dr Ellis McTaggart, speaking at a meeting on 8 December 1910. Quoted in *Cambridge University Reporter* (13 December 1910), p. 406.
60. Dr Mayo, speaking at a meeting on 8 December 1910. Quoted in *Cambridge University Reporter* (13 December 1910), p. 406.
61. Tillyard, *Muse Unchained*, p. 26.
62. Ibid.
63. Ibid., pp. 41–3.
64. Palmer, *Rise*, p. 76.
65. Examiners' Reports on the Honour School of English Language and Literature for 1913–16 record a growing dissatisfaction with students' performance, with many candidates avoiding questions that required 'an exact knowledge of Old and Middle English grammar and philology', and showing a 'vague, rambling and inaccurate' grasp of literary history (Oxford University Archive (hereafter OUA), FA 4/10/2/1, pp. 6, 50). A committee founded to discuss the future of the Honour School recommended in 1917 that candidates should show more knowledge of English social and political history, and that Old and Middle English texts should be treated as pieces of literature rather than as material for philological study. The new Honour School proposed by this committee consisted of papers on the philology and history of the English Language; the history of English literature, criticism and style; prescribed authors; the history of England during the periods of literature studied; and a special subject drawn from a list that included Gothic and Old Saxon, Old Icelandic, ballad poetry, political satire and periodical literature (ibid., pp. 60, 68).
66. E. A. Freeman, quoted in Palmer, *Rise*, p. 96; see also Potter, *Muse in Chains*, p. 194.
67. OUA, FA 4/5/2/1, p. 57.
68. OUA, FA 4/5/2/6, p. 86.
69. Memo of 31 January 1922, in OUA, FA 4/10/2/2, p. 6.
70. OUA, FA 4/10/2/1, p. 60.
71. Ibid., p. 50.
72. Ibid., p. 35.
73. Ibid., p. 50.
74. In 1913, for example, examiners noted students' unwillingness to tackle questions requiring 'an exact knowledge of Old and Middle English grammar and philology', stating that 'the Language course offers difficulties which very few candidates are prepared to face'. Ibid., p. 6.
75. OUA, FA 4/10/2/3, p. 100.
76. Ian MacKillop, *F. R. Leavis: A Life in Criticism* (London: Penguin, 1995), pp. 54, 56.
77. Ibid., p. 54.
78. Chadwick eventually recognised that his subject had little part to play in the new English Tripos, and requested that it be transferred to the Faculty of Archaeology and Anthropology, a move that took place in 1926. See MacKillop, *Leavis*, p. 93.

79. John Gross, *The Rise and Fall of the Man of Letters: English Literary Life since 1800* (London: Penguin, [1969] 1991), p. 201.
80. Comment on behalf of the Oxford English Faculty on the Government's Norwood Report on the secondary curriculum, 1944. OUA, FA 4/5/2/7, p. 164.
81. Tillyard, *Muse Unchained*, p. 82.
82. MacKillop, *Leavis*, p. 57.
83. *Cambridge University Examination Papers* (1918–19), p. 599.
84. Ibid., p. 606.
85. Such questions are present throughout Cambridge's exam papers. In 1918, for example, students were asked to 'examine the quality of Shakespeare's Humanism in connection with his attitude to racial particularism', and to debate Shaw's opinion that 'in Shakespeare's plays the woman always takes the initiative. In his problem plays and his popular plays alike the love interest is the interest of seeing the woman hunt the man down.' In 1919, questions included 'For what reasons, epical and other than epical, are we inclined to sympathise with Milton's Satan, and, on the whole, with the "bad" rather than with the "good" characters in *Paradise Lost?*' and 'Illustrate, account for, and criticise the Romantic aloofness from contemporary realities of much Victorian poetry' (*Cambridge University Examination Papers* (1917–18), pp. 398–9; (1918–19), pp. 602–3).
86. Sir Arthur Quiller-Couch, *Studies in Literature: Third Series* (Cambridge: Cambridge University Press, [1929] 1948), pp. 149–50.
87. Ibid., p. 156.
88. Ibid.
89. Sir Arthur Quiller-Couch, *On the Art of Reading* (Cambridge: Cambridge University Press, [1920] 1947), p. 24.
90. Ibid., p. 21.
91. Ibid., p. 33.
92. Ibid., pp. 34–5.
93. 'Come to us – to your professors and readers as well as to your supervisors of studies [...] our oaks are seldom sported against anyone in search of what counsel we can give. There is a good and ancient phrase up here, "I am reading with so-and-so": and it truly indicates the tradition of the place which we, in our Tripos, would carry on. I beg you to remember that our justification is bound up in your promise, and that men (say) of my age, or considerably younger, may take much heart from hope in younger men who intrude on our shyness as friends.' Quiller-Couch, *Studies in Literature: Third Series*, pp. 162–3.
94. See Rothblatt, *Revolution of the Dons*.
95. Sir Arthur Quiller-Couch, *Q Anthology*, ed. F. Brittain (London: J. M. Dent, 1948), p. 211.
96. Quiller-Couch, *Studies in Literature: Third Series*, p. 159.
97. Ibid., pp. 153–4.
98. *Student's Handbook to Cambridge, 1917–18* (Cambridge: Cambridge University Press, 1917), p. 405.
99. Tillyard, *Muse Unchained*, pp. 82–3.
100. Ibid., p. 82.
101. *Cambridge University Examination Papers* (1918–19), p. 603.
102. Ibid., p. 624.

103. *Cambridge University Examination Papers* (1919–20), p. 899.
104. D. Nichol Smith, 'The Degree of Doctor of Philosophy', paper delivered at Edinburgh on 8 July 1931. OUA, FA 4/5/2/3, p. 140. Nichol Smith succeeded Sir Walter Raleigh and George Gordon as Merton Professor in 1929.
105. OUA, FA 4/5/2/1, p. 63.
106. OUA, FA 4/5/2/2, p. 84.
107. OUA, FA 4/10/2/1, p. 32.
108. OUA, FA 4/10/2/2, p. 175.
109. OUA, FA 4/10/2/3, pp. 17, 62, 101.
110. OUA, FA 4/10/2/2, pp. 12, 61.
111. OUA, FA 4/10/2/3, p. 128.
112. OUA, FA 4/5/2/6, p. 56.
113. OUA, FA 4/5/2/7, p. 8.
114. OUA, FA 4/10/2/1, p. 32.
115. OUA, FA 4/10/2/3, p. 62.
116. Tillyard, *Muse Unchained*, p. 87. The foundation of a separate English Faculty in 1926, and the subsequent reform of the English Tripos, were seen by F. R. Leavis as marking the end of a truly liberal approach to English at Cambridge: After these reforms, teaching and administration in the English Tripos became much more systematic, regulated and centralised. These changes, according to Francis Mulhern, 'induced a significant shift in the intellectual climate of the school', with an emphasis on factual scholarship replacing the creativity of the original Tripos. A central figure in this shift, so Mulhern claims, was F. L. Lucas, a newly appointed lecturer in the English Faculty, who criticised the 'organized orgies of opinion' into which he claimed English had descended, and stated of the English Faculty that 'we are not training reviewers'. See Leavis, *English Literature in Our Time*, pp. 19–23; Francis Mulhern, *The Moment of 'Scrutiny'* (London: Verso, [1979] 1981), pp. 29–31.

3   Critics and professors

1. Wallace Martin, 'Criticism and the Academy', in *The Cambridge History of Literary Criticism*, vol. 7: *Modernism and the New Criticism*, ed. A. Walton Litz, Louis Menand and Lawrence Rainey (Cambridge: Cambridge University Press, 2000), p. 279.
2. Laurel Brake, *Subjugated Knowledges: Journalism, Gender and Literature in the Nineteenth Century* (London: Macmillan, 1994).
3. Ibid., pp. 1–3.
4. Leslie Stephen, 'Charlotte Brontë', *Cornhill Magazine*, 36 (1877), 723–9; quoted in Brake, *Subjugated Knowledges*, p. 6.
5. These periodicals were aimed at differing audiences and had widely differing editorial policies. The *Cornhill Magazine*, edited in the nineteenth century by both W. M. Thackeray and Leslie Stephen, aimed to cultivate popular taste while combining this with high-quality literary reviews. *Macmillan's Magazine*, meanwhile, contained more serious articles, with contributors including the academics Adolphus William Ward (Professor of English Literature and History at Manchester), George Webbe Dasent (Professor of

English Literature and Modern History at King's College) and A. C. Bradley. Some periodicals aimed at breadth of coverage: Others sought to offer lengthy articles on a small number of topics. See Walter E. Houghton (ed.), *The Wellesley Index to Victorian periodicals, 1824–1900*, 5 vols. (Toronto: University of Toronto Press; London: Routledge & Kegan Paul, 1966–1989); Sullivan, *British Literary Magazines*.

6. Joanne Shattock, *Politics and Reviewers: The 'Edinburgh' and the 'Quarterly' in the Early Victorian Age* (London: Leicester University Press, 1989), p. 13.

7. For details of these processes, see Altick, *The English Common Reader*; Clive Bloom (ed.), *Literature and Culture in Modern Britain, I, 1900–1929* (London: Longman, 1993); John Carey, *The Intellectuals and the Masses: Pride and Prejudice among the Literary Intelligentsia, 1880–1939* (London: Faber & Faber, 1992); Gross, *Rise and Fall of the Man of Letters*; Josephine M. Guy and Ian Small, 'The British "man of letters" and the rise of the Professional', in *The Cambridge History of Literary Criticism*, vol. 7: *Modernism and the New Criticism*, ed. A. Walton Litz, Louis Menand and Lawrence Rainey (Cambridge: Cambridge University Press, 2000); Wallace Martin, 'Criticism and the Academy'; Jeremy Treglown and Bridget Bennett (eds), *Grub Street and the Ivory Tower: Literary Journalism and Literary Scholarship from Fielding to the Internet* (Oxford: Oxford University Press, 1998).

8. These processes are detailed in Brake, *Subjugated Knowledges*; Guy and Small, *Politics and Value in English Studies* and 'The British "man of letters" '; Heyck, *Transformation of Intellectual Life*; Levine, *The Amateur and the Professional*; Ian Small, *Conditions for Criticism: Authority, Knowledge and Literature in the Late Nineteenth Century* (Oxford: Clarendon Press, 1991).

9. Anonymous review of David Masson's *The Life of John Milton*, *Athenaeum*, no. 2732 (6 March 1880), p. 303.

10. James Spedding, 'The Story of *The Merchant of Venice'*, *Cornhill Magazine*, 41 (1880), pp. 276–9.

11. Brake, *Subjugated Knowledges*, p. 43.

12. Anonymous review of Rhoda Broughton's *Second Thoughts*, *Athenaeum*, no. 2745 (5 June 1880), p. 725. Laurel Brake has offered a different account of the forms taken by literary criticism in Victorian periodicals, arguing that criticism was shaped by the 'house styles' of different periodicals, rather than by abstract principles of professionalisation. Writers therefore had to honour the distinctions between these different styles, adopting a range of authorial personae that varied from one publication to another. For Brake, then, Victorian criticism had its origins 'in the sway and bustle of the market-place' rather than the ivory tower. See Brake, *Subjugated Knowledges*, pp. 8–13, 32. However, this does not explain the coexistence of such varied forms of criticism as the articles from the *Athenaeum* that I have discussed here, published within the same year, yet exemplifying markedly different approaches.

13. A. W. Ward, quoted in Houghton, *Wellesley Index*, I, p. 322.

14. Sullivan, *British Literary Magazines*, pp. 3–6.

15. Ibid., pp. xx, 346.

16. See Carey, *The Intellectuals and the Masses*.

17. Virginia Woolf, *A Room of One's Own* (London, 1928: Grafton, 1977), p. 32.

18. Potter, *Muse in Chains*, p. 37.

19. Stanley Leathes, *The Teaching of English at the Universities* (English Association pamphlet no. 26, October 1913), p. 9.
20. John Churton Collins, 'English Literature at the Universities', *Quarterly Review*, 163 (1886), pp. 300, 313–14.
21. Edmund Gosse, *A Short History of Modern English Literature* (London: Heinemann, [1897] 1925), p. 106.
22. W. P. Ker, *On Modern Literature: Lectures and Addresses*, ed. Terence Spencer and James Sutherland (Oxford: Clarendon Press, 1955), p. 182.
23. Ibid., pp. 183–4.
24. George Saintsbury, *A History of Nineteenth Century Literature* (London, 1896: Macmillan, 1906), pp. 445, 461.
25. Ibid., pp. 478–80.
26. Martin, 'Criticism and the Academy', pp. 273, 283.
27. Stefan Collini, *Arnold* (Oxford: Oxford University Press, 1988), p. 19.
28. Small, *Conditions for Criticism*, p. 59.
29. Arnold, *Culture and Anarchy*, pp. 54, 7, 147.
30. Ibid., p. 45.
31. See George Watson, *The Literary Critics: A Study of English Descriptive Criticism* (London: Penguin, 1962), pp. 15–16.
32. Arnold, *Culture and Anarchy*, pp. 54, 69, 68.
33. Baldick, *Social Mission*, p. 30.
34. Matthew Arnold, *On Translating Homer* (London, 1861: Routledge, 1905), pp. 248–9.
35. Walter Pater, *Appreciations: With an Essay on Style* (London: Macmillan, [1889] 1931), p. 14.
36. Walter Pater, *The Renaissance: Studies in Art and Poetry* (London: Macmillan, [1873] 1919), p. ix.
37. Pater, *Appreciations*, p. 10.
38. Ibid., p. 14.
39. Ibid., p. 15.
40. Ibid., pp. 5–7.
41. Pater, *The Renaissance*, p. x.
42. Adam Phillips, introduction to Walter Pater, *The Renaissance: Studies in Art and Poetry*, ed. Adam Phillips (Oxford: Oxford University Press, 1986), p. ix.
43. Pater, *The Renaissance*, pp. 235–6. This Conclusion was withdrawn from the second edition of *The Renaissance* (published in 1877) due to its perceived hedonism and 'moral negligence' (Phillips (ed.), *The Renaissance*, p. xiii). See also Small, *Conditions for Criticism*, pp. 58–9.
44. Phillips (ed.), *The Renaissance*, p. ix.
45. Small, *Conditions for Criticism*, p. 93.
46. Baldick, *Social Mission*, pp. 77, 79.
47. Walter Raleigh, *Shakespeare* (London: Macmillan, 1907), p. 109.
48. Gordon, *Discipline of Letters*, p. 16.
49. Ibid., pp. 3–4.
50. Ibid., p. 12.
51. Ker, *On Modern Literature*, p. 150.
52. Ibid., p. 155.
53. Ibid., p. 158.
54. Ibid., p. 162.

55. Pater, *The Renaissance*, pp. xxix–xxx.
56. Bradley, *Oxford Lectures on Poetry*, p. 4.
57. Ibid., pp. 4–5.
58. Ibid., pp. 22–4.
59. Ibid., p. 26.
60. Eric S. Robertson, *Life of Henry Wadsworth Longfellow* (London: [n.p.], 1887), 'Introductory Note'. Quoted in Guy and Small, 'The British "man of letters" ', pp. 381–2.
61. Edmund Gosse, *Gray* (London: Macmillan, [1882] 1909), pp. v–vii.
62. W. J. Courthope, *A History of English Poetry*, I (London: Macmillan, 1895), pp. 3–4, n. 1; p. xxiii; p. 70, n. 1.
63. Ibid., p. xx.
64. Ibid., pp. 247–9, 252.
65. Advertising material in endpapers of Raleigh, *Shakespeare*.
66. Gosse, *Short History of Modern English Literature*, p. v.
67. George Saintsbury, *History of Nineteenth Century Literature*, p. vii.
68. Ibid., pp. 12–13.
69. Ibid., pp. 13, 55, 275, 351.
70. Gosse, *Short History of Modern English Literature*, p. v.
71. Ibid., pp. 103–4.
72. Ibid., p. 104.
73. Ibid., p. 123.
74. *KCC* (1880–1), p. 647; (1883–4), p. 630; (1886–7), p. 689.
75. Raleigh, *Shakespeare*, pp. 7, 18.
76. A. C. Bradley, *Shakespearean Tragedy* (London: Macmillan, [1904] 1958), p. 13.
77. L. C. Knights, *Explorations: Essays in Criticism Mainly on the Literature of the Seventeenth Century* (London, 1946: Penguin, 1964), pp. 15, 27.
78. Edward Dowden, *Shakspere: A Critical Study of His Mind and Art* (London: Kegan Paul, Trench, Trübner, [1875] 1900), pp. xiv, 5.
79. Bradley, *Shakespearean Tragedy*, p. xiii.
80. Ibid.
81. Ibid., p. 10.
82. Ibid., p. 36.
83. Ibid., pp. 37–8.
84. Ibid., p. 95.
85. Ibid., pp. 90, 96–102, 91.
86. Ibid., pp. 130–1.
87. Ibid., pp. 102, 139.
88. Ibid., p. 230.
89. Ibid., pp. 406–13.
90. Ibid., p. viii.
91. Raleigh, *Shakespeare*, p. 153.
92. Ibid., p. 156.
93. Sir Walter Raleigh, *On Writing and Writers*, ed. George Gordon (London: Arnold, 1926), p. 215.
94. Quoted in Gross, *Rise and Fall of the Man of Letters*, p. 196.
95. Raleigh, *Shakespeare*, p. 3.
96. Ibid., p. 20.
97. Ibid., p. 3.

98. Ibid., p. 7.
99. Ibid., pp. 44–55.
100. Ibid., pp. 97–107.
101. Arnold, *Culture and Anarchy*, p. 109.
102. *VUC* (1910–11), p. lxiii.
103. Pater, *The Renaissance*, p. x.

4   Criticism and the modernists: Woolf, Murry, Orage

1. Brake, *Subjugated Knowledges*, p. 3; see also pp. 4–7.
2. As documented in Chapter 3, many of the great Victorian periodicals folded in the first few decades of the twentieth century: the *Westminster Review* in 1914, the *Athenaeum* in 1921, the *Fortnightly Review* in 1924. These decades also saw the emergence of 'little magazines' such as the *English Review* (founded in 1908), *Rhythm* (1911), *The Egoist* (1914) and the *Criterion* (1922).
3. A. R. Orage, quoted in Wallace Martin, *Orage as Critic* (London: Routledge & Kegan Paul, 1974), p. 74.
4. 'Modernism' is, of course, an extremely contentious term which has been defined in a number of ways. Malcolm Bradbury and James McFarlane, in *Modernism: A Guide to European Literature 1890–1930* (London, 1976: Penguin, 1991), draw attention to both its significance and its multiplicity of forms: it was 'an upheaval of [...] cataclysmic order' (p. 20), yet is also 'subject to many interpretations [...] Perhaps the most any account can offer is a personal or at least partial version of an overwhelmingly complex phenomenon, an individual selection from the infinity of detail' (p. 21). This complexity leads Bradbury and McFarlane to offer a general definition of Modernism as 'a new consciousness, a fresh condition of the human mind' (p. 22) – a description conveniently wide enough to encompass the wide range of literary and artistic movements and philosophies contained in Bradbury and McFarlane's text. Louis Menand and Lawrence Rainey, however, challenge this notion of cataclysmic change by pointing to Andreas Huyssen's distinction between modernism and the avant-garde: 'In modernism art and literature retained their traditional 19th-century autonomy from every day life [...] the traditional way in which art and literature were produced, disseminated, and received, is never challenged by modernism but maintained intact', whereas 'the avant-garde [...] attempted to subvert art's autonomy, its artificial separation from life, and its institutionalization as "high art"' (Andreas Huyssen, quoted in Louis Menand and Lawrence Rainey, Introduction to *The Cambridge History of Literary Criticism*, vol. 7: *Modernism and the New Criticism*, ed. A. Walton Litz, Louis Menand and Lawrence Rainey (Cambridge: Cambridge University Press, 2000), p. 4). This sense of the autonomy of modernist art underwrites John Carey's treatment of Modernism in *The Intellectuals and the Masses*, in which modernist art is seen as a 'hostile reaction' to the introduction of universal elementary education: 'The purpose of modernist writing [...] was to exclude these newly educated [...] readers, and so to preserve the intellectual's seclusion from the "mass"' (p. vii). Carey's definition of Modernism as concerned with difficulty and exclusivity has been widely criticised: Stefan Collini points

to the fact that not all of the writers Carey cites were actually Modernists, and questions his suggestion that we should see their disparagement of popular newspapers and tinned food as being characteristic of intellectuals during this period (Collini, *English Pasts*, pp. 289–97). Nevertheless, it is fair to say that Woolf, Murry and Orage all saw art (particularly literature) as being difficult and that much of their criticism focuses on the problems involved in reading 'properly' – a task that was often performed not by the academic, but by the possessor of a more mysticised set of skills and qualities. It is important to point out that in analysing the work of these three critics, I will focus less on the 'difficulty' and formal experimentation associated with Modernist literature itself, as with the difficulty these critics imputed to the correct interpretation of *any* literature: Orage, in particular, was opposed to some aspects of Modernism's stylistic difficulty.

5. Herbert Read, quoted in Bradbury and McFarlane, *Modernism*, p. 20.
6. Carey, *The Intellectuals and the Masses*, p. 9.
7. Ibid., pp. 17, 21.
8. John Middleton Murry, 'Northcliffe as Symbol', *Adelphi*, 1 (October 1930), pp. 16, 18.
9. Virginia Woolf, *The Common Reader: Second Series* (London: Hogarth, [1932] 1986), p. 44; A. R. Orage, quoted in Martin, *Orage as Critic*, p. 140.
10. While it is true that the realist fiction produced for the newly literate mass audience was criticised by many Modernist writers, the availability of cheap editions of the classics was also a source of disquiet.
11. Wallace Martin, *'The New Age' under Orage* (Manchester: Manchester University Press, 1967), p. 3.
12. Matthew Arnold, 'The Function of Criticism at the Present Time', in *The Complete Prose Works of Matthew Arnold*, vol. III: *Lectures and Essays in Criticism*, ed. R. H. Super (Ann Arbor: University of Michigan Press, 1962), p. 270.
13. Virginia Woolf, *The Common Reader* (London: Hogarth, [1925] 1929), p. 189.
14. Rachel Bowlby, *Virginia Woolf: Feminist Destinations* (Oxford: Basil Blackwell, 1988), pp. 12–13.
15. Hermione Lee, *Virginia Woolf* (London: Vintage, 1997), pp. 415–16.
16. Maria DiBattista, 'Virginia Woolf', in *The Cambridge History of Literary Criticism*, vol. 7: *Modernism and the New Criticism*, ed. A. Walton Litz, Louis Menand and Lawrence Rainey (Cambridge: Cambridge University Press, 2000), pp. 126, 135.
17. Virginia Woolf, *A Room of One's Own* (London, 1929: Grafton, 1977), p. 31.
18. DiBattista, 'Virginia Woolf', pp. 127–8.
19. Anne Olivier Bell and Andrew McNeillie (eds), *The Diary of Virginia Woolf*, 5 vols (London: Penguin, 1979–85), 2, p. 248.
20. Elena Gualtieri, *Reading Virginia Woolf's Essays: Sketching the Past* (London: Macmillan, 2000), pp. 4–5.
21. Ibid., pp. 5–6.
22. Ibid., p. 16.
23. Leila Brosnan, *Reading Virginia Woolf's Essays and Journalism* (Edinburgh: Edinburgh University Press, 1997), p. 88.
24. Bell and McNeillie, *The Diary of Virginia Woolf*, 1, p. 197; 3, p. 33.
25. Brosnan, *Reading Virginia Woolf's Essays and Journalism*, p. 40.
26. Ibid., p. 139.

27. Brosnan argues, for instance, that the control exercised over London's literary journalism by figures such as Desmond MacCarthy, John Maynard Keynes, David Garnett and Leonard Woolf (who from 1923 to 1930 was literary editor of the *Nation* and the *Athenaeum*) meant that Woolf, far from being an outsider, was virtually 'guaranteed access to places of publication': her network of relations and acquaintances meant that her entry into journalism was a far smoother experience than those of less well connected writers, both male and female. This concurs with DiBattista's view that Woolf's depiction of herself as an outsider was partly disingenuous, as she had an insider's knowledge of how the literary world worked. See Brosnan, *Reading Virginia Woolf's Essays and Journalism*, pp. 46–8; DiBattista, 'Virginia Woolf', p. 128.

28. Brosnan, *Reading Virginia Woolf's Essays and Journalism*, p. 98.

29. Ibid., p. 100. Rylands had graduated from Cambridge in 1924 after taking Part I of his Tripos in English and Part II in Classics; he worked as a tutor in English and a Fellow of King's College, Cambridge before his appointment as University Lecturer in English in 1935.

30. Woolf, *A Room of One's Own*, p. 100.

31. Bell and McNeillie, *The Diary of Virginia Woolf*, IV, pp. 178–9.

32. Nigel Nicolson and Joanne Trautmann (eds): *The Letters of Virginia Woolf*, 6 vols (London: Chatto & Windus, 1975–80), 5, p. 450.

33. Woolf, *A Room of One's Own*, pp. 32, 28–9.

34. Bell and McNeillie, *The Diary of Virginia Woolf*, 4, p. 179.

35. Woolf, *The Common Reader: Second Series*, pp. 266–7.

36. Woolf, *The Common Reader*, pp. 171–2.

37. Ibid., p. 270.

38. Pater, *Appreciations*, p. 13.

39. Ibid., p. 8.

40. Woolf, *The Common Reader*, p. 211.

41. Ibid., p. 189.

42. DiBattista, 'Virginia Woolf', p. 128.

43. Small, *Conditions for Criticism*, p. 93.

44. Ibid., p. 103.

45. Woolf, *The Common Reader*, p. 11. Woolf's decision to use masculine pronouns to refer to her common reader is seen by Hermione Lee as fuelled by 'her keenness to avoid autobiographical self-exposure' (Lee, *Virginia Woolf*, p. 414). However, the way in which Woolf feminises the act of reading – and her speech about reading at Hayes Court Girls' School, later published as 'How Should One Read a Book?' – mean that this use of masculine pronouns should not be seen as an indication that the 'common reader' was always male.

46. Woolf, *The Common Reader*, pp. 11–12.

47. Woolf, *The Common Reader: Second Series*, p. 263.

48. First published in *Times Literary Supplement* on 29 September 1910; then in *Books and Portraits* (London, 1977: Triad Panther, 1979).

49. Ibid., p. 414.

50. Q. D. Leavis, *Fiction and the Reading Public* (London, 1932: Bellew, 1990), p. 35.

51. Quoted in Lee, *Virginia Woolf*, p. 415.

52. Q. D. Leavis, *Fiction and the Reading Public*, pp. 48–9.

53. Ibid., p. 49.

54. Quoted in Q. D. Leavis, *Fiction and the Reading Public*, p. 49.

55. Woolf, *The Common Reader*, p. 11.
56. Virginia Woolf, *The Death of the Moth and Other Essays* (London, 1942: Penguin, 1961), p. 153.
57. Ibid., p. 154. Woolf's description carries the interesting implication that it is the 'highbrows' who create the art enjoyed by the masses – a very different situation to that described by the Leavises.
58. Ibid., p. 155.
59. Ibid.
60. Ibid., pp. 156, 158.
61. Arnold, *Culture and Anarchy*, pp. 101–2.
62. Woolf, *A Room Of One's Own*, p. 32.
63. Ibid., pp. 158, 156.
64. Guy and Small, 'The British "man of letters"', p. 386.
65. John Middleton Murry, *Between Two Worlds* (London: Jonathan Cape, 1935), pp. 362–3, 193.
66. John Middleton Murry, *The Problem of Style* (London: Oxford University Press, [1922] 1975), p. 1.
67. John Middleton Murry, *Pencillings: Little Essays on Literature* (London: Collins, 1923), p. 185.
68. Guy and Small, 'The British "man of letters"', p. 382.
69. Murry, *Pencillings*, pp. 39–40.
70. Bell and McNeillie, *The Diary of Virginia Woolf*, II, p. 242.
71. Ibid., p. 120.
72. Small, *Conditions for Criticism*, p. 6.
73. Pater, *The Renaissance* ([1873] 1919), pp. ix–x.
74. This use of the language of psychology is discussed in Small, *Conditions for Criticism*, Chapter 3. Small points out that the emergence of the discipline of psychology enabled aesthetics to be discussed in terms of a theory of perception, rather than as a theory of art.
75. Woolf, *The Common Reader: Second Series*, p. 259.
76. Ibid., pp. 260–1.
77. In 'Middlebrow', Woolf claims to 'ask nothing better than that all reviewers, for ever, and everywhere, should call me a highbrow [...] If any human being, man, woman, dog, cat or half-crushed worm dares call me "middlebrow" I will take my pen and stab him, dead'. Woolf, *The Death of the Moth*, p. 160.
78. Ibid., p. 158.
79. Orage, quoted in Martin, *Orage as Critic*, pp. 41, 65.
80. Ibid., pp. 63, 65.
81. Murry, *Problem of Style*, pp. 30–1.
82. Ibid., pp. 20, 32, 47, 92.
83. Orage, quoted in Martin, *Orage as Critic*, p. 38.
84. Ibid., p. 39.
85. Martin, *Orage as Critic*, p. 1.
86. Orage, quoted in Martin, *Orage as Critic*, p. 46.
87. See Martin, 'The New Age' under Orage, pp. 1–16.
88. Max Plowman and Richard Rees, editorial, *Adelphi*, 1 (October 1930), pp. 2–3.
89. Stefan Collini, 'Lament for a lost culture: How the twentieth century came to mourn the seriousness of the nineteenth', *Times Literary Supplement* (19 January 2001), pp. 3–5.

90. Plowman and Rees, editorial, *Adelphi*, 1 (October 1930), p. 1.
91. Max Plowman, review of John Middleton Murry, *Discoveries* and *Studies in Keats*, *Adelphi*, 1 (November 1930), p. 165.
92. Ibid., pp. 165–6.
93. Ibid., p. 167.
94. Ibid.
95. John Middleton Murry, 'Hamlet Again', *Adelphi*, 1 (January 1931), pp. 347, 342.
96. Orage, quoted in Martin, *Orage as Critic*, p. 45.
97. Ibid., p. 36.
98. Ibid., p. 40.
99. Guy and Small, 'The British "Man of Letters" ', p. 384.
100. Ibid., p. 77.
101. Orage, quoted in Martin, *Orage as Critic*, pp. 77–9.
102. Significantly, while Orage acknowledged that such readers were 'literate', he denied that they could be 'cultured'. Martin, *Orage as Critic*, p. 66.
103. Murry, *Problem of Style*, p. 1.
104. Ibid., p. 7.
105. Ibid., p. 68.
106. Ibid., pp. 16–17.

5 Methods and institutions: Eliot, Richards and Leavis

1. Baldick, *Social Mission*, p. 15; Eagleton, *Literary Theory*, pp. 30–1.
2. Pamela McCallum, *Literature and Method: Towards a Critique of I. A. Richards, T. S. Eliot and F. R. Leavis* (Dublin: Gill and Macmillan, 1983), pp. 3–7.
3. Baldick, *Social Mission*, pp. 3, 159.
4. Mulhern, *Moment of 'Scrutiny'*, p. ix.
5. T. S. Eliot, *The Use of Poetry and the Use of Criticism* (London: Faber & Faber, [1933] 1964), p. 14; I. A. Richards, *Principles of Literary Criticism* (London, 1924: Routledge, 1948), p. 4; Leavis, *English Literature in Our Time*, p. 2.
6. Louis Menand, 'T. S. Eliot', in *The Cambridge History of Literary Criticism*, vol. 7: *Modernism and the New Criticism*, ed. A. Walton Litz, Louis Menand and Lawrence Rainey (Cambridge: Cambridge University Press, 2000), pp. 55, 19–20.
7. Paul H. Fry, 'I. A. Richards', in *The Cambridge History of Literary Criticism*, vol. 7: *Modernism and the New Criticism*, ed. A. Walton Litz, Louis Menand and Lawrence Rainey (Cambridge: Cambridge University Press, 2000), pp. 182–3; MacKillop, *F. R. Leavis*, pp. 48–60.
8. Mulhern, *Moment of 'Scrutiny'*, pp. 22–7.
9. John Paul Russo, *I. A. Richards: His Life and Work* (Routledge: London, 1989), p. 535.
10. Menand, 'T. S. Eliot', p. 20.
11. Graham Hough, 'The Poet as Critic', in *The Literary Criticism of T. S. Eliot*, ed. David Newton-De Molina (London: Athlone, 1977), p. 45.
12. Eliot, *The Use of Poetry*, pp. 35–36.
13. T. S. Eliot, *The Sacred Wood: Essays on Poetry and Criticism* (London: Methuen, [1920] 1969), pp. 14–15; Eliot, *The Use of Poetry*, p. 35.
14. T. S. Eliot, *The Selected Prose of T. S. Eliot*, ed. Frank Kermode (London: Faber & Faber, 1975), p. 73.

15. Eliot, *Selected Prose*, p. 74.
16. T. S. Eliot, *On Poetry and Poets* (London: Faber & Faber, 1957), pp. 27–8.
17. Ibid., p. 27.
18. T. S. Eliot, *Milton: Two Studies* (London: Faber & Faber, [1936] 1968), pp. 23–4.
19. Eliot, *Sacred Wood*, pp. 3–7.
20. Ibid., pp. 17, 20–1. For Eliot, Swinburne was 'an appreciator and not a critic' (ibid., p. 19). Eliot's comments about Swinburne's 'undisciplined' style are borne out by Swinburne's description of *Doctor Faustus*: 'the sublimity of simplicity in Marlowe's conception and expression of the agonies endured by Faustus under the immediate imminence of [his] doom gives the highest note of beauty, the quality of absolute fitness and propriety, to the sheer straightforwardness of speech in which his agonising horror finds vent ever more and more terrible from the first to the last equally beautiful and fearful of that tremendous monologue which has no parallel in all the range of tragedy'. *The Age of Shakespeare* (1908), reprinted in *The Complete Works of Algernon Charles Swinburne, Prose Works: I*, ed. Sir Edmund Gosse and Thomas James Wise (London: Heinemann, 1926), p. 272.
21. *Sacred Wood*, pp. 37–8.
22. Eliot, *Use of Poetry*, p. 19.
23. Pater, *The Renaissance* ([1873] 1919), p. viii.
24. Ibid., p. viii.
25. Eliot, *Sacred Wood*, pp. 123–4; see also A. H. Cruickshank, *Philip Massinger* (Oxford: Blackwell, 1920).
26. Eliot, *Selected Prose*, pp. 68, 57.
27. Eliot, *Milton*, p. 47.
28. Eliot, *Use of Poetry*, p. 15.
29. Eliot, *Sacred Wood*, p. ix.
30. Ibid., p. 91.
31. Eliot, *Milton*, pp. 16, 18–19.
32. Ibid., p. 11.
33. See Shattock, *Politics and Reviewers*, pp. 9–10, 109–12.
34. F. W. Bateson, 'Criticism's Lost Leader', in *The Literary Criticism of T. S. Eliot*, ed. Newton De Molina (London: Athlone, 1977), p. 17.
35. Eliot, *Sacred Wood*, pp. 126–7.
36. Ibid., p. 139.
37. J. Hillis Miller, *Poets of Reality* (London: Oxford University Press, 1966), p. 160. Quoted in McCallum, *Literature and Method*, p. 121.
38. Eliot, *Use of Poetry*, p. 17.
39. Eliot, *On Poetry and Poets*, p. 27.
40. Ibid., p. 77.
41. It is significant, of course, that Eliot chose an academic setting – that of the Charles Eliot Norton lectures at Harvard – to present himself in such a way. His strategy here is similar to that of John Middleton Murry, who, as we saw in Chapter 4, used his lectures at Oxford to consolidate a critical authority that was somewhat at odds with that of professional scholarship.
42. Eliot, *Use of Poetry*, p. 89.
43. Baldick, *Social Mission*, p. 131.
44. Tillyard, *Muse Unchained*, p. 100.
45. Eliot, *Use of Poetry*, p. 150.

46. Eliot, *Selected Prose*, p. 75.
47. Ibid., p. 56.
48. Eliot, *On Poetry and Poets*, pp. 105, 107, 109.
49. Ibid., p. 114.
50. Ibid., p. 105.
51. I. A. Richards, quoted in Russo, *Richards*, p. 735.
52. Russo, *Richards*, p. 273.
53. John Constable, 'I. A. Richards, T. S. Eliot and the Poetry of Belief', *Essays in Criticism*, 40 (1990), 222–43; accessed online at http://www.btinternet.com/~j1837c/jbc/iartse/html.
54. Eliot, *Use of Poetry*, pp. 131–4.
55. T. S. Eliot, 'Literature, Science and Dogma', *The Dial*, 82 (1927). Quoted in Constable, 'Richards, Eliot and the Poetry of Belief'.
56. Quoted in Constable, 'Richards, Eliot and the Poetry of Belief'.
57. Eliot, *Use of Poetry*, p. 19.
58. Eliot, *Sacred Wood*, p. ix; T. S. Eliot, *To Criticize the Critic* (London: Faber & Faber, 1965), pp. 25–6.
59. Richards, *Principles of Literary Criticism*, p. 35.
60. I. A. Richards, *Practical Criticism: A Study of Literary Judgment* (London: Routledge & Kegan Paul, [1929] 1978), p. 334.
61. Ibid., pp. 337–8.
62. I. A. Richards, journal entry of 17 December 1969; *Complementarities: Uncollected Essays*, ed. John Paul Russo (Cambridge, Massachusetts: Harvard University Press, 1976), p. 266. Quoted in Russo, *Richards*, pp. 216, 734–5.
63. Richards, *Principles of Literary Criticism*, pp. 11–18, 36–7.
64. Ibid., p. 36.
65. Ibid., pp. 36–7.
66. Mulhern, *Moment of 'Scrutiny'*, p. 28.
67. MacKillop, *F. R. Leavis*, p. 62.
68. I. A. Richards, *Poetries and Sciences* (first published as *Science and Poetry*, London: Routledge & Kegan Paul, [1926] 1970), p. 18.
69. Ibid., pp. 100–4.
70. Ibid., pp. 23–8.
71. Richards, *Practical Criticism*, pp. 348–9.
72. Quoted in Richards, *Practical Criticism*, p. 350.
73. McCallum, *Literature and Method*, p. 62.
74. Richards, *Practical Criticism*, pp. 13–15.
75. Ibid., p. 309.
76. Ibid., p. 333.
77. Russo, *Richards*, pp. 35, 203. In *So Much Nearer: Essays towards a World English* (1968), Richards corrected Shelley's 'Poets are the unacknowledged legislators of the world' to 'Po*ems* are the unacknowledged legisla*tion*'. Quoted in Russo, *Richards*, p. 203.
78. Ibid., p. 92.
79. Ibid., p. 89.
80. Martin, 'Criticism and the academy', pp. 307–8.
81. Richards, *Practical Criticism*, p. 12.
82. Ibid., p. 321.

83. Such a need is summarised in the words of F. L. Lucas, a lecturer in the English Faculty at Cambridge in the 1920s, who criticised the 'organized orgies of opinion' into which he claimed English had descended. See Mulhern, *Moment of 'Scrutiny'*, pp. 29–31.
84. MacKillop, *Leavis*, pp. 93–5.
85. Mulhern, *Moment of 'Scrutiny'*, p. 33.
86. F. R. Leavis, 'The Literary Mind', *Scrutiny*, 1 (1932–3), p. 24; quoted in Mulhern, *Moment of 'Scrutiny'*, p. 76.
87. Mulhern, *Moment of 'Scrutiny'*, p. 28.
88. The foundation of an independent English Faculty in 1926 led to the disbanding of the 'freelance' tutors on whom the teaching of English had previously depended, and the establishment of 'much more formal and centralized structures of teaching and administration' (Mulhern, *Moment of 'Scrutiny'*, p. 29). Mulhern notes that 'this "consolidation" of the English school was achieved partly at the expense of its "creative" sources' (ibid.).
89. Leavis, *English Literature in Our Time*, p. 14.
90. Ibid., pp. 11–12.
91. Ibid., p. 12.
92. Ibid., pp. 23–4.
93. Ibid., p. 3.
94. Ibid., p. 3.
95. Ibid., p. 7.
96. Ibid., pp. 7–8.
97. Ibid., p. 8.
98. Eliot, *Selected Prose*, p. 69.
99. Eliot, *Use of Poetry*, p. 27.
100. F. R. Leavis, 'The Literary Racket', *Scrutiny*, 1 (1932–3), p. 166.
101. Leavis, *Education and the University*, pp. 51–64; MacKillop, *Leavis*, p. 38.
102. Leavis, *Education and the University*, pp. 58–9.
103. MacKillop, *Leavis*, p. 239.
104. Leavis, *English Literature in Our Time*, p. 2.
105. F. R. Leavis, quoted in MacKillop, *Leavis*, p. 239.
106. Leavis, *Education and the University*, pp. 7, 11.
107. Leavis, *English Literature in Our Time*, p. 17.
108. Ibid., p. 3.
109. Ibid., p. 5.
110. Ibid., pp. 17, 20.
111. F. R. Leavis, 'Mr. Pryce-Jones, the British Council and British Culture', *Scrutiny*, 18 (1951–2), p. 228.
112. The creation of the new Faculty involved the appointment of 12 full-time, tenured lecturers. However, Leavis was not a successful candidate. He was given a two-year probationary lectureship in January 1927, but it was to be another 20 years before he finally gained a full-time university appointment. See MacKillop, *Leavis*, pp. 92, 225–6.
113. R. P. Bilan, *The Literary Criticism of F. R. Leavis* (Cambridge: Cambridge University Press, 1979), p. 149. Quoted in McCallum, *Literature and Method*, p. 196.
114. MacKillop, *Leavis*, p. 171.

115. F. R. Leavis, *Revaluation: Tradition and Development in English Poetry* (London, 1936: Penguin, 1972), p. 252.
116. F. R. Leavis, *The Great Tradition* (London, 1948: Penguin, 1962), p. 51.
117. McCallum, *Literature and Method*, pp. 184–5.
118. Eliot, *Selected Prose*, p. 56.
119. Russo, *Richards*, p. 735.
120. Leavis, *English Literature in Our Time*, p. 11.
121. Collins, 'The Universities in Contact with the People', p. 583.
122. Baldick, *Social Mission*, p. 197.

6 Revising English: Theory and practice

1. C. L. Mowat, 'Cleavage and Culture', *Critical Quarterly*, 2 (1960), p. 232.
2. Lionel Trilling, quoted in Richard Hoggart, 'The Difficulties of Democratic Debate', *Critical Quarterly*, 5 (1963), p. 210.
3. Mowat, 'Cleavage and Culture', p. 227.
4. A. E. Dyson, Editorial, *Critical Quarterly*, 2 (1960), p. 197.
5. Terence Hawkes, General Editor's Preface to 'New Accents' series, in Catherine Belsey, *Critical Practice* (London: Methuen, 1980), p. vii.
6. Terence Hawkes, *Structuralism and Semiotics* (London: Routledge, [1977] 2003), pp. 139–40.
7. Hayden White, 'The Absurdist Moment in Contemporary Literary Theory', in *Directions for Criticism: Structuralism and its Alternatives*, ed. Murray Krieger and L. S. Dembo (Madison: University of Wisconsin Press, 1977), p. 85.
8. For one attack on radical literary theory and its place in the universities, see Peter Washington, *Fraud: Literary Theory and the End of English* (London: Fontana, 1989).
9. *English: The National Curriculum for England* (Department for Education and Employment/Qualifications and Curriculum Authority, QCA/99/459, 1999), pp. 35–6.
10. Brian Cox, *Cox on the Battle for the English Curriculum* (London: Hodder & Stoughton, 1995), p. 75; see also Brian Cox, *Cox on Cox: An English Curriculum for the 1990s* (London: Hodder & Stoughton, 1991).
11. Cameron, *Verbal Hygiene*, pp. 78–115.
12. Peter Hollindale, 'War-weary sides call for truce', *Times Educational Supplement* (12 January 1996), accessed online at http://www.tes.co.uk/search/search_display.asp?section+Archive&sub_section=Friday&id=25359&Type=0.
13. This system was intended to make post-16 education more inclusive, rigorous and internationally competitive, providing for the needs of employers as well as universities. It was originally hoped that the broader first year of sixth-form studies would encourage science students to continue learning a foreign language and humanities specialists to pursue additional studies in mathematics or a science. These hopes were fuelled by concerns (expressed throughout the 1980s and 1990s) that the UK was not producing enough engineers or scientists, and that its existing scientists lacked the ability to compete in global and European markets.
14. Remark made at the English Association Spring Conference for Teachers, St Catherine's College, Oxford, March 1999.

15. GCE Advanced Subsidiary and Advanced Level Specifications: Subject Criteria for English Literature.
16. Ibid.
17. Ibid.
18. OCR: English Language and Literature, Mark Scheme for the Components/ Modules, June 2001 (OCR, 2001), report on units 9000/1 and 4481, section 7.
19. Jenny Stevens, 'The new 'A' Levels: Critical Theory in the Sixth Form Classroom: A Very, Very Short Introduction', *The Use of English*, 52 (2000), p. 1.
20. Robert Eaglestone, 'Active voice! Responding to Adrian Barlow on the new English Literature A-levels', *English Association Newsletter*, 166 (2001), pp. 6–7.
21. *A Language for Life: Report of the Committee of Inquiry* (DES, 1975), paragraph 1.3. Quoted in Bethan Marshall, *English Teachers – The Unofficial Guide: Researching the Philosophies of English Teachers* (London: RoutledgeFalmer, 2000), p. 4.
22. Cox, *Cox on Cox*, pp. 21–2.
23. See Marshall, *English Teachers – The Unofficial Guide*, 'A Rough Guide to English Teachers' (after p. 56), also pp. 70–129.
24. J. Dover Wilson, *Milestones on the Dover Road* (1969), pp. 252–53. Quoted in Baldick, *Social Mission*, p. 96.
25. *English: The National Curriculum for England* (1999), pp. 8–9.
26. Marshall, *English Teachers – The Unofficial Guide*, pp. 25–7, 91.
27. Nick Peim has commented on the fact that such texts have never been part of the accepted English canon: they 'are not, according to any formalized or traditional view, official texts of English Literature'. Nick Peim, *Critical Theory and the English Teacher: Transforming the Subject* (London: Routledge, 1993), p. 74.
28. See David Holbrook, *English for Maturity* (Cambridge: Cambridge University Press, 1967).
29. Peim, *Critical Theory and the English Teacher*, pp. 4–5.
30. Marshall, *English Teachers – The Unofficial Guide*, pp. 109–10.
31. Ibid., pp. 109, 91.
32. Peter Griffiths, *English at the Core* (Buckingham: Open University Press, 1992), p. 18. Quoted in Marshall, *English Teachers – The Unofficial Guide*, p. 9.
33. Jay Snow, 'On the Subject of English', *English in Education*, 25 (1991), p. 23. Quoted in Marshall, *English Teachers – The Unofficial Guide*, p. 10.
34. Melanie Phillips, *All Must Have Prizes* (London: Warner, [1996] 1998), p. 121.
35. Ibid., pp. 121–2, 120–1.
36. Such figures include David Pascall, appointed head of the National Curriculum Council in 1991 and responsible for the 1993 revision of Cox's original National Curriculum for English; John Marenbon, chair of the NCC's English Committee; and John Marks, chair of its Mathematics Committee and secretary of the education study group of the Centre for Policy Studies, a right-wing think tank. Pascall was a former BP oil executive who reputedly 'had no interest in or knowledge of the National Curriculum' until his appointment to the NCC; Marenbon was a specialist in medieval philosophy at Trinity College, Cambridge. See Cox, *Cox on the Battle for the English Curriculum*, pp. 26–7, 98–9.
37. John Marks, speech entitled 'The National Curriculum and Primary School Method', delivered at the Institute of Economic Affairs, November 1992.

Quoted in Cox, *Cox on the Battle for the English Curriculum*, p. 32. The 1989 version of the National Curriculum stated that teachers should 'give pupils the opportunity to gain some experience of the works of Shakespeare', but deliberately left teachers free 'to use their professional judgment in selecting texts suitable for the needs of their own pupils', and encouraged an exploratory approach in which pupils were able to 'discuss the themes, settings and characters of the texts they read in order to make a personal response to them' (Cox, *Cox on Cox*, pp. 68, 194). In contrast, the NCC's revised version made the teaching of Shakespeare compulsory by introducing questions on Shakespeare in the Key Stage 3 tests in English, although less able pupils were not required to study a complete play.

38. Bob Bibby, former Inspector in English for Dudley, quoted in Cox, *Cox on the Battle for the English Curriculum*, p. 104.
39. Cox, *Cox on the Battle for the English Curriculum*, pp. 34–5.
40. Pamela Bickley, 'The New A-Level: What Will It Mean?', paper given at the English Association Conference for Higher Education, April 2000, accessed online at http://www.le.ac.uk/engassoc/info/se1.html.
41. OCR: English Language and Literature, Mark Scheme for the Components/ Modules, June 2001 (OCR, 2001).
42. See AQA English Literature, Specification A: Advanced Subsidiary GCE 5741/ Advanced GCE 6741 (AQA, 1999; hereafter AQA Specification A), pp. 14–22.
43. Frank Myszor and Jackie Baker, *Living Literature: Exploring Advanced Level English Literature*, ed. George Keith and John Shuttleworth (London: Hodder & Stoughton, 2000), pp. vi–vii.
44. Barbara Dennis, *The Victorian Novel* (Cambridge: Cambridge University Press, 2000), rear cover.
45. Myszor and Baker, *Living Literature*, p. 6.
46. Rob Pope, *The English Studies Book* (London: Routledge, 1998), p. 197.
47. Ibid., p. 37.
48. Edexcel Advanced Subsidiary GCE in English Literature (8180)/Advanced GCE in English Literature (9180): Teachers' Guide (Edexcel, 2000), p. 13.
49. AQA English Literature, Specification A: Report on the Examination, GCE 2001, Advanced Subsidiary (5471), June Series (AQA, 2001; hereafter AQA Examiners' Report), p. 17.
50. AQA English Literature, Specification A: GCSE 3712 (AQA, 2004), p. 12.
51. AQA English Literature, Specification A: Specimen Units and Mark Schemes (AQA, 1999), pp. 91, 96, 102, 106.
52. Simon Dentith, 'English and the Audit Culture: An Introduction', *English Subject Centre Newsletter*, 3 (May 2002), accessed online at http://www.english.ltsn.ac.uk/ resources/general/publications/newsletters/newsissue3/dentith.htm.
53. AQA Examiners' Report (June 2001), p. 23.
54. Ibid., pp. 25, 29.
55. AQA Specification A, p. 25.
56. AQA English Literature: General Certificate of Education, June 2002, Advanced Level Examination, Specification A, Unit 4 (Monday 10 June 2002), p. 3.
57. AQA Specification A, p. 11.
58. AQA English Literature: 5741/6741 Newsletter, AS/A2 English Literature Specification A, 'Essential Information for the Urgent Attention of the Head of English' (AQA, March 2002), p. 12.

59. OCR: Advanced Subsidiary GCE in English Literature (3828)/Advanced GCE in English Literature (7828) (OCR, 2000), p. 48.
60. Mike Craddock, 'Idealism, Theory, Practice and the New "A" Levels', *The Use of English*, 52 (2001), p. 108.
61. Richard Hoyes, 'Richard Hoyes puts the fun back into Eng Lit', *Friday* magazine, *Times Educational Supplement* (11 February 2000), p. 5. It is interesting to note that Hoyes's comment echoes I. A. Richards's complaint about 'books-about-books-about-books', referred to in Chapter 5.
62. Mike Craddock, 'Curriculum 2000: A Teacher's Verdict', *The Use of English*, 54 (2003), p. 115.
63. Ibid., p. 113.
64. Ibid., p. 112.
65. Craddock, 'Idealism, Theory, Practice and the New "A" Levels', 108.
66. AQA History: Advanced Subsidiary GCE 5041/Advanced GCE 6051 (AQA, 2002), pp. 13, 25.
67. AQA Religious Studies: Advanced Subsidiary GCE 5061/Advanced GCE 6061 (AQA, 2002, hereafter AQA Religious Studies), pp. 10, 31.
68. Derek Attridge, *The Singularity of Literature* (London: Routledge, 2004).
69. AQA Religious Studies, p. 10.
70. Elaine Showalter, *Teaching Literature* (Oxford: Blackwell, 2003), p. vii.
71. Philip Smallwood, ' "More Creative than Creation": The Idea of Criticism and the Student Critic', *Arts and Humanities in Higher Education*, 1 (2002), p. 64.
72. Chrissie Boughey, 'From Equity to Efficiency: Access to Higher Education in South Africa', *Arts and Humanities in Higher Education*, 2 (2003), p. 67.
73. Amis, *The War against Cliché*, pp. xiii–xiv.
74. Natasha Walter, 'Can We Win the War against Cliché?', *The Independent* (23 April 2001), accessed online at http://www.independent.co.uk/story.jsp?story=68134.
75. Amis, *The War against Cliché*, p. xiii.
76. Lawrence Rainey, 'The most uncommon reader', *The Independent* (21 April 2001), accessed online at http://www.independent.co.uk/story.jsp?=67826.
77. Bloom, *How to Read and Why*, p. 23.
78. Ibid.
79. Ibid., p. 28.
80. Ibid., p. 21.
81. Carey, *Pure Pleasure*, p. xii.
82. Bloom, *How to Read and Why*, p. 21.
83. Ibid., pp. 22, 19.
84. Carey, *Pure Pleasure*, pp. x–xi.
85. Bloom, *How to Read and Why*, p. 150.
86. Carey, *Pure Pleasure*, pp. 3, 19.
87. Bloom, *How to Read and Why*, p. 79.
88. Ibid., p. 159.
89. Anthony Kearney, 'What to Read and Why: A View of John Carey's *Pure Pleasure*', *Use of English*, 53 (2001), p. 49.
90. Jim Sait, summary of lecture delivered by John Sutherland at the University of Sydney, accessed online at http://www.usyd.edu.au/publications/news/2K0810News/1008_briefly.html.

91. John Sutherland, *Is Heathcliff a Murderer? Puzzles in 19th-Century Fiction* (Oxford: Oxford University Press, 1996), p. ix.
92. Charlotte Brontë, *Jane Eyre* (London: Penguin, [1847] 2002), rear cover.
93. Carey, *Pure Pleasure*, p. xi; Walter, 'Can We Win the War against Cliché?', p. 5; Bloom, *How to Read and Why*, p. 23.

Conclusion

1. Arnold, *On Translating Homer*, p. 249.
2. Collins, 'The Universities in Contact with the People', p. 583.
3. Collini, *English Pasts*, p. 313.

Bibliography

Archive material

From the archives of the University of Oxford (held at Oxford University Archives, Bodleian Library)

Minutes of meetings of the Board of the Faculty of Literae Humaniores, 1883–1924: OUA, FA 4/7/1/1–3.

Reports of the meetings of the Board of the Faculty of Literae Humaniores, 1899–1913: OUA, FA 4/7/2/1.

Minutes of the meetings of the Board of the Faculty of Medieval and Modern Languages and Literature, 1913–28: OUA, FA 4/10/1/1.

Reports of the Faculty of Medieval and Modern Languages and Literature, 1913–27: OUA, FA 4/10/2/1–3.

Minutes of the meetings of the Board of the Faculty of English Language and Literature, 1926–46: OUA, FA 4/5/1/1.

Reports of the Board of the Faculty of English Language and Literature, 1926–45: OUA, FA 4/5/2/1–7.

From the archives of the University of Cambridge (held at Cambridge University Library)

Cambridge University Reporter, 1910–19.

Cambridge University Examination Papers, 1917–26: L952.b.5.

Student's Handbook to Cambridge, 1917–18 (Cambridge: Cambridge University Press, 1917): Cam.d.1.11.

'Guard Book' containing information on the King Edward VII Professorship of English Literature: University Archives, CUR 39.46.

From the archives of King's College, London

Minutes of Special Committee Meetings held at King's College, London: KA/CS/M1–2.

Calendar of King's College, London: editions dated 1836–37, 1880–1930.

From the archives of the University of Nottingham (held at the Hallward Library, University of Nottingham)

University College, Nottingham: Calendars for sessions 1882–1901, 1909–21: Not. 5. A2.

From the archives of the University of Manchester (held at the John Rylands Library, University of Manchester)

Owens College Calendar, editions dated 1880–86, 1900–01: UA/19.

Victoria University of Manchester Calendar, editions dated 1900–11, 1920–21, 1930–31, 1940–41: UA/21.

Documents relating to the teaching of English in secondary schools

English: The National Curriculum for England (Department for Education and Employment/Qualifications and Curriculum Authority, QCA/99/459, 1999).

GCE Advanced Subsidiary and Advanced Level Specifications: Subject Criteria for English Literature (Department for Education and Employment/Qualifications and Curriculum Authority, QCA 991680144, 1999).

AQA English Literature, Specification A: Advanced Subsidiary GCE 5741/Advanced GCE 6741 (AQA, 1999).

AQA English Literature, Specification A: Specimen Units and Mark Schemes (AQA, 1999).

AQA English Literature, Specification A: Report on the Examination, GCE 2001, Advanced Subsidiary (5471), June Series (AQA, 2001).

AQA English Literature: 5741/6741 Newsletter, AS/A2 English Literature Specification A, 'Essential Information for the Urgent Attention of the Head of English' (AQA, March 2002).

AQA English Literature: General Certificate of Education, June 2002, Advanced Level Examination, Specification A, Unit 4 (Monday 10 June 2002).

AQA English Literature, Specification A: GCSE 3712 (AQA, 2004).

AQA History: Advanced Subsidiary GCE 5041/Advanced GCE 6051 (AQA, 2002).

AQA Religious Studies: Advanced Subsidiary GCE 5061/Advanced GCE 6061 (AQA, 2002).

Edexcel Advanced Subsidiary GCE in English Literature (8180)/Advanced GCE in English Literature (9180): Teachers' Guide (Edexcel, 2000).

OCR: Advanced Subsidiary GCE in English Literature (3828)/Advanced GCE in English Literature (7828) (OCR, 2000).

OCR: English Language and Literature, Mark Scheme for the Components/Modules, June 2001 (OCR, 2001).

Published material

Primary sources

Anonymous. Review of David Masson's *The Life of John Milton, Athenaeum*, 2732 (1880), 303.

——. Review of Rhoda Broughton's *Second Thoughts, Athenaeum*, 2745 (1880), 725.

Arnold, Matthew. *On Translating Homer* (London, 1861: Routledge, 1905).

——. *Culture and Anarchy* (London, 1869: Cambridge University Press, 1932).

——. 'The Function of Criticism at the Present Time', in *The Complete Prose Works of Matthew Arnold*, vol. III: *Lectures and Essays in Criticism*, ed. R. H. Super (Ann Arbor: University of Michigan Press, 1962), 258–85.

Barry, Alfred. 'The Good and Evil of Examination', *Nineteenth Century*, 3 (1878), 647–66.

Bell, Anne Olivier and McNeillie, Andrew (eds). *The Diary of Virginia Woolf*, 5 vols (London: Penguin Books, 1979–85).

Bennett, Arnold. *Literary Taste* (London: Hodder & Stoughton, 1909).

Bloom, Harold. *How to Read and Why* (London: Fourth Estate, [2000] 2001).

Board of Education, Committee on English in the educational system of England: *The Teaching of English in England* (London: HMSO, 1921).

Bradley, A. C. *Shakespearean Tragedy* (London: Macmillan, [1904] 1958).

———. *Oxford Lectures on Poetry* (London: Macmillan, 1941).

Brontë, Charlotte. *Jane Eyre* (London, 1847: Penguin, 2002).

Butcher, Henry. Presidential Address to the British Academy, delivered 27 October 1909, *Proceedings of the British Academy* (1909–10), 23.

Carey, John. *Pure Pleasure: A Guide to the 20th Century's Most Enjoyable Books* (London: Faber & Faber, 2000).

Collins, John Churton. 'English Literature at the Universities', *Quarterly Review*, 163 (1886), 289–329.

———. 'Can English Literature be Taught?', *Nineteenth Century*, 22 (1887), 642–58.

———. 'The Universities in Contact with the People', *Nineteenth Century*, 26 (1889), 561–83.

Courthope, W. J. *A History of English Poetry*, I (London: Macmillan, 1895).

Cruickshank, A. H. *Philip Massinger* (Oxford: Blackwell, 1920).

Dowden, Edward. *Shakspere: A Critical Study of his Mind and Art* (London: Kegan Paul, Trench, Trübner, [1875] 1900).

Dyson, A. E. Editorial, *Critical Quarterly*, 2 (1960), 195–9.

Eliot, T. S. *The Sacred Wood. Essays on Poetry and Criticism* (London: Methuen, [1920] 1969).

———. *Homage to John Dryden* (London: Hogarth, 1924).

———. *The Use of Poetry and the Use of Criticism* (London: Faber & Faber, [1933] 1964).

———. *On Poetry and Poets* (London: Faber & Faber, 1957).

———. *To Criticize the Critic* (London: Faber & Faber, 1965).

———. *Milton: Two Studies* (London: Faber & Faber, 1968).

———. *The Selected Prose of T. S. Eliot*, ed. Frank Kermode (London: Faber & Faber, 1975).

Garrod, H. W. *The Profession of Poetry and Other Lectures* (Oxford: Clarendon Press, 1929).

Gordon, George. *The Discipline of Letters* (Oxford: Clarendon Press, 1946).

Gosse, Edmund. *Gray* (London: Macmillan, [1882] 1909).

———. *A Short History of Modern English Literature* (London: Heinemann, [1897] 1925).

Hoggart, Richard. 'The Difficulties of Democratic Debate', *Critical Quarterly*, 5 (1963), 197–212.

Ker, W. P. *On Modern Literature: Lectures and Addresses*, ed. Terence Spencer and James Sutherland (Oxford: Clarendon Press, 1955).

Knights, L. C. *Explorations: Essays in Criticism Mainly on the Literature of the Seventeenth Century* (London: Penguin, [1946] 1964).

Lang, Andrew. Letter, *Academy*, 27 (20 June 1885), 438–9.

Leathes, Stanley. *The Teaching of English at the Universities* (English Association pamphlet no. 26, October 1913).

Leavis, F. R. 'The Literary Racket', *Scrutiny*, 1 (1932–3), 166–8.

———. *New Bearings in English Poetry* (London, 1932: Penguin, 1963).

———. *Revaluation: Tradition and Development in English Poetry* (London, 1936: Penguin, 1972).

———. 'Literary Criticism and Philosophy: A Reply', *Scrutiny*, 6 (1937–8), 59–70.

———. *Education and the University: A Sketch for an 'English School'* (London: Chatto & Windus, 1943).

——. *The Great Tradition* (London, 1948: Penguin, 1962).

——. 'Mr. Pryce-Jones, the British Council and British Culture', *Scrutiny*, 18 (1951–2), 224–8.

——. *The Common Pursuit* (London: Chatt & Windus, 1952).

——. *English Literature in Our Time and the University* (Cambridge: Cambridge University Press, 1969).

Leavis, Q. D. *Fiction and the Reading Public* (London, 1932: Bellew, 1990).

——. 'Professor Chadwick and English Studies' (published anonymously), *Scrutiny*, 14 (1946–7), 204–8.

Martin, Wallace. *Orage as Critic* (London: Routledge & Kegan Paul, 1974).

Mowat, C. L. 'Cleavage and Culture', *Critical Quarterly*, 2 (1960), 223–32.

Murry, John Middleton. *Fyodor Dostoevsky: A Critical Study* (London: Secker, 1916).

——. *The Problem of Style* (London: Oxford University Press, [1922] 1975).

——. *Pencillings: Little Essays on Literature* (London: Collins, 1923).

——. *Keats and Shakespeare* (Oxford: Oxford University Press, 1925).

——. 'Northcliffe as Symbol', *Adelphi*, 1 (October 1930), 15–18.

——. 'Hamlet Again', *Adelphi*, 1 (January 1931), 341–47.

——. *Between Two Worlds* (London: Jonathan Cape, 1935).

Myszor, Frank, and Baker, Jackie. *Living Literature: Exploring Advanced Level English Literature*, ed. George Keith and John Shuttleworth (London: Hodder & Stoughton, 2000).

Nicolson, Nigel, and Trautmann, Joanne (eds). *The Letters of Virginia Woolf*, 6 vols (London: Chatto & Windus, 1975–80).

Pater, Walter. *The Renaissance: Studies in Art and Poetry* (London: Macmillan, [1873] 1919).

——. *Appreciations: With an Essay on Style* (London: Macmillan, [1889] 1931).

——. *The Renaissance: Studies in Art and Poetry*, ed. Adam Phillips (Oxford: Oxford University Press, 1986).

Plowman, Max. Review of John Middleton Murry, *Discoveries* and *Studies in Keats, Adelphi*, 1 (November 1930), 165–8.

Plowman, Max, and Rees, Richard. Editorial, *Adelphi*, 1 (October 1930), 1–3.

Quiller-Couch, Sir Arthur. *On the Art of Reading* (Cambridge: Cambridge University Press, [1920] 1947).

——. *Studies in Literature: Third Series* (Cambridge: Cambridge University Press, [1929] 1948).

——. *Q Anthology*, ed. F. Brittain (London: Dent, 1948).

Raleigh, Sir Walter. *Shakespeare* (London: Macmillan, 1907).

Raleigh, Sir Walter. *On Writing and Writers*, ed. George Gordon (London: Arnold, 1926).

Richards, I. A. *Principles of Literary Criticism* (London: Routledge & Kegan Paul, [1924] 1948).

——. *Poetries and Sciences* (first published as *Science and Poetry*, London: Routledge & Kegan Paul, [1926] 1970).

——. *Practical Criticism: A Study of Literary Judgment* (London: Routledge & Kegan Paul, [1929] 1978).

——. *How to Read a Page* (London: Kegan Paul, 1943).

Saintsbury, George. *Miscellaneous Essays* (London: Percival, 1892).
——. *A History of Nineteenth Century Literature 1780–1900* (London: Macmillan, [1896] 1906).
Skeat, W. W. Letter, *Academy*, 27 (18 April 1885), 275.
Spedding, James. 'The Story of *The Merchant of Venice*', *Cornhill Magazine*, 41 (1880), 276–9.
——. 'Why did Shakespere write Tragedies?', *Cornhill Magazine*, 42 (1880), 153–72.
Stephen, Leslie. *Hours in a Library* (London: Smith, Elder, 1874).
Sutherland, John. *Is Heathcliff a Murderer? Puzzles in 19th-Century Fiction* (Oxford: Oxford University Press, 1996).
Sweet, Henry. Letter, *Academy*, 27 (25 April 1885), 294–5.
——. Letter, *Academy*, 27 (9 May 1885), 331.
——. Letter, *Academy*, 27 (13 June 1885), 422.
——. Letter, *Academy*, 27 (27 June 1885), 457.
Swinburne, Algernon Charles. *The Age of Shakespeare*, in *The Complete Works of Algernon Charles Swinburne, Prose Works: I*, ed. Sir Edmund Gosse and Thomas James Wise (London: Heinemann, 1926), 267–480.
Thompson, J. W. Letter, *Academy*, 27 (27 June 1885), 457.
Tillyard, E. M. W. *The Muse Unchained: An Intimate Account of the Revolution in English Studies at Cambridge* (London: Bowes & Bowes, 1958).
Vaughan, C. E. *Types of Tragic Drama* (London: Macmillan, 1908).
Vigfussun, G. Letter, *Academy*, 27 (2 May 1885), 312.
Wilde, Oscar. *The Complete Works of Oscar Wilde* (London: HarperCollins, 1991).
Woolf, Virginia. *The Common Reader* (London: Hogarth, [1925] 1929).
——. *A Room of One's Own* (London: Grafton, [1929] 1977).
——. *The Common Reader: Second Series* (London: Hogarth, [1932] 1986).
——. *The Death of the Moth and Other Essays* (London, 1942: Penguin, 1961).
——. *Books and Portraits* (London, 1977: Triad Panther, 1979).

Secondary sources

Altick, Richard D. *The English Common Reader: A Social History of the Mass Reading Public 1800–1900* (Chicago: University of Chicago Press, 1957).
Amis, Martin. *The War against Cliché: Essays and Reviews 1971–2000* (London: Jonathan Cape, 2001).
Annan, Noel. *The Dons: Mentors, Eccentrics and Geniuses* (London: HarperCollins, 1999).
Ashcroft, Bill, Griffiths, Gareth and Tiffin, Helen. *The Empire Writes Back: Theory and Practice in Post-Colonial Literatures* (London: Routledge, 1989).
Attridge, Derek. *The Singularity of Literature* (London: Routledge, 2004).
Bacon, Alan. 'English Literature Becomes a University Subject: King's College, London as Pioneer', *Victorian Studies*, 29 (1986), 591–612.
Baldick, Chris. *The Social Mission of English Criticism 1848–1932* (Oxford: Clarendon Press, 1983).
Barry, Peter. 'Is English Safe?', *English Association Newsletter*, 170 (2002), 1–2.
Bateson, F. W. 'Criticism's Lost Leader', in *The Literary Criticism of T.S. Eliot*, ed. David Newton-De Molina (London: Athlone, 1977), 1–19.
Benjamin, Walter. 'The Work of Art in the Age of Mechanical Reproduction', *Illuminations* (New York, 1968: HarperCollins, 1992), 211–44.

Bickley, Pamela. 'The New A-Level: What Will It Mean?', paper given at the English Association Conference for Higher Education, April 2000, accessed online at http://www.le.ac.uk/engassoc/info/se1.html.

Bloom, Clive. *Literature, Politics and Intellectual Crisis in Britain Today* (Basingstoke: Palgrave, 2001).

——(ed.). *Literature and Culture in Modern Britain*, I, 1900–1929 (London: Longman, 1993).

Boughey, Chrissie. 'From Equity to Efficiency: Access to Higher Education in South Africa', *Arts and Humanities in Higher Education*, 2 (2003), 65–71.

Bowlby, Rachel. *Virginia Woolf: Feminist Destinations* (Oxford: Blackwell, 1988).

Bradbury, Malcolm and McFarlane, James (eds). *Modernism: A Guide to European Literature 1890–1930* (London: Penguin, [1976] 1991).

Brake, Laurel. *Subjugated Knowledges: Journalism, Gender & Literature in the Nineteenth Century* (London: Macmillan, 1994).

Brake, Laurel and Small, Ian (eds). *Pater in the 1990s* (Greensboro, North Carolina: ELT, 1991).

Brosnan, Leila. *Reading Virginia Woolf's Essays and Journalism* (Edinburgh: Edinburgh University Press, 1997).

Cain, William E. *The Crisis in Criticism: Theory, Literature and Reform in English Studies* (Baltimore: Johns Hopkins University Press, 1984).

——. *Reconceptualizing American Literary/Cultural Studies: Rhetoric, History, and Politics in the Humanities* (New York: Garland, 1996).

Cameron, Deborah. *Verbal Hygiene* (London: Routledge, 1995).

Carey, John. *The Intellectuals and the Masses: Pride and Prejudice among the Literary Intelligentsia, 1880–1939* (London: Faber & Faber, 1992).

Charles, Prince of Wales. Annual Shakespeare Birthday Lecture, 22 April 1991, accessed online at http://193.36.68.132/speeches/education_22041991.html.

Collini, Stefan. *Arnold* (Oxford: Oxford University Press, 1988).

——. *English Pasts: Essays in History and Culture* (Oxford: Oxford University Press, 1999).

——. 'Lament for a Lost Culture: How the Twentieth Century Came to Mourn the Seriousness of the Nineteenth', *Times Literary Supplement* (19 January 2001), 3–5.

Constable, John: 'I. A. Richards, T. S. Eliot and the Poetry of Belief', *Essays in Criticism*, 40 (1990), 222–43; accessed online at http://www.btinternet.com/~j1837c/jbc/iartse/html.

Court, Franklin. *Institutionalizing English Literature: The Culture and Politics of Literary Study* (Stanford: Stanford University Press, 1992).

Cox, Brian. *Cox on Cox: An English Curriculum for the 1990s* (London: Hodder & Stoughton, 1991).

——. *Cox on the Battle for the English Curriculum* (London: Hodder & Stoughton, 1995).

Craddock, Mike: 'Idealism, Theory, Practice and the New "A" Levels', *The Use of English*, 52 (2001), 107–11.

——. 'Curriculum 2000: A Teacher's Verdict', *The Use of English*, 54 (2003), 110–19.

Crawford, Robert. *Devolving English Literature* (Oxford: Clarendon Press, 1992).

——. *The Scottish Invention of English Literature* (Cambridge: Cambridge University Press, 1998).

Dennis, Barbara. *The Victorian Novel* (Cambridge: Cambridge University Press, 2000).

Dentith, Simon. 'English and the Audit Culture: An Introduction', *English Subject Centre Newsletter*, 3 (May 2002), accessed online at http://www.english.ltsn.ac.uk/resources/general/publications/newsletters/newsissue3/dentith.htm.

DiBattista, Maria. 'Virginia Woolf', in *The Cambridge History of Literary Criticism*, vol. 7: *Modernism and the New Criticism*, ed. A. Walton Litz, Louis Menand and Lawrence Rainey (Cambridge: Cambridge University Press, 2000), 122–37.

Don Vann, J. and VanArsdel, Rosemary T. (eds). *Victorian Periodicals and Victorian Society* (Aldershot: Scolar, 1994).

Dowling, Linda. *Language and Decadence in the Victorian Fin de Siècle* (Princeton: Princeton University Press, 1986).

Doyle, Brian. *English and Englishness* (London: Routledge, 1989).

Eaglestone, Robert. *Doing English: A Guide for Literature Students* (London: Routledge, 2000).

——. 'Active voice! Responding to Adrian Barlow on the new English Literature A-levels', *English Association Newsletter*, 166 (2001), 6–7.

Eagleton, Terry. *Literary Theory: An Introduction* (Oxford: Blackwell, 1983).

——. *The Function of Criticism* (London: Verso, [1984] 1996).

Fish, Stanley. *Professional Correctness: Literary Studies and Political Change* (Cambridge, Massachusetts: Harvard University Press, 1995).

Fry, Paul H. 'I. A. Richards', in *The Cambridge History of Literary Criticism*, vol. 7: *Modernism and the New Criticism*, ed. A. Walton Litz, Louis Menand and Lawrence Rainey (Cambridge: Cambridge University Press, 2000), 181–99.

Garber, Marjorie. *Academic Instincts* (Princeton: Princeton University Press, 1999).

Gervais, David. 'Literary Criticism and the Literary Student', *English*, 41 (1992), 149–61.

Good, Graham. *The Observing Self* (London: Routledge, 1988).

Gordon, Lyndall. *Virginia Woolf: A Writer's Life* (Oxford: Oxford University Press, 1984).

Graff, Gerald. *Professing Literature: An Institutional History* (Chicago: University of Chicago Press, 1987).

Graff, Gerald and Warner, Michael (eds). *The Origins of Literary Studies in America: A Documentary Anthology* (London: Routledge, 1988).

Griffith, Peter. *English at the Core: Dialogue and Power in English Teaching* (Milton Keynes: Open University Press, 1992).

Gross, John. *The Rise and Fall of the Man of Letters: English Literary Life since 1800* (London: Penguin, [1969] 1991).

Gualtieri, Elena. *Reading Virginia Woolf's Essays: Sketching the Past* (London: Macmillan, 2000).

Guillory, John. 'The Ideology of Canon-Formation: T. S. Eliot and Cleanth Brooks', in *Canons*, ed. Robert von Hallberg (Chicago: University of Chicago Press, 1984), 337–62.

——. *Cultural Capital: The Problems of Literary Canon Formation* (Chicago: University of Chicago Press, 1993).

Guy, Josephine M. and Small, Ian. *Politics and Value in English Studies: A Discipline in Crisis?* (Cambridge: Cambridge University Press, 1993).

——. 'The British "man of letters" and the rise of the Professional', in *The Cambridge History of Literary Criticism*, vol. 7: *Modernism and the New Criticism*, ed. A. Walton Litz, Louis Menand and Lawrence Rainey (Cambridge: Cambridge University Press, 2000), 377–88.

Hamilton, Ian. 'Evil Days', *London Review of Books* (23 July 1992), 9–10.

Hawkes, Terence. *Structuralism and Semiotics* (London: Routledge, [1977] 2003).

——. General Editor's Preface to 'New Accents' series, in Catherine Belsey, *Critical Practice* (London: Methuen, 1980), pp. vi–vii.

Heyck, T. W. *The Transformation of Intellectual Life in Victorian England* (London: Croom Helm, 1982).

Hoggart, Richard. *The Uses of Literacy* (London: Penguin, 1958).

Holbrook, David. *English for Maturity* (Cambridge: Cambridge University Press, 1967).

Hollindale, Peter. 'War-weary sides call for truce', *Times Educational Supplement* (12 January 1996), accessed online at http://www.tes.co.uk/search/search_display.asp?+section+Archive&sub section=Friday&id=25359&Type=0.

Hough, Graham. 'The Poet as Critic', in *The Literary Criticism of T. S. Eliot*, ed. David Newton-De Molina (London: Athlone, 1977), 42–63.

Houghton, Walter E. (ed.). *The Wellesley Index to Victorian periodicals, 1824–1900*, 5 vols (Toronto: University of Toronto Press; London: Routledge & Kegan Paul, 1966–1989).

Hoyes, Richard. 'Richard Hoyes puts the fun back into Eng Lit', *Friday* magazine, *Times Educational Supplement* (11 February 2000), 5.

Kearney, Anthony, 'What to Read and Why: A View of John Carey's *Pure Pleasure*', *The Use of English*, 53 (2001), 49–56.

Kent, Christopher. 'The *Academy*', in *British Literary Magazines: The Victorian and Edwardian Age, 1837–1913*, ed. Alvin Sullivan (Westport, Connecticut: Greenwood, 1984), pp. 3–6.

Knight, Roger, 'Some "Contextual Influences" on the New "A" Levels', *The Use of English*, 52 (2001), 97–106.

Lee, Hermione. *Virginia Woolf* (London: Vintage, 1997).

——. ' "Crimes of Criticism": Virginia Woolf and Literary Journalism', in *Grub Street and the Ivory Tower: Literary Journalism and Literary Scholarship from Fielding to the Internet*, ed. Jeremy Treglown and Bridget Bennett (Oxford: Clarendon Press, 1998), 112–34.

Levine, Philippa. *The Amateur and the Professional: Antiquarians, Historians and Archaeologists in Victorian England, 1838–1886* (Cambridge: Cambridge University Press, 1986).

McCallum, Pamela. *Literature and Method: Towards a Critique of I. A. Richards, T. S. Eliot and F. R. Leavis* (Dublin: Gill and Macmillan, 1983).

MacKillop, Ian. *F. R. Leavis: A Life in Criticism* (London: Penguin, 1995).

McMurtry, Jo. *English Language, English Literature: The Creation of an Academic Discipline* (London: Mansell, 1985).

Marshall, Bethan. *English Teachers – The Unofficial Guide: Researching the Philosophies of English Teachers* (London: RoutledgeFalmer, 2000).

Martin, Wallace. *'The New Age' under Orage* (Manchester: Manchester University Press, 1967).

——. 'Criticism and the Academy', in *The Cambridge History of Literary Criticism*, vol. 7: *Modernism and the New Criticism*, ed. A. Walton Litz, Louis Menand and Lawrence Rainey (Cambridge: Cambridge University Press, 2000), 269–321.

May, Derwent. *Critical Times: The History of the Times Literary Supplement* (London: HarperCollins, 2001).

Menand, Louis. 'T. S. Eliot', in *The Cambridge History of Literary Criticism*, vol. 7: *Modernism and the New Criticism*, ed. A. Walton Litz, Louis Menand and Lawrence Rainey (Cambridge: Cambridge University Press, 2000), 17–56.

Menand, Louis, and Rainey, Lawrence. Introduction to *The Cambridge History of Literary Criticism*, vol. 7: *Modernism and the New Criticism*, ed. A. Walton Litz, Louis Menand and Lawrence Rainey (Cambridge: Cambridge University Press, 2000), 1–14.

Moody, David. 'Where is the Literature? Responding to Robert Eaglestone on the new English Literature A-levels', *English Association Newsletter*, 168 (2001), 2.

Morrison, James, and Johnson, Andrew. 'Inside Prince Charles' Literary Think Camp', *Independent on Sunday* (6 October 2002), 5.

Mulhern, Francis. *The Moment of 'Scrutiny'* (London: Verso, [1979] 1981).

Palmer, D. J. *The Rise of English Studies* (Oxford: Oxford University Press, 1965).

Parrinder, Patrick. 'A View from the Bench', *English Association Newsletter*, 165 (2000), 1–2.

Peim, Nick. *Critical Theory and the English Teacher: Transforming the Subject* (London: Routledge, 1993).

Phillips, Melanie. *All Must Have Prizes* (London: Warner, [1996] 1998).

Pope, Rob. *The English Studies Book* (London: Routledge, 1998).

Potter, Stephen. *The Muse in Chains: A Study in Education* (London: Jonathan Cape, 1937).

Rainey, Lawrence. 'The most uncommon reader', *The Independent* (21 April 2001), accessed online at http://www.independent.co.uk/story.jsp?=67826.

Rose, Jonathan. *The Intellectual Life of the British Working Classes* (New Haven and London: Yale University Press, 2001).

Rothblatt, Sheldon. *The Revolution of the Dons: Cambridge and Society in Victorian England* (London: Faber & Faber, 1968).

Russo, John Paul. *I. A. Richards: His Life and Work* (Routledge: London, 1989).

Sait, Jim. Summary of lecture by John Sutherland at the University of Sydney, accessed online at http://www.usyd.edu.au/publications/news/2K0810News/1008_briefly.html.

Scholes, Robert. *The Rise and Fall of English: Reconstructing English as a Discipline* (New Haven and London: Yale University Press, 1998).

Shattock, Joanne. *Politics and Reviewers: The 'Edinburgh' and the 'Quarterly' in the early Victorian age* (London: Leicester University Press, 1989).

Showalter, Elaine. *Teaching Literature* (Oxford: Blackwell, 2003).

Simpson, David. *The Academic Postmodern and the Rule of Literature: A Report on Half-Knowledge* (Chicago: University of Chicago Press, 1995).

Small, Ian. *Conditions for Criticism: Authority, Knowledge and Literature in the Late Nineteenth Century* (Oxford: Clarendon Press, 1991).

Smallwood, Philip. 'Criticism, Valuation and Useful Purpose', *New Literary History*, 28 (1997), 711–22.

——. ' "Outside the Academic Fold": Criticism, Theorists and the Men of Letters', *English*, 47 (1998), 41–52.

——. ' "More Creative than Creation": The Idea of Criticism and the Student Critic', *Arts and Humanities in Higher Education*, 1 (2002), 59–71.

Stevens, Jenny. 'The new "A" Levels: Critical Theory in the Sixth Form Classroom; a very, very short introduction', *The Use of English*, 52 (2000), 1–11.

Sullivan, Alvin (ed.). *British Literary Magazines: The Victorian and Edwardian Age, 1837–1913* (Westport, Connecticut: Greenwood, 1984).

Treglown, Jeremy, and Bennett, Bridget (eds). *Grub Street and the Ivory Tower: Literary Journalism and Literary Scholarship from Fielding to the Internet* (Oxford: Oxford University Press, 1998).

Treharne, Elaine. 'Balancing the English Degree Programme', *English Association Newsletter*, 166 (2001), 3–4.

Walter, Natasha. 'Can we win the war against cliché?', *The Independent* (23 April 2001), accessed online at http://www.independent.co.uk/story.jsp?story=68134.

Washington, Peter. *Fraud: Literary Theory and the End of English* (London: Fontana, 1989).

Watson, George. *The Literary Critics: A Study of English Descriptive Criticism* (London: Penguin, 1962).

White, Hayden. 'The Absurdist Moment in Contemporary Literary Theory', in *Directions for Criticism: Structuralism and its Alternatives*, ed. Murray Krieger and L. S. Dembo (Madison: University of Wisconsin Press, 1977), 85–110.

Widdowson, Peter. *Re-Reading English* (London: Methuen, 1982).

——. *Literature* (London and New York: Routledge, 1999).

Williams, Raymond. *Culture and Society 1780–1950* (London: Hogarth Press, 1958).

Index

Printed in the United States
69601LVS00001B/124-126